Unassigned Frequencies

Laurence Lieberman

Unassigned Frequencies

AMERICAN POETRY IN REVIEW, 1964–77

UNIVERSITY OF ILLINOIS PRESS

Urbana Chicago London

Special thanks to the following journals,
in which most of these essays originally
appeared:

> *American Poetry Review*
> *Antioch Review*
> *Far Point*
> *Hudson Review*
> *Poetry*
> *Yale Review*

LIBRARY OF CONGRESS CATALOGING IN PUBLICATION DATA

Lieberman, Laurence.
  Unassigned frequencies.

  Includes index.
  1. American poetry — 20th century — Addresses, essays,
lectures. 2. American poetry — 20th century — Book
reviews. I. Title.
PS325.L5   811'.5'409   77-10072
ISBN 0-252-00477-9

for JOHN E. PALMER

Contents

Preface   ix

PART I

John Ashbery: UNASSIGNED FREQUENCIES: WHISPERS OUT OF TIME   3
A. R. Ammons: OF MIND AND WORLD   62
James Dickey: THE WORLDLY MYSTIC   74
James Dickey: THE DEEPENING OF BEING   83
Jean Garrigue: THE BODY OF THE DREAM   107
Richard Howard: THE ARCHEOLOGIST POET   116
W. S. Merwin: THE CHURCH OF ASH   122
Howard Moss: BITTER AND SWEET, DREAD AND DESIRE   133
Mark Strand: THE BOOK OF MOURNING   140
David Wagoner: THE COLD SPEECH OF THE EARTH   152
James Wright: WORDS OF GRASS   182

PART II

W. H. Auden   193
Michael Benedikt   195
Robert Duncan   196
David Galler   198
Paul Goodman   199
Arthur Gregor   201
John Holmes   203
Edwin Honig   206
Katherine Hoskins   207
Langston Hughes   208
Richard Hugo   209
Galway Kinnell   212
Stanley Kunitz   214
Archibald MacLeish   217

Josephine Miles   220
Vassar Miller   222
W. R. Moses   223
Howard Nemerov   225
John Peck   227
Theodore Roethke   230
Muriel Rukeyser   232
Karl Shapiro   233
W. D. Snodgrass   235
Peter Viereck   237
Robert Watson   238
Theodore Weiss   239
Reed Whittemore   243
Miller Williams   245

PART III

James Dickey and A. R. Ammons: THE UNBROKEN FLOW   249
M. B. Tolson and A. R. Ammons: BOOK-LENGTH POEMS   252
W. S. Merwin and Anthony Hecht: RISKS AND FAITHS   257

John Berryman, William Stafford, and James Dickey: THE
    EXPANSIONAL POET: A RETURN TO PERSONALITY   263
William Stafford and Frederick Morgan: THE SHOCKS OF
    NORMALITY   272
Derek Walcott and Michael S. Harper: THE MUSE OF HISTORY   284

Preface

While the present selection from my readings of American poetry published in the last dozen years can hardly purport to be inclusive—for every important poet discussed, perhaps two of equal merit have been bypassed—I do wish to suggest that this gathering of essays and shorter reviews is, in its limited way, *representative* of the remarkable variety and sweep of poetry in the United States today. The book cannot begin to accomplish an overview of contemporary American poetry—the function, say, of a good anthology or survey—but I hope the frequent tendency here to follow up successive volumes by many of the poets who have published repeatedly and advanced their art impressively during the dozen years following the death of Theodore Roethke (who, in my view, rounded out the most prodigiously developed career of any American poet who came into prominence after World War II) may suggest something of the rigorous health and genius for survival exhibited by an unfashionably high ratio of the most gifted poets of our present generation in America, a generation often mistakenly characterized by its handful of suicides.

Much of the work in this book was written on assignment, confined to cramped word limits and magazine deadlines. For years I felt uneasy with the grueling restrictions of the reviewer's task, but in time I grew to regard the narrow work space as a welcome and vivid challenge. I knew it would never be possible for me to write a conventional book review, or *notice*, though editors who invited me to write brief commentaries on current books were contented to classify my finished product as reviews, despite the many discrepancies from standard practice, and they hospitably urged me to write more criticism for their reviewing columns. If they were happy with my first diffident excursions into the critical enterprise, perhaps I should take heart, and continue to give a generous allotment of my best creative energies to developing a craft I little understood at first, but which felt mysteriously and indissolubly linked to the progress of my own poetic art. Though I felt, consistently, that my work in poetry was dominant, the criticism subordinate—if complementary—to my verse, at intervals, my critical prose seemed to usurp a disproportionate share of my primary creative resources. I found, to my surprise, that I was becoming wholly preoccupied with exploring the *mode* of the short review-essay. The medium itself demanded a kind of total absorption in the shaping of form and symmetries of style. To struggle to fashion and refine this critical instrument, I discovered, was to mold a full-fledged art genre in its own right.

Whenever an editor sent me the current assortment of poetry volumes for an omnibus review, I invariably felt that the few books I selected to write about, culled from the unmanageably diverse grab-bag, had somehow chosen me, rather than I them. It seemed as if the indispensable books and I joined hands in a zone outside the contract between editor and reviewer, outside any job assignment. A force like Necessity, perhaps, governed our matings—the currents of feeling that passed between reader and writer traveled, it would seem, on *unassigned* word frequencies.

Increasingly, I was drawn to books which kept me perpetually in training as reader, those works which demanded many re-readings as I sought to come perfectly into their measure, to adjust the scale of my cerebral ear to the pitch of each author's voice. Often, the strongest books completely resisted my intelligence on first reading, seeming impenetrable. Their special music left me feeling tone deaf. But glimmerings of the distinctive nuance of voice commanded me to acquire new skills in learning to read. I found, again and again, that the books I craved most were the ones that compelled me to stretch myself beyond my usual limits, to cultivate unexplored faculties of readership. These books humbled me, renewing wholly my passion to become again a student, an apprentice-reader in faithful tutelage to each new mentor in turn. Though I often found myself passing over books that were perhaps among the most expertly written in a given season, I adopted early on the policy of dealing only with those books which somehow spoke to the purity of being in me, knowing that, as often as not, the reasons for my feeling a deep personal affinity for some good books, and not for others, were private and ineffable—not to say enigmatic. But I had begun writing criticism with the conviction that I was one reader whose commentaries about books would always lack authority, much less consequentiality, unless my personal demon seemed to connect deeply with the spirit of the poet's vision, or to resonate with the tenor of his style.

In the last few years I have been troubled repeatedly by a dilemma intrinsic to the reviewer's enterprise. Finding myself to be allured by one surpassingly good book and, at last, swept away by the beauty and power of its vision, I felt it would be impossible to do justice to the work in any grouping with the other strong books of the quarter which demanded my attention. The single outstanding volume was intractable—it could not be manipulated into a context beyond that dictated by its own internal logic and organic symmetry. The master-work, in each case, prompted me to write a highly specialized elucidation, as in the extended studies of Strand, Merwin, Wagoner, and Ashbery. (In 1967, a similar conflict had spurred me to undertake a commission to write a monograph on James Dickey's work—"The Deepening of Being"—to accompany a volume of his selected poems.)

This book's arrangement in three sections is designed, in part, to call special attention to a number of poets who, from volume to volume, have most conspicuously mobilized their talents, slowly galvanizing the lavish resources of early career into a masterful artistry. Hence, the first part comprises longer essays, often joining two or more pieces that deal with different stages in a developing author's career. The middle section gathers together shorter pieces, arranged alphabetically, which formerly appeared in round-up reviews. In the course of writing numerous poetry chronicles on assignment for various publications, I found that occasionally my responses to two or three volumes by different poets became happily wedded into self-contained units, most notably the piece "The Muse of History," linking black poets Derek Walcott and Michael S. Harper. A third and final section, therefore, contains the longer pieces which, in the hybrid mode of the review-essay, consolidate discussions of two or more poets.

—L. L.

PART I

John Ashbery

UNASSIGNED FREQUENCIES:
WHISPERS OUT OF TIME

How desperately, today, we need a poetry that will shame the slovenly readership out of us. Poetry must demand more from us if it is to make of us the kind of audience who will demand, in turn, loftiest vision—a readership who will settle for nothing less than to be up-lifted in ardor of collaborative appreciation. John Ashbery is our gadfly. His new poetry creates discomforts, snares, inconveniences for readers to sting them into a more responsible mode of readership. Perhaps Marianne Moore is the only other major American poet of this century who, recognizing to her surprise—in mid-career—how unmanageable her gourmet sensibility had grown to most reader's intellectual palates, took as strenuous measures as Ashbery to render her obscurities clear. How she struggled for utmost transparency, and undertook to guide readers to develop the reading skills needed to surmount near-insuperable obstacles to comprehension! Hence, her delectably readable footnotes.

I have lived with John Ashbery's "Self-Portrait in a Convex Mirror" as with a favorite mistress for the past nine months. Often, for whole days of inhabiting *the room* of its dream, I have felt that it is the only poem—and Ashbery the only author—in my life. It is what I most want from a poem. Or an author. To those many readers of poetry who perennially will not be bothered with surmounting the difficulties—both technical and cognitive—necessitated by any careful reading of Ashbery's work, I would reply, if questioned about the grounds for my monomaniacal fixations in reading, no poem is worth my time of life that does not so exhaustively challenge me and absorb me as to come wholly into possession of my dream-life. I would con-fine my ardent readership to those few authors who command me to learn how to read all over again, to rediscover the reading process and discipline as if I am encountering the great adventure for the first time. Beyond this appetite of mine, which Ashbery satisfies immoder-ately, I find that when I put this poem down I catch myself in the act of seeing objects and events in the world as if through different—

This essay considers *Self-Portrait in a Convex Mirror,* by John Ashbery. (Viking Press, 1975.) Bibliographical information for the volumes considered in each subsequent essay appears at the foot of the first page of that essay.

through amazingly novel *other*—eyes: the brilliantly varied other life of surfaces has been wonderfully revivified, and I take this transformation to be an accurate index of the impact of Ashbery's poetry upon the modus operandi of my perception.

Ashbery, in dramatizing himself as a student of Parmigianino's mirror-portrait, undertakes to diagram an exemplar of the ideal interaction between reader and writer, the poem a disguised map of good reading of his own poems. Much as Parmigianino has disciplined and trained Ashbery's faculties as participating enthusiast, Ashbery would now train his readers to cultivate the necessary receptive faculties:

> We have surprised him
> At work, but no, he has surprised us
> As he works. The picture is almost finished,
> The surprise almost over, as when one looks out,
> Startled by a snowfall which even now is
> Ending in specks and sparkles of snow.
> It happened while you were inside, asleep,
> And there is no reason why you should have
> Been awake for it, except that the day
> Is ending and it will be hard for you
> To get to sleep tonight, at least until late.

Poet and painter, reader and writer, encounter one another by a succession of surprises. Two satellites, they travel in separate and distinct orbits, taking snatched glimpses of the same core—or globe—of reality, like two moons circling a planet. They interrupt each other's go-by, intermittently; first the one, then the other taking the lead, initiating the surprise. When the interaction between them has run its course, the reader will find himself plunged into trance. He is the dumbfounded witness in Ashbery's remarkable snowfall metaphor.

I, too, am that witness, that reader. The drama envisioned by this emblematic picture closely duplicates the stages of my own allurement in reading Ashbery's poem:

(1) I learn to read and re-read slowly enough for the vision to relaxedly sink into my waiting sleep-centers. The dream guides me into avoiding a premature frontal engagement with the poem's visionary architecture. I pause and pause, holding my full commitment to the poem in abeyance for months, waiting for the poem to come back to me from inside my own shadow-life.

(2) Before I recognize the presence of snowfall covering the whole landscape before me—which occurred in my absence—the last few "specks and sparkles" of snow are falling. The end traces register

upon my full waking consciousness and shock me into a revelation of my own absent witnessing, rendered possible by a necessary obliqueness in my readership.

(3) Now I can hardly believe how massive the poem's impact has been, my conscious response lagging far behind the ravishment of my dream-life. The poem has worked upon me, devastatingly, by way of my sleeping being. The abrupt change in myself as reader-human sweeps over me.

I

It was inevitable that John Ashbery—of all contemporaries—would find himself in a very special dilemma when he came to write his self-portrait, or to grapple with the contemporary world directly in the poem. In previous work, Ashbery usually presented the modern city, or the present age, as if it were some unfamiliar and forgotten ancient city, casting a hypnotic spell over us with flashes of familiarity, as in "These Lacustrine Cities." In Ashbery's vision, we were repeatedly surprised to discover that the society and urban landscape presented as a foreign locale were shrewdly disguised versions of our own. It would seem that we have better perspective in relation to the past, or to the future, than to the present: "Tomorrow is easy, but today is uncharted." My own face, my own city, my own country, my own era—these are the most difficult and intractable landscapes. But a self-portraitist must, of necessity, illumine the enigmas of his own corpus, his America, his New York, his 1974.

Even so, Ashbery finds that he must be constantly nourished by interaction with images out of the past to renew his power to stay alive in the present. *Self-Portrait* is a laboratory in which past and present, yesterday and today, cross-fertilize each other. The alternating rhythm of withdrawal and arrival, the pendulum swing between past and present, is the mode of life that graphs the underlying blueprint of this poem's wavelike grand sweep, its ample span of experience. In the opening passages of *Self-Portrait,* the painter's hand, face, and soul drift toward and away, toward and away "in a recurrent wave of arrival." This oscillating movement defines the poem's architecture:

> As Parmigianino did it, the right hand
> Bigger than the head, thrust at the viewer
> And swerving easily away, as though to protect
> What it advertises . . .
> > The soul establishes itself.
> But how far can it swim out through the eyes
> And still return safely to its nest? . . .

> One would like to stick one's hand
> Out of the globe, but its dimension,
> What carries it, will not allow it . . . .
> It must join the segment of a circle,
> Roving back to the body of which it seems
> So unlikely a part.

The body is so "unlikely" a mate for the hand, the reasoning brain so unlikely a prison for the soul, America so unlikely a country to have been Ashbery's birthplace, the U.S. citizenry so unlikely a readership for Ashbery to address himself to, the seventies so unlikely a decade for him to inhabit.

Exiles, self-banishments from these unpropitious sites, for Ashbery have been the beginning of wisdom and identity; arrival and fulfillment have been concomitant with repatriations to all the abandoned sites, a full—if conditional—return to home ground. No other contemporary poet's return from exile has generated so shattering an impact on our whole scheme of values; no other has flooded our vague, ambiguous, and over differentiated literary climate with so bold and disaffiliated a voice, or with so rich a blend of seminal new possibilities for the future health of our art. Ashbery's unexpected arrival in his power to fully embrace the present moment, which explodes in a number of key passages in the last pages of *Self-Portrait,* unleashes great affirmative energies. He had given himself up, unconditionally, to the world of the great past. Total severance from the present day appears to have purified him, released him from all bondage to the past, ultimately, and freed him to be whole and totally present in the world of today. His voyaging into the past prepared him, obliquely, to spring alive into the present, as never before; much as living for many years in exile and sequestration in France, or in seclusion at home, finally mellowed him into a preparedness to embrace his America; or indeed, much as avoiding any obligation to cultivate a wide readership for so many years of his publishing career predisposed him, by indirection, by a roundabout course, to feel a messianic calling and mission to connect with American readers.

*

For fifteen years, John Ashbery had been haunted by Francesco Parmigianino's self-portrait—which he first encountered in Vienna in the summer of 1959—before he undertook to write his most ambitious poem. The transfigured face of the portrait loomed in Ashbery's memory: in time, the face grew apparitional, its features shimmering with hallucinatory intensity. Like the saintly-Promethean struggling faces of Beethoven and Mahler, Francesco's face is beautifully anguished and radiantly ecstatic, by turns:

> ... the face
> Riding at anchor, issued from hazards, soon
> To accost others, "rather angel than man" (Vasari).

It is the face of a man triumphing in his struggle to cope with all the complexities of the dream-life. It is the emblematic face of the lone solitary spirit, *sequestered* in its grapplings with itself; and more, the spirit returning intermittently from Byzantium to brave "the fury and the mire of human veins," riding the Yeatsian dolphin over "that dolphin-torn, that gong-tormented sea." In this major poem, more than in all of his other work taken together, Ashbery rides that dolphin, engaged profoundly with both the life of dreams and the public life of today. In our day, we must struggle to retrieve the institution of dreaming from our culture's rubbish heap, since our age is more impoverished than most by neglect and outright scorn of the world of dreams; hence, the necessity for Ashbery to go foraging in a past age for a heroic model to be held in the timeless mind's eye as reminder, emblem, and finally, as blood-linked totem. The totemic stage is the condition of apotheosis for the work of art. For Ashbery to infuse the language of poetry with totemic force is to raise the poem, once again, into a sphere of communal grace in which the confluence of our whole human clan's—or tribe's—shared dream-life can find its meeting ground, and all scattered tributaries of our dreaming can trace their way back to a common parent stream in "the waters of life."

Parmigianino's portrait survives as an immortal totem of the dream. Ashbery finds that this exquisitely crafted mirror-portrait, which was nourished continually by our mutual dream-life during its prolonged composition, is, finally, indistinguishable from our own lost face of dreaming. If we approach a depth of absorption in studying the painting—or in reading a poem—that matches the uttermost submergence of the artist in the act of creation, we shall come upon a face inescapably recognized to have been "ours once," a face we hardly knew we had lost until the moment that it is revealed to be a map of our own features rearranged, our lost dream-life restored to us:

> Perhaps an angel looks like everything
> We have forgotten, I mean forgotten
> Things that don't seem familiar when
> We meet them again, lost beyond telling,
> Which were ours once.

Throughout the composing of his masterwork, Ashbery finds that to dwell upon Parmigianino's angel face is to be fortified in his arduous crafting. The portrait repeatedly shocks him out of mental lapses, moments of partial amnesia to the task of vision, and steels him in resuming the service of the dream.

The extraordinary relationship that develops between Ashbery and Parmigianino in the course of this poem strikes me as being unprecedented in contemporary letters. The poem begins in a spirit of arbitrariness, happy accident, as if the Parmigianino self-portrait were simply one sample chosen at random from a large available repertoire of works in this genre, any one of which might have sufficed for Ashbery's purposes. But we grow to learn—along with the author—that the poem's choice of subject, and indeed, the poet's choice of heroic model and mentor, was somehow enigmatically fated, predetermined, "chosen, meant for me, and materialized in the disguising radiance of my room." The drama that unfolds, we are to understand, has been guided by the hand of Providence. The author finds that he has been inexplicably re-routed by *necessity*:

> ... imagining
> He had a say in the matter and exercised
> An option of which he was hardly conscious,
> Unaware that necessity circumvents such resolutions
> So as to create something new
> For itself, that there is no other way,
> That the history of creation proceeds according to
> Stringent laws ...

Ashbery begins his own self-portrait by describing Parmigianino's self-portrait. The portrayal of Francesco Parmigianino is one way to sidle up to his own identity by avoiding it, by examining the other man's identity, by controlled indirection. Since Parmigianino has successfully mirrored his own dream-life, the careful spectator—by responding empathetically to the painting—will penetrate the exterior face and find his way to the interior, in which one man's otherness is found to be magically interlocked with another's. Thus, a good reader may find his way across the isthmus to the territory of his own lost dark side, his inner face, by unraveling the enigmas of a visionary author's works. When this miracle occurs, it is felt to be a unique experience like falling in love, and it is only partially initiated—or controlled—by the reader. It is a gift thrust upon him by the world outside with the irresistible force of a visitation. The experience is dizzying, a cosmic punch. It shakes him to the roots of his being.

So began this strange kinship across the centuries between Ashbery and Parmigianino to act out an unfinished life history. Ashbery hints—toward the end of the poem—that the marvelous interaction between a man alive today and his mysterious brother-spirit, "mate-

rialized" out of the distant past, both partakes of and transcends the
heightened intensity of sexual love. It is a cosmic romance, an un-
earthly love affair, which evolves through much the same stages as a
sexual-erotic encounter:

> To be serious only about sex
> Is perhaps one way, but the sands are hissing
> As they approach the beginning of the big slide
> Into what happened. This past
> Is now here, the painter's
> Reflected face, in which we linger, receiving
> Dreams and inspirations on an unassigned
> Frequency...

Francesco Parmigianino had to wait out many centuries until the
one exactly right pair of eyes would accurately comprehend his self-
portrait, be exalted by it, and transfigure it, in turn, by its clairvoyant
beholding. John Ashbery is that greatly inspired witness and inter-
preter who has translated the painting's genius, making it accessible to
us today, freeing the work to ripen into a classic, its place in world
history correctly defined for the first time. Ashbery becomes Parmigia-
nino's co-creator. His role is equivalent to that of a conductor's dis-
covery and restoration of an unjustly neglected symphonic master-
piece. Collaboration of the amazed spectator is the marriage of minds
that implements "the portrait's will to endure." This poem's drama
clearly attests that a painting's—or poem's—beholder can immortalize
the artist, advancing his soul's orbit thousands of miles around the
planet, thousands of years in time. Beyond this, a fellow artist who
inherits and builds upon the vision reanimates the mode of the origi-
nal. If he completes the vision and enables it to "hasten out of style,"
he may both assassinate and canonize the ancestor. The old mode is
rendered fatally obsolete and laid to rest, so to say; it loses its con-
temporaneity, finally, as the new mode plunders its residue of still
useable resources ("another life is stocked there"), then drives it
under, into the dust. The painting takes its place in the empyrean of
classics. The artist is sainted.

*

The vicissitudes of an age's fashions, trends, fads are perceived by
Ashbery—increasingly, as the poem proceeds—to be the arch-enemy
of the artist. Today, perhaps more than in any previous age, the artist
needs to cultivate stolidity, impassivity, the temperament—indeed, the
metabolism—of corporeal unwaveriness. A more stable new physiol-
ogy is needed to counteract, or neutralize, today's hysterias, the imagi-

nation of nervous hyperactivity:

> My guide in these matters is your self,
> Firm, oblique, accepting everything with the same
> Wraith of a smile...

Francesco Parmigianino's stance is one of poised stoicism, an intellectual prepossession that is so fully realized—so consummate—it pervades his temperament, his body's rhythms, his metabolism, and his dream's postures. All this is revealed to the poet by the shifting moods of the self-portrait, evoked by a remarkable blend of diverse tones and shades. The figure in the portrait wears a guise that is both "restive" and "serene"; it appears to "protect what it advertises"; it balances "embrace" with "warning," "affirmation" with "restraint":

> ... there is in that gaze a combination
> Of tenderness, amusement and regret so powerful
> In its restraint that one cannot look for long.
> The secret is too plain. The pity of it smarts,
> Makes hot tears spurt: that the soul is not a soul,
> Has no secret, is small, and it fits
> Its hollow perfectly: its room, our moment of attention...
> You will stay on, restive, serene in
> Your gesture which is neither embrace nor warning
> But which holds something of both in pure
> Affirmation that doesn't affirm anything.

Parmigianino is a man who has shorn himself of all false comforts, all illusions. He has gritted his teeth and taken the hard look at the worst. He has accepted, in full, the tragic limits and tragic cost of mortality. He has, centuries before his time, successfully and irrevocably deflated the romantic myths, and has survived triumphantly in spirit, despite the acknowledged losses.

In the poem's opening passages, Parmigianino sounds tragically handicapped, a cripple, an object of pathos. The keynote is entrapment, alienation, detention, as the prevailing condition of the artist. Ironically, his superb craft and sense of humor both defeat him. His smile is a mere "pinpoint," a "perverse light"—it can never release pain in a catharsis of laughter. Mirrored here is Ashbery's frustration in having chosen a medium which consistently deflates peak moments of intense emotion to guarantee the sustained mild radiance of the whole form:

> One would like to stick one's hand
> Out of the globe, but its dimension,
> What carries it, will not allow it.
> No doubt it is this, not the reflex

> To hide something, which makes the hand loom large
> As it retreats slightly . . .
> Roving back to the body of which it seems
> So unlikely a part, to fence in and shore up the face
> On which the effort of this condition reads
> Like a pinpoint of a smile, a spark
> Or star one is not sure of having seen.
> As darkness resumes. A perverse light whose
> Imperative of subtlety dooms in advance its
> Conceit to light up; unimportant but meant.
> Francesco, your hand is big enough
> To wreck the sphere, and too big,
> One would think, to weave delicate meshes
> That only argue its further detention.

How the hand tries to escape its human size, to outleap its human orbit! But the hand—like the soul—recognizes that its orbit is bounded fixedly: it can stretch its limits, borders, only to a degree allowed by the mirror's convexity. The hand, like the trapped soul, registers helplessness and frustration; its human confines have been fatally defined, once and for all time, and there is no turning back from the revelation of smallness and boundedness. Neither hand nor soul can escape from the curved surface of Francesco's halved sphere. All of life is "englobed." All moments and events are equalized, flattened to the one plane, the single dimension of rounded surface:

> But your eyes proclaim
> That everything is surface. The surface is what's there
> And nothing can exist except what's there.
> There are no recesses in the room, only alcoves . . .

Nothing can be secret, or hidden, since everything must occur on the surface. For the artist to utterly accept the harsh, cold lesson of all life being confined to outer surfaces—our body's skin, the globe's crust (paint on the canvas, black words on white paper)—is to exorcize the demon/angel, soul, by a succession of deflations until "the balloon pops." Flat. Flat. The explosion is followed by a ferocity of void, a tremendous negative energy like that of a vacuum tube from which all the air has been removed, and Ashbery knows how to hold this inverse pregnancy in suspension, many tons of minus pressure—a fierce suction—building to pull something into the churning vacancy. (Ashbery's great pauses are the longest waits this side of action—the plot of the story—of any major writer in English since Henry James.)

The exorcism of the soul is an emblem, for Ashbery, of the dethronement of the several divinities of nineteenth-century Romanticism in the arts: tonality in music, the natural image ("aping nature")

in painting, and rational cognition in poetry. What is lost, irretriev-
ably, is the emotional amplitude and intensity of the Romantic Age.
Farewell to ecstatic peaks of feeling. Farewell to the grand climaxes.
The possibilities of transcendence, at first felt to be nullified or re-
duced to infinitesimal scale, are later perceived to be relocated, spread
out in a thin film covering all surfaces. Slowly, a new vision of mental
freedom and expansiveness develops, taking the form of a linear
unfolding of "fertile thought associations"—all of approximately
equal weight and import—emanating a thin, mild, but persistent
radiance, a multiverse of sparkles as from a starry night sky. (The new
mode seems to be roughly the poetic equivalent of serial form in
Schönberg's music, or the evenly distributed spattering of epiphanies
in a Jackson Pollock painting.) The artist's crafting hand seems to
have supplanted—or superseded—his soul. Only the hand can trace,
and keep in step with, the multiversity of life crowding the surface.

Francesco Parmigianino perpetuates a total affirmative vision by
slowly erecting a sturdy aesthetic edifice upon the cornerstone of
modest good workmanship, which unexpectedly grew—in the course
of a lifetime of unflagging commitment to his reductive vision—into a
method and mode that could sustain the mind's thirst for utmost
belief, counterbalancing the losses endured by the depreciated myth
of the soul, his faith now grounded in "secrets of wash and finish that
took a lifetime to learn." His unquenched cravings for immortality are
re-channeled into the portrait's genius for survival, its rage of longev-
ity, a force of mind and spirit so viable that it spreads its wings over
today, overshadowing our accomplishments in the modern age: "Our
time gets to be veiled, compromised/ by the portrait's will to endure."
Francesco's new mode is a religion of art that formulates, or codifies,
its creed upon elegant preciosities of style and craft. Details are all
low-keyed, mildly radiant epiphanies. The medium, in and of itself, is
exalted. Francesco's piety, his devoutness, takes the form of constancy
and fidelity to the unending succession of details.

What a revelation, then, about the art of self-portraiture! Due to the
controlled distortions of the convex mirror, all facts of nature tran-
scribed as details of his self-portrait are altered, adorned, twisted
"slightly and profoundly" by his dream-life. In the shifting ex-
pressions of the face (in Ashbery's poem, the equivalent would be
shifting associations of memory in the mind's free play), all "postures
of the dream" are captured, expressed. The portrait knows how to
contain and register *as* expression all of the dream's fluctuations and
waverings. The paint—and indeed, the paint of words, word-paint—
is a broad enough palette, the workman in colors expert enough at his
craft to make the changing expressions of the face reveal to a trained
spectator/reader the whole dream-life, which is to say, all of the

higher reality. If painter and spectator both do their jobs with assiduity, nothing will be left out. Everything will be included. No shred of reality will elude the painter's inclusive grasp. But what about the tragic cost, the punctured balloon of the soul? Knowing how to lose, knowing what to give up, is the key to all that we can gain. Ashbery's career has vacillated between two poles, two opposite aesthetics—the rage to leave everything out, the rage to put everything back in. Significantly, Ashbery mastered in early career the powerful restraint in leaving out, as carried to the *unreadable*—yet cryptically apprehensible—extreme of poems in *The Tennis Court Oath*, a book whose ambitious failure I now perceive to have been an indispensable detour that precipitated, finally, the elevated vision of Ashbery's recent work. Knowing how to leave things out, paradoxically, evolved into the disposition of the poem's art in which everything is mysteriously found to have been put back in—in some other form.

The paradox exhibited by these milestones in Ashbery's career mirrors the fate of Sören Kierkegaard's Knight of Faith in *Fear and Trembling*. Abraham's utmost purity of heart, demonstrated by his readiness to sacrifice the life of his son Isaac to prove the steadfastness of his faith, won him both Isaac's life and his soul's salvation. My quest, in this long essay, is to surround and penetrate many of the images of Ashbery's poem in an ambience of total surgical autopsy as exhaustive, say, as Kierkegaard's elucidation of biblical images in *Fear and Trembling*.

*

What shall constitute the self-portrait of a "man of words," a man whose best life has been granted to him through language, a man whose identity—whose very substance of selfhood—is recognized by mid-career to be dominated by word-ingredients? A man-soul and man-body composed chiefly of words? Since the beginning of Ashbery's career, he has been obsessed with devising poetic forms whose compositional mold would be broad enough to accommodate and contain all key dimensions of contemporary reality. Whereas, in Ashbery's earlier work, he espoused the metaphysics of radical immaterialism, treating all external bodies—including words—as being of the essence of mind; in the advanced work of his new poetry, he explores the full-fledged doctrine of radical corporealism. All of reality—including words—may be perceived and experienced as body-surface:

> The body is what this is all about and it disperses
> In sheeted fragments, all somewhere around,
> But difficult to read correctly since there is

No common vantage point, no point of view
Like the "I" in a novel.
(from "No Way of Knowing")

Though much of the poem's apparatus is comprised of ideas—"fertile thought associations"—they, too, are perceived to be fragments of body in a different form, "accidents scarring" the mind's surface. Ideas are simply additional items in the make-up of the poem's compositional furnishings. They are equivalent, as repositories of truth, to all other components of the poem's architecture: imagistic, anecdotal, descriptive, narrational. This poetry carries a burden of revelation that can appropriate into nuances of style data received from every material surface that catches the light:

Everything is surface. The surface is what's there,
And nothing can exist except what's there . . . It [the surface] is not
Superficial but a visible core.

Not that everything *is* surface, but everything—for the artist—may be translated into, mirrored as, surface. The invisible world, the world of the dream, may be surprised into total visibility. Surface is a disguised two-dimensional metaphor for the invisible depths, a reversal of the usual metaphoric relation between mind and body. Body mirrors the dream. The planet skin mirrors its core, the surface becoming a "magma of interiors." We start out to explore the lineaments of our epidermis—our outermost living layers—only to discover we are transcribing a disguised graph of our intestinal linings, our innermost cavities, caves in the self. Outsides and insides reverse. Reality, itself, is composed of all disguises. Merely by looking closely, then, at the exterior surfaces of things, we come to know the invisible world that the surfaces of this world disguise.

We forget that every time we look at the world's gay and colorful surfaces, we see the magic world mirrored. The *other* world of our dreams is totally reflected in the mirror of *this* world of visible forms. Hence, if the poem attends with scrupulous eye and ear and fingertip to the velleities of surface, it will obliquely project life at the core. As the poem assembles more and more fragmentary glimpses of the natural world, grasped in concert with the fecund succession of ideas fluttering across the mind's surface, the lengthening verse will gradually embrace all of the magic world of dreams.

II

Is the process of self-portraiture necessarily solipsistic, or narcissistic? To come purely to terms with *the self*, must the poet become a hermit, a recluse in exile—shutting out other lives, cutting himself off from all human fellows "too far removed from our closed-in state"? In composing autobiography, does the poet become so self-infatuated, so self-preoccupied, that he becomes oblivious to the joys and agonies of another?

The confessional poet revealed the diaristic milestones of his private life. His mode was chiefly exhibitionistic, vacillating between the poles of self-glorification and self-condemnation. Too close to the scandal sheet, vitas, memoirs, diaries, reminiscences are all found to be equally suspect:

> Another directory form to be corrected.
> Henry did one years & years agone for *Who's Who*,
> Wasn't that enough?
> Why does the rehearsal of the public events of his life
> Always strike him as a list of failures, pal?
> (from #343, *The Dream Songs*, by John Berryman)

Ashbery is the first major contemporary poet to advance the autobiographical mode beyond John Berryman. The theory of the self-portrait advanced by Ashbery's poem has special relevance to both Berryman's *Dream Songs* and Lowell's *Notebook*. Berryman's single aspiration (avowedly emulated by Lowell), from *Homage to Mistress Bradstreet* to *The Dream Songs*, was to provide a map of the "whole dream-life" by producing an all-inclusive succession of sketches, miniature self-portraits. Neither Berryman nor Lowell seemed to entertain, even in passing, Ashbery's tenet that to embrace the whole of reality, you must know what to leave out, or, in the words of a contemporary much closer to Ashbery in spirit—as well as in age—A. R. Ammons, "how much revelation concealment necessitates."

John Berryman tried to surmount the built-in limitations of the confessional mode by inventing Henry, a disguised autobiographical persona. Henry, Berryman's grand metaphor for illuminating the self, operated as a mirror wherein the poet's dream-life transfigured and disguised the pedestrian data of his personality and day-to-day experiences. For Ashbery, the true story of our lives is to be sought in disclosures of enigmas in the self. They must be gently coaxed to reveal themselves, obliquely. The enigmas in our being are at the core of our identity. We do not know what they are, since we cannot encounter them directly, but we may hope to *reflect* them in the "accumulating mirror" of a poem which assembles chains of "fertile thought associations" that are spontaneously generated in a trance of creative reverie. Francesco Parmigianino studied his face in the convex mirror and copied with infinite care the details precisely distorted

there—the distortions, by indirection, captured the nuances, over-
tones, shades, the play of lights and shadows, of his continually shift-
ing dream-life. Hence, the self-portrait is an even truer likeness of the
inner man than of the exterior man, the physiognomy of his cor-
poreal face a fleshly mask for the interior mythic face lurking under
the surface of skin and bones. The visible face is the disguise, veiling
the invisible face which flares out—by flashes and glints—at the ex-
terior feature's margins, curves, edges, arcs, contours. All the por-
trait's borders—the alternating bumps and hollows, rises and
valleys—shimmer with hints of the other face lurking beneath, the
enigmatic face of our otherness.

Ashbery sets out to imitate Parmigianino's method in this broad
canvas, but he can share the painter's mirror for a limited time only;
then he must improvise an equivalent convex mirror of his own.
What, finally, is to be Ashbery's mirror? To begin with, he doesn't
know. I read the opening pages of this poem as Ashbery's quest for a
viable substitute for Parmigianino's mirror.

The author, who sets out to paint his own self-portrait in words, has
gotten himself calculatedly sidetracked. His method is to be one of
obliqueness, indirection. At first, he will assiduously ignore his own
person, his own country, his own century, giving his whole "moment
of attention" to the self-exploration of another man. Ashbery, who
dramatizes himself as Francesco's heir and apprentice in the contem-
porary world, is an ideal collaborator with the artist. He would give
himself up absolutely to the ancestor, soaking up every droplet of his
vision of the world, which, in Francesco's case, is found to be con-
tained in his visionary portrait of himself. Ashbery adopts the role of a
spiritual anemiac receiving a blood transfusion from his donor. When
he first wakens, however briefly, from the trance, the haze slowly
unblurs, and he finds that he has begun to see the world as if through
the painter's eyes, to touch objects as if with the other man's sensory
receptors, and he is flung into a dizzying new grasp of himself:

> The balloon pops, the attention
> Turns dully away. Clouds
> In the puddle stir up into sawtoothed fragments.
> I think of the friends
> Who came to see me, of what yesterday
> Was like. A peculiar slant
> Of memory that intrudes on the dreaming model
> In the silence of the studio as he considers
> Lifting the pencil to the self-portrait.
> How many people came and stayed a certain time,
> Uttered light or dark speech that became part of you

Like light behind windblown fog and sand,
Filtered and influenced by it, until no part
Remains that is surely you. Those voices in the dusk
Have told you all and still the tale goes on
In the form of memories deposited in irregular
Clumps of crystals. Whose curved hand controls,
Francesco, the turning seasons and the thoughts
That peel off and fly away at breathless speeds
Like the last stubborn leaves ripped
From wet branches? I see in this only the chaos
Of your round mirror which organizes everything
Around the polestar of your eyes which are empty,
Know nothing, dream but reveal nothing.
I feel the carousel starting slowly
And going faster and faster: desk, papers, books,
Photographs of friends, the window and the trees
Merging in one neutral band that surrounds
Me on all sides, everywhere I look.
And I cannot explain the action of leveling,
Why it should all boil down to one
Uniform substance, a magma of interiors.

"Clouds in the puddle," recent events in his own day-to-day life, had fallen into abeyance—held in suspension, while he gave himself up to his mentor's vision. Now he finds himself seesawing from past to present, his center of perception shifting from the mind of the portrait to the mind of the poem:

My guide in these matters is your self,
Firm, oblique, accepting everything with the same
Wraith of a smile, and as time speeds up so that it is soon
Much later, I can know only the straight way out,
The distance between us.

As the poem's drama unfolds, Ashbery learns to mediate with force and mastery between the two uniquely differentiated intelligences—that of painting, that of poetry—and he cross-breeds a hybrid aesthetic, a novel coupling of plastic and verbal arts; moreover, he draws lavishly, if secretively, upon the art of cinematography in molding this long poem's architecture.

Memory, then, is to be the poet's mirror. As Ashbery tries to make out the details of his identity reflected in the mirror, he finds he cannot look at himself directly. No man can look squarely into his own eyes. He must behold his image by glancing a little to one side of the present. The minimal remove of day-old memories will suffice: for

Ashbery, this time-shunt constitutes the mirror's slight convexity. The creation of our self-image from residues and fragments of memory is a process that goes on of itself continually in our dream-life, and for the poem to take a hand in this process that is preponderantly controlled and guided by the forces of necessity in our otherness, our subconscious psyches, is for the poem to become allied to profound depths of mind which operate in a dimension outside our individual wills, egos, or personalities. "Sawtoothed fragments" suggests that the jigsaw clusters of recent memory return to full consciousness with a supernatural clarity and conciseness, the margins around each fragment shimmering with fresh meaning and nuance; each fragment, returned from forgetting, is strangely altered by its incubation and fertilization in our dreamscape. The stark particularity of detail in each is amazing. "Sawtoothed edges" denotes a precision of unmistakable clean outlines, both in remembered events and in meanings laden in each vessel of fact. The payloads of significance and private insight carried by each fragment burst open as we take them up and place them in the lines of the poem for inspection, "memories deposited in irregular clumps of crystals." To investigate these "clumps of crystals" is to discover that the artist can proceed to explore the living substance of his experience—at one memory remove—with all the authority and surety of touch, the exactitudes born of *necessity*, that we ordinarily ascribe, say, to the professional chemist in the laboratory.

As we recall, the longest autobiographical poem in Ashbery's previous collection of poems was entitled "Fragment," the most accomplished work in a continuing cycle of poems advancing Ashbery's remarkable theory that our wholeness of self can be assembled and contained in a poem by isolating a single fragment of our lives, a living sample evoking the whole life of which it is the emblem. What is included resonates with what is left out to suggest the wholeness of being incarnated in our most characteristic human gestures and speech patterns. Or by inspecting a freely scattered assortment of fragments selected from a few hours—or days—of a life, gradually, the continuity of the whole inner life is added up and, at some unexpected, chance moment in the trance of composition, emerges complete. We cannot trace, clearly, any conventional ascension toward climax and denouement in the poem's drama, since the form operates as a monochromatic linear chain, modeled after the mode of the atonal twelve-tone scale in music. The form does not peak, but slowly accumulates epiphanies, all of about the same weight and mild radiance, all the fragments of experience flattened to the same common denominator of equalizing value; then, puzzlingly, the poem's finish occurs as an unexpected fulfillment, rising suddenly from within—surfacing, weightless and free, like a cork bobbing at the top of a pool—at an unanticipated moment. We inexplicably know that it feels like arrival, or fulfillment, so we surmise that must be what it is.

How shatteringly difficult it is to take an undistorted and non-habituated look at the self, to see with a fresh, unbiased eye, divested of conditioned response, the naked likeness of *the person me*. The poem's first shunted moment of turning to look—as if in a truck's right-hand side-mirror that one hadn't noticed before—at the private life of the author takes a reader by surprise:

> I think of the friends
> Who came to see me, of what yesterday
> Was like. A peculiar slant
> Of memory that intrudes on the dreaming model
> In the silence of the studio as he considers
> Lifting the pencil to the self-portrait.

To re-enter the cryptic and foreign mental environment of the five-hundred-year-old painter was an effortlessly simple task, so eager was Francesco Parmigianino to welcome Ashbery into the cosmos of his vision. But to look back into his own day-old memoryscape, the so-called familiar mental environment, is to be engulfed in dizzying perplexities. Ashbery takes the first gingerly, sidelong look at himself with a "painter's deep mistrust" of the probity of all that he sees. Like a photographer experimenting with a quirky new model of camera, he refuses to trust the actuality of any scene to be represented by, or synchronized with, the picture that meets his eyes. He knows that no matter how short the time lapse, memory distorts, as does Parmigianino's convex mirror, and he must train himself to translate with fidelity into the lines of his word portrait the images and ideas filtered to his explorative reverie by "a peculiar slant of memory."

It is all but impossible to locate in the exact phrasing and rhythms the technical means whereby the tempo of the poem creates a hushed urgency of quiet, enveloping these first lines that advance, haltingly, into the life events of the poet. The power of Ashbery's restraint in holding back from speaking out directly of himself and his friends until he is assured of the necessary tone and accents of plain speech evokes for readers the miracle of awakening. We encounter the usual everyday events, nothing out of the ordinary, and find all possible strangeness and mystery therein. It is all the magical novelty of first-look-taking, first glancings about in the moments of slow awakening from a deep sleep: transparencies, lucidities, mysteries are everyplace he looks. With X-ray wizardry, he finds he can look clean through his own day-old skull, posed in trance of remembering. His remarkable disembodied eye sees piercingly into the head from which it has eerily strayed, wandered, irradiating his own brain of a "dreaming model/in the silence of the studio as he considers/ lifting the pencil to the self-portrait." The self is instantly reborn, transfigured. To Ashbery's newly acquired mode and organ of sight—the transplanted eye of the past—it appears to be a strange, unfamiliar cosmos, an interior land-scape of enigmas. His amazement is signaled by the emergence of naïveté, the asking of questions of the most radical innocence and artlessness:

> How many people came and stayed a certain time,
> Uttered light or dark speech that became part of you
> Like light behind windblown fog and sand,
> Filtered and influenced by it, until no part
> Remains that is surely you. Those voices in the dusk
> Have told you all and still the tale goes on
> In the form of memories deposited in irregular
> Clumps of crystals. Whose curved hand controls,
> Francesco, the turning seasons and the thoughts
> That peel off and fly away at breathless speeds
> Like the last stubborn leaves ripped
> From wet branches?

As Ashbery views the flickerings of his self-image in the mirror of day-old memory, of "yesterday," his reflection—variegated with stun-ning facets of jeweled transparencies—displays all supposedly ousted lives in the world outside the solipsist-poet, other people and nature, which, by an odd reversal of mirror images, are now declared to be all that is most valuable and enduringly serious to this poet. The self, then, is filtered through memory, wherein it is demonstrated to have under-gone metamorphosis into a repository which receives and selects and assimilates—as by osmosis—the voices of other lives that touch our sensorium. Human memory, in itself, is revealed to be a marvelous organ covered with the mental equivalent of thousands of sense re-ceptors working strenuously to *program* all of the wonderful human impressions of each day into the self's memory bank ("a magma of interiors"). The seat of the poet's identity, allowing for its own total conversion into the world of received impressions, has attained the elevated spiritual plane in which mere private wishes and agonies have been purged, flushed out of the self to give place to the superior marvelous inrush of radiant other lives. *They* suddenly come to com-prise the foreground of Ashbery's self-portrait, since they have been reconstituted by memory into integral fragments of his composite self:

> I feel the carousel starting slowly
> And going faster and faster: desk, papers, books,

Photographs of friends, the window and the trees
Merging in one neutral band that surrounds
Me on all sides, everywhere I look.
And I cannot explain the action of leveling,
Why it should all boil down to one
Uniform substance, a magma of interiors.

*

Only now, and never before this moment in his career, shall
Ashbery have been ready to find voice to speak the portrait of himself.
Following his many years of withdrawal and seclusion, a period of
slow mellowing, this exactly appointed occasion has been granted to
him. A reader feels he can bodily sense an immense weight lifting, as
if Ashbery has been relieved, suddenly, of the burden of guilt and
bewilderment of two decades of self-imposed ostracism to which his
choice of direction as artist (guided by inner necessity, but no less a
willed and earned choice for that) had condemned him, years of
lonely waiting to connect with a viable audience, and to expedite
human good fellowship with a widespread community of readers.
From the years of apostleship to Wallace Stevens' "High Renaissance"
art—eventuating in early mastery of his own distinctive idiom—to his
most recent triumphs, he repeatedly had sought to be reassured that
his solipsistic pose was not destined to confine him to a permanent rift
of alienation from the human community. How could he have for-
given himself if he should awaken one day—in late career—to find
that he'd sold himself a phony aesthetic bill of lading, and carried an
artificial freight of loneliness; that the "brilliant contraption" of his
poem (as a recent critic has pejoratively dubbed it) was destined to
mature into a piece of elegant superior machinery, eternally useless to
others except as an expensive hand-crafted rarefied curiosity item,
hollow at the core; and that his grim isolationist ars poesy and
obscurantism had been, at bottom, no more than a defensive strategy
of revenge provoked by a hostile readership, and hence a self-
betrayal, an act of unconscious high treason against his mission and
calling, the back-bending toil of his chosen trade and all-demanding
"task of vision," as voiced in the fatally eloquent prophecy of his
recent chilling poem, "Fear of Death":

>   . . . fear of growing old
> Alone, and of finding no one at the evening end
> Of the path except another myself

> Nodding a curt greeting: "Well, you've been awhile
> But now we're back together, which is what counts."

These fears of inured and irreversible disaffiliation from the larger human community are transferred, by emotional sublimation, to Ashbery's characterization of Francesco in the opening pages of *Self-Portrait* as a spiritual amputee, a victim of insular metaphysics:

> The soul has to stay where it is,
> Even though restless . . . It must stay
> Posing in this place. It must move
> As little as possible. This is what the portrait says.

Thus, the shock of unanticipated early triumph in the poem's second movement. Ashbery discovers, as he *crests* into mid-career, that he can now join the human community as a full-fledged citizen bearing prodigal gifts of his advanced civilization. What emerges here is the revelation that the years of steadfastness, the unremitting fidelity to his isolationist personal ethic, provided the scaffolding for a compassionately humane artistry.

How much it has cost this author to reach the point in his art at which he can openly give voice to the astonishing enigmas hidden in the plainest everyday exchanges with friends, just as he readies himself—in poised restraint of language—to articulate a discovery that has perhaps been building toward codification in his mature work for years. His self-enchantment, though it grew into a near-perfect solipsism, shocked even its author by exploding, finally, into a disguised mode of embracing the entire human community which he had consistently repulsed from the *surface* preoccupations of his art. His solipsism proved to be a mask worn by a deep and abiding compassionateness for others, which, in the concluding pages of this poem, grows into a messianic passion to change the whole face of his culture, and indeed, to initiate a cultural revolution by a revolutionizing of his poetics. He advances the creed—recalling Ezra Pound at his early best—that potent changes in language arts will germinate matching changes in the whole fabric of our country's mass sensibility, from the ground of common speech up, and thereby revive the nation's capacity to embrace its mission and stand up to shoulder its full burden of the collective dream-life of unbroken civilization, the harvest of thousands of years of accumulating health of spirit which floods into our present homeland today, and on through us into the future, whether or not we train ourselves to find and fill our best potential niche in the unstoppable creative evolution of mankind:

> It is civilization that counts, after all, they seem
> To be saying [generations of the dead],
>   and we are as much a part of it as anybody else
> Only we think less about it, even not at all . . . until some
> Fool comes shouting into the forest at nightfall

News of some thing we know and care little of
As the distant castle rejoices to the joyous
Sound of hooves releasing rooks straight up into the faultless air
And meanwhile weighs its shadow ever heavier on the mirroring
Surface of the river, surrounding the little boat with three figures in it.
(from "Voyage in the Blue")

The single artist, to begin with, must discover and accomplish his own full "mansize quotient" in that ageless stream of acculturation, and thereby become a heroic model and guide for his age to emulate. Ashbery's vision of himself as quixotic gift-bearer and rescuer of the city-bound dreamless citizenry, first hinted at in this passage in "Voyage in the Blue," finally sweeps into the center of *Self-Portrait*'s drama. His integral self—swept clear of melodrama, the news-hawking debris of personality, all the detritus comprising the stock in trade of the confessional poets' school—converts to a map, a blueprint of this poet's United States, the myth of its people and culture. To read the book of his self, then, would be to engage the marvels of his friends' lives, as well as to unlock the riddles of America's mythos.

John Ashbery's central aspiration and triumph in this poem is to have sired a new species of self-portraiture, whereby the poet's portrayal of self—rivaling, say, the magazine cover photos of the aging W. H. Auden—shall reveal, enigmatically, the social and cultural topography of the life outside him. Every crease, groove, wrinkle, haunted gulley in the details of Auden's face grew to represent—as an emblem represents—major crises, setbacks, and advances for the human spirit in the historical moment of his age. The intense soaring life of the man's soul etched the disgraces and glories of his epoch in the geography of his face. Ashbery has invented a mode of autobiographical poem which carves into the details of its stylistic lineaments, and engraves upon the architectural contours of its form, a towering Audenesque visage.

*

As in the great passages of delicate first touchings upon the pulse of the mystery in the best novels and stories of Henry James, passages that have been slowly ripened over a wide expanse of fastidiously crafted nuances and rhythms, we note the remarkable succession of attunements by which Ashbery harmonizes and blends his art medium to predispose it for the drama that is to follow. He instills the language, as it slowly collects in the work's spacious mold, with a timbre of heightened alertness, a power of intensest listening held firm over a wide sweep of purely visceral writing: the linings of viscera and intestinal walls of language, in place of the customary shell of skins, are everywhere exposed and given voice—"a visible core." A prolonged wave of musical resonances and overtones, of an aural magnitude that can be produced only by the most refined and exquisitely tuned poetic instruments, slowly accumulates. We can feel the excitement of one embarking on a unique new species of human adventure shuddering in the sinews of the lines, lines which will dare to anatomize—to surgically dissect—the tissues of our dreaming process. Ashbery makes forced entry into "the dreaming model's" formative chain of consciousness, exposing through his incision into the body of the dream the miraculous process of transmutation of self into bits and pieces of experience of the world which have invaded his utterly naked and vulnerable sensibility:

> How many people came and stayed a certain time,
> Uttered light or dark speech that became part of you
> Like light behind windblown fog and sand,
> Filtered and influenced by it, until no part
> Remains that is surely you. Those voices in the dusk
> Have told you all and still the tale goes on
> In the form of memories deposited in irregular
> Clumps of crystals.

Musing over these lines, dreaming my slow drift of reader indolence lazingly into them, the only way I know to come into possession of their gift of meaning, I'm reminded that Ashbery—as one other commentator has observed publicly before me—is a man who is exploring "places where no one has ever been." While others clearly have experienced these psychic transformations, no other writer of my acquaintance has ever been able to locate, anatomize, and profoundly articulate this process that occurs just near enough to our full waking consciousness to seem familiar, hovering at the subliminal thresholds of ordinary pedestrian awareness, but too commonplace to appear to merit the serious and persevering attention Ashbery has given it; it is far enough away to both elude our grasp and trick the mind, by the many disguises it wears, into thinking it has already been perfectly apprehended many times before. After all, the dreaming goes on in us in one form or another at all times—waking, sleeping, or wakeful sleep—so of course we must know all about it by now, though we suppose we have assimilated the wisdom so completely we've forgotten the difficult first steps we took, stumblingly, as in learning to walk or talk. Thus, we absently go about deceiving ourselves in a haze of blind know-it-all-ness about a central experience of our cerebration.

   Observe with Ashbery the remarkable steps in the process of inundation and transmutation of self. At first, he follows the guidelines of his mentor, Francesco Parmigianino:

> I see in this only the chaos
> Of your round mirror which organizes everything
> Around the polestar of your eyes which are empty,
> Know nothing, dream but reveal nothing.

(1) He empties himself of all private emotions and cherished ideas, completely disencumbering his psyche of the trappings and furnishings of ego.

(2) He opens himself to an unstoppable flood of daily occurrences, welcoming the inundation of his psyche by chance events, rushing in to fill the void left by the evicted personality: the voices of his friends, sinking into his exposed and perfectly impressionable sensory apparatus, merge with the substance of their container ("became part of you").

(3) Two distinct elements—the poet's sensibility ("windblown fog and sand"), the friends' voices ("light")—interact, as in a chemistry laboratory, resulting in the test-tube disintegration of the form of each, followed by fusion into a new compound element, an alloy of the two original ingredients ("no part/ remains that is surely you").

(4) The resultant compound is very hardy, durable, and may be stored indefinitely—though consciously forgotten—in the memory bank ("memories deposited in irregular/ clumps of crystals").

All this is a life process, not an art process yet, antedating by whatever time-lapse the taking up again of the "clumps" which insulate and protect the memory deposits, letting them play out their second growth in the word shapes of a poem:

> Those voices in the dusk
> Have told you all and still the tale goes on . . .

The imbibed samples are found to contain all of reality, so to have swallowed them is to be inhabited by the whole truth of our existence today. It is to embrace the best life in the world outside us in ideal forms deposited within us ("we shall be inhabited/ in the old way, as ideal things came to us"). But though we have been told everything that can be known by those voices that fill us, nothing of our essential reality having been left out, or left unrecorded by our interior memory-computer, this supreme vision of reality will remain the sole purchase and profit of a recluse, a hermit-solipsist, unless it is projected into a poem's metaphor in which readers may be included, find its life, and share its communion. The artist's relentless self-discipline, realized first as a living process of ingesting the world and transmuting it into the self, is subsequently translated by no less rigorous and scrupulous a discipline into the human community of the poem's form.

When the poet returns to the memory deposits in the act of composition, they become resolved once more, breaking up into new constituent elements, now issuing forth as layers and layers of thought associations that are peeled off the clusters of memory and snatched—grabbed on the fly, so to speak—by the poet/maker's hand as he crafts them swiftly into the unfolding images and details of the poem:

> Whose curved hand controls,
> Francesco, the turning seasons and the thoughts
> That peel off and fly away at breathless speeds
> Like the last stubborn leaves ripped
> From wet branches?

To cope with this new aesthetic, Ashbery must become very adept at adjusting the poetry's pace to synchronize words, images, and lines of verse to abrupt changes of tempo in the release of ideas from exploded memory clumps. The process is evidently close to the watercolorist's art, the color flow of ideas speeding up and slowing down and seeping into the canvas as the density of the fluid base varies from thin to thick.

The forces of nature partook of the voices that invaded the poet's psyche, inhabited his mental life, and were finally transmuted into never-to-be-regurgitated parts of himself, crystalline memory deposits. The voices were carried inside him on twilight currents, taken into the mind's climate as if clothed in a seasonal attire. Since the speech of his friends was drenched in nature, the seasonal cycles embedded in their accents, his stream of ideas feeding out into the lines of verse during the creation of a poem—a discharge from the voices preserved and stored in "clumps of crystals"—emerges, trailing the winds and gray light, thought garbed in the dusky climate of its source. The idea chains are borne aloft upon the same wind that delivered them to the poet. In this vision, ideas sweep into the poet's mental orbit on the wind, spilling out of nature into mind. His ideas travel on the puffs and gusts like leaves, stir up, churn around in a whirlpool, then die out as the breeze dies. When the ideas slacken and wane, they resemble leaves that have grown "diluted, bleached":

> The fertile
> Thought-associations that until now came
> So easily, appear no more, or rarely. Their
> Colorings are less intense, washed out
> By autumn rains and winds, spoiled, muddied . . .

Perhaps this tracing of the steps in Ashbery's creative process may account for his remarkable ingenuity of exhibiting ideas in his new poetry as *a form of nature,* as if ideas are themselves endowed with biological properties: chemical make-up, geological density, or geographical topography. They are "windblown fog and sand," they are "irregular clumps of crystals," they are "last stubborn leaves ripped/ from wet branches"—they are anything but just ideas. Our free flow of thought associations soaks up the passing events, mingles them with memory images, pictures. This idea flux draws constituents into its labyrinth from all sources, human and terrestrial, present and past. The voltage of feeling running through the charged network of ideas is the form of energy that sustains the mind of this poem's to and fro swervings between yesterday and today.

III

Two central questions are interlaced through seams of the poem's developing argument and drama: (1) What is today, and how large is today's promise? (2) How grand and sweeping are the possibilities of the artist's medium, and what are the limits of pure medium—of form and style, in and of itself? In the third movement, Ashbery sees these two dimensions—the size of the present, the capacities of his medium—as rival factions, each competing for a larger share of his best energies; and, despite the suggestion of a hostile relation between them, clearly, too, some mutual interdependency between his art mode and his social milieu is operating. But at this stage of the drama, it is conceded that the claims upon his human energies made by the medium are superior, a higher priority, while the rival claims made by today—by the life of his own age, country, human community—may have to be forgone, or held in abeyance for an indefinite pause in his career, to insure that "the even stronger possibilities" of his medium "can remain/ whole without being tested." Evidently, Ashbery feels that he must attain a full measure of authority and imperial stature for his canvas, and reach the far point in his vision of insuring utmost credence—a preponderance of faith—in the body of his art mode to hold its own against his age's monolithic indifference to artists and their enterprise.

Following his years of service as executive editor of *Art News* (1965-72), it is not surprising that Ashbery's aesthetic canons are tempered by the professional art critic's inveterate suspiciousness of standards, trends, prevailing fashions, with strong predilections for standards of austerity and elegance derived from the timeless classics. It appears that Ashbery's skeptical bent of mind spreads from the art world to every other sector of contemporary life. Hence, the circuitous and roundabout tactics by which he maneuvers into position to grapple with his own life in the present age. Following elaborate rituals of delay and postponement, he approaches the grand moments of headlong encounter with today—for Ashbery, this is evidently the most difficult and unnatural direction for the art of the poem to pursue, and, as such, the most arduous challenge for the author to undertake. By a succession of exquisite shifts of stance, Ashbery negotiates his passage through the "long corridor" of vision ("the 'poetic' straw-colored space") from Parmigianino's painting back to the present day, a voyage beset with snares, hazards, traps which must be circumvented by the most delicate maneuvers. Ashbery finds that to accomplish his own unique rapprochement with the present, he must improvise the most exacting strategy of feints and passes, rearguard checks and balances. The peaceable iconoclast braces himself to advance into a revolutionary vanguard.

John Ashbery's mission, awakening him to the necessity of taking an increasing role in public life, has driven him from the comfortable sanctuary of the dream. He has recognized himself to be one of a dwindling handful of spokesmen who can accurately elucidate the special quarrels of today's artist with his culture, and one of the indispensable few who can lead a vanguard to surmount the near-insuperable obstacles to a towering visionary career carried to its limits. He must, *of necessity* (the divinity and muse who guides his craft, his task of vision), come to terms with his today, meeting his hostile milieu on the adversary's own home ground to invite revolutionary search and inquiry on both sides. That is his honorable quest.

In the previous movement, Ashbery re-envisaged his human identity. His mythic face, discovered to be the real seat of his identity, had been submerged by his known—deceptively familiar—human face. Consequently, he wedded himself to the unknown mask of his otherness lurking behind the features, or lineaments, of his visible and public face. In this movement, he advances across immense distance in the field of the dream to encounter, obliquely, the world of the present. Firmly anchored in the past and his art medium, he takes his first hesitant steps, preliminary gropings, toward the great stranger, the most cryptic foreign country, the enigma of enigmas, the unknown—and perhaps gravely unknowable—here and now:

> Tomorrow is easy, but today is uncharted,
> Desolate, reluctant as any landscape
> To yield what are laws of perspective
> After all only to the painter's deep
> Mistrust, a weak instrument though
> Necessary.

The painstakingly difficult years of nurturing and refining his "deep mistrust," that "weak instrument," have provided Ashbery with the austere discipline necessary to strip away the familiar bland face of today and search out the hidden mask, the mythic reality. The visible face of the present is the disguise, the invisible mask the reality, "uncharted, desolate." Ashbery's unyielding skepticism, a tool first cultivated in his development of new modes of writing, now turns its obdurate, cool sights upon human society. Perhaps the unyielding landscape of the present has met its match, an artist's eye, unflinching, that has stared into the bottomless abyss of the dream-pit, without deviation, without deflection, and will address itself to the landscape of the present with the same unwavering steadfastness, thereby restoring to our day its lost magic, its lost other face.

Two landscapes are polarized—today, the field of the dream. The poet must live in both, by turns, and must discover the "laws of perspective" in each. Despite our time's lacks, an artist can find privacy in seclusion ("today enough of a cover burnishes"). This safeguard gives him fortitude to risk brief forays, attacks against the city's fortress of indifference. His first incursions upon the battlements of the present are promptly repulsed, and as Ashbery recoils from his collisions with the walls of the city fortress, it is his pain of exile—a mild irony and bitterness—that is released, articulated. For now, the only virtue he will attribute to today's climate is that the landscape affords the artist sanctuary in which to hide.

Following brief interludes, side trips out into the city's "jungle," the poet returns promptly to the homestead of his medium, where his "house is built in tomorrow":

> Some day we will try
> To do as many things as are possible
> And perhaps we shall succeed at a handful
> Of them, but this will not have anything
> To do with what is promised today, our
> Landscape sweeping out from us to disappear
> On the horizon. Today enough of a cover burnishes
> To keep the supposition of promises together
> In one piece of surface, letting one ramble
> Back home from them so that these
> Even stronger possibilities can remain
> Whole without being tested.

The poet allows himself to be pulled two ways. As he vacillates between cityscape and poemscape, the radius of oscillations—narrow at first—slowly widens, and each return to home ground results in fresh insights about the remarkable elasticity and boundlessness of his chosen medium, form, mode. By a succession of grand illuminating metaphors, at graduated moments in the poem's cyclic progression—disguisedly cyclic, despite Ashbery's counter-romantic thrust for a monochromatic serial layout—he defines the invincibility and amazing comprehensiveness of his medium.

> (1) I feel the carousel starting slowly
>   And going faster and faster: desk, papers, books,
>   Photographs of friends, the window and the trees
>   Merging in one neutral band that surrounds
>   Me on all sides, everywhere I look.
>   And I cannot explain the action of levelling,
>   Why it should all boil down to one
>   Uniform substance, a magma of interiors:

The medium is a perfect solvent. All phenomena, solutes that can be dissolved in the one solution, are reduced swiftly to "one/ uniform substance."

> (2) The skin of the bubble-chamber's as tough as
>   Reptile eggs; everything gets "programmed" there
>   In due course: more keeps getting included
>   Without adding to the sum:

The medium is a bottomless container. It is limitlessly inflatable. Also, it is unshatterable. Everything in it connects to everything else in unbreakable chains: the process of branchings—from image to image, idea to idea—is perfectly continuous.

> (3) So the room contains this flow like an hourglass
>   Without varying in climate or quality
>   (Except perhaps to brighten bleakly and almost
>   Invisibly, in a focus sharpening toward death—more
>   Of this later):

The medium is a timeless zone, seasonless. It creates its own special unwavering climate, its own time-count. It triumphs over the seasonal cycles, but as the parenthesis explains, it does not quite triumph over death; however, it postpones death, and numbs death's sting by spreading it out, distributing it evenly to all points of the vast surface. (Ironically, Ashbery's observations about the nature of death in the timeless visionary world of art are given only casual notice, here, in a parenthesis. Did he forget this aside? He never picks up the thread, overtly, for which a reader may hunt in vain; rather, the poem's whole finale—the symphonic last movement of seven pages—dramatizes the "focus sharpening toward death" in immortal art.)

(4)   What should be the vacuum of a dream
        Becomes continually replete as the source of dreams
        Is being tapped so that this one dream
        May wax, flourish like a cabbage rose,
        Defying sumptuary laws, leaving us
        To awake and try to begin living in what
        Has now become a slum:

The medium is prodigal in abundance. Its resources are inexhaustible.

In this anticipatory passage, oddly linking the art medium with contemporary society, the self-portraitist first hints at the character of today. It is a landscape of desolation. Cityscape is depicted as the mirror-opposite of poemscape, or dreamscape. In this vision, the artwork has a grotesque monopoly on the world of dreams. The artist maintains a stranglehold on the dream-market, while the modern city languishes in destitution of dream-bankruptcy. The metaphor which defines the schism between art and life today shrewdly translates the variables of the imagination into those of economics and marketing ("defying sumptuary laws"), an index of human shortages of food and housing. The city's plight, today, is one of depletion of natural resources. While ecologists try to salvage and conserve the dwindling remains of environmental assets, Ashbery registers the dearth of imaginative assets, the paucity of dreams, a central and indispensable human resource whose steady diminution has passed unnoticed. No other resource has been so heedlessly squandered. To our technological age's calipers, the national treasure of dreams had seemed "inconsequential until one day/ we notice the hole they left." To Ashbery, the economic and residential slum is a facade behind which looms a cultural slum, the strip-mined landscape of the spirit. Every form of human waste has become a stigma of public shame, the outcry for its restitution a cue for civic pride, except the despoilment of our dream-life. This peculiar imbalance—the absolute discrepancy between owning up to loss of resources for technology and the failure to own up to loss of resources for the country's health of imagination—is unique to our own bizarre moment in history. It is a freakish condition, the body of our American dream mutilated, but we maintain a false pose of enlightenment. Ashbery's poem holds a mirror up to this least-recognized form of squandered national treasure. His aspiration and compulsion in his art—even in those passages which turn aside, face away in dazed abhorrence from these conditions—is to create an interior cosmos which will provide an antidote to the disease of the culture.

No other poet of our day has so profoundly mirrored and illumi-
nated our time's duplicities, evasions, apostasies—the outright
fraudulence of its neglect of resources of America's dream-life, rang-
ing from the mecca of the fine arts to pop art, and finally, to play-
grounds for children ("'Play' is something else;/ It exists, in a society
specifically/ Organized as a demonstration of itself"). No other poet
has struggled so unremittingly to create in the body of the poem a
cosmos strong enough to resist and massively conteract the perils, the
"urgency," of our anti-cultural climate. If the dream-centers of the
city have gone bankrupt, those of the artist's medium rage for a
radical and uncompromising aesthetic of self-replenishment. Ashbery
is creating a medium which both exhibits by its craft and elucidates by
the marvelous labyrinth of its intellectual content and dramatic struc-
ture the inexhaustibility of its dream-resources, the gorgeous foun-
taining of fresh images and novel ideas begotten in the poet by the
cross-fertilizing of his own imagination with "dreams and inspira-
tions" delivered to him on waves generated, periodically, by Par-
migianino's painting:

> This past
> Is now here: the painter's
> Reflected face, in which we linger, receiving
> Dreams and inspirations on an unassigned
> Frequency.

The wellspring of the past—gushing into the present—continually
re-stocks Ashbery's dream-reservoir, creating, for a time, the illusion
of infinite bounty. His art medium militates against the depletion of
its resources, to perpetuity, by improvising a mode of delivery that
simulates perpetual motion, the poem's structural machinery imitat-
ing a perpetuum mobile.

In earlier books of verse, Ashbery had devised similar contraptions,
most notably "Clepsydra," a work of near-perfect symmetries. The
earlier masterpiece brought to culmination Ashbery's slow-building
prepossession, persisting from early career, for producing forms that
achieved a semblance of ideal beauty, coupled with a variety of con-
tents that oddly resisted their author's emotional involvement; taken
together, they attested, rather, to his emotional withdrawal from the
materials of his art. At its most extreme, this tendency grew into a
tonal ambience of utmost disaffection from the solid quantities lifted
from human experience and spliced—or welded—into the serial chain
of the poem's scrupulously architected layout. "Clepsydra" achieved a
chilled, test-tube perfection. Ashbery might well have recalled the
icy solipsisms of "Clepsydra" when he finally repudiated the aesthetic

of Parmigianino's self-portrait, which he perhaps identified with the
fastidious exotica of the earlier period in his own career:

> Once it seemed so perfect—gloss on the fine
> Freckled skin, lips moistened as though about to part
> Releasing speech, and the familiar look
> Of clothes and furniture that one forgets.
> This could have been our paradise: exotic
> Refuge within an exhausted world.

In "Clepsydra," Ashbery's refining of exquisite symmetries of his
waterwheel—the poem's single inclusive metaphor—was the highest
priority of his craft, and perhaps the only one to which he felt he
owed a complete allegiance.

But in *Self-Portrait*, Ashbery forecloses irrevocably on the mortgage
to an *ars poetica* which conceives the poem as an "exotic refuge," and
advances to an aesthetic which carries a full burden of mirroring the
age's ills. His new art mode achieves a powerful re-engagement with
the human community. The poem is viewed as a vast storehouse of
squandered dreams, conserving the magnitude of all useless things—
rejects, dream things, play things—in a commodious reservoir which
salvages the wasted provisions of the community's neglect. The poem
is a sentinel of our idle hours: idling along, it would instruct us in how
to use our spare time and free dreaming spaces. It would re-focus our
monomaniacal consumer intelligence, our marketing supply-and-
demand obsessive mentality, lifting the mind and spirit out of the
desolation, the voids, left by excessive heedless consumptions, depre-
dations of irreplaceable raw materials. The poem would school the
mind in economics of the dream, the imagination's market, in which
supply is always equal to demand since the source of dreams is bound-
less. The poet has discovered a miracle of economics, and holds up an
ironic mirror to a culture which is rapidly exhausting its unearned
treasures, indispensable supplies depleted to inflate the synthetic bal-
loon of commodities, subsidies. The bluntly stated paradox of the
economics of the dream ("defying sumptuary laws, leaving us/ to
awake and try to begin living in what/ has now become a slum") makes
a mockery of the social milieu it mirrors, a milieu which has been
horribly victimized by ironclad edict of those very uncompromising
laws. The abrupt shock of awakening from paradise of art medium to
inferno of city slum suggests more than a hint of the world of dreams
taking vengeance upon the human community which has virtually
banished the artist-dreamers from the kingdom of municipal city-
states; and indeed, the revenge motif is elaborated in prophesied
dooms of the poem's final pages.

The poet—a perpetual traveler between inner and outer land-
scapes, the abrupt voyages resembling sudden awakenings from a
deep sleep—perfects the dreamscape of the poem's medium, only to
awaken to the bewildering contrast with the dreamless wasteland of
the cityscape, the "slum." He is helpless, perplexed, as he fumbles in
his preliminary attempts to mediate between the two worlds, to build a
viable bridge between the poem and the culture that ignores its
brother, its mirror, its "darkening opposite":

> No previous day would have been like this.
> I used to think they were all alike,
> That the present always looked the same to everybody
> But this confusion drains away as one
> Is always cresting into one's present.
> Yet the "poetic," straw-colored space
> Of the long corridor that leads back to the painting,
> Its darkening opposite—is this
> Some figment of "art," not to be imagined
> As real, let alone special? Hasn't it too its lair
> In the present we are always escaping from
> And falling back into, as the waterwheel of days
> Pursues its uneventful, even serene course?

For Parmigianino, there was "no way out of the problem of pathos vs.
experience," so he remained isolated in his hermitage. But Ashbery
ventures out into the public life, committed in dead earnest to finding
his own "man-size quotient" in the present day. Consequently, the last
pages of this poem are much preoccupied with evolving a conversion
table for extrapolating gains from the visionary dreamscape of the
poem into commensurate gains in the human community:

> Why be unhappy with this arrangement, since
> Dreams prolong us as they are absorbed?
> Something like living occurs, a movement
> Out of the dream into its codification.

Indeed, the arrangement had grown to be a thorn in the side of
Ashbery's earlier work, a source of frustration and unhappiness, since
the codification of the dream had been confined to the sealed-off
cubicle of the perfected art-gadget. But in Ashbery's advanced new
mode, he engineers periodic maneuvers, pilgrimages into the teeming
life of the city's techno-oligarchy ("a movement/ out of the dream"),
ruled by the machine and the business monopoly. If the exile in
poetry's elegant retreat, its exclusive devotion to preciosities of the
dream-machinery, acted formerly as a refuge unmanning the
dreamer, leaving him unfit to grapple with the machinery of today,
the present; now "codification" must extend from the poem's rarefied

beauties, its hothouse-flower art, to the everyday world. However, a viable interaction between artist and community must be re-negotiated if the codified dream of the poem is to "prolong" the poet's capacity for worldly living, as well as to enable him to revive and enhance the community's capacity for unworldly dreaming. This two-phased public mission is the essential new burden that the medium of Ashbery's poetry is required to carry in his new book, which contains a poem bearing the *not* ironic title, "The One Thing That Can Save America."

*

> New York
> Where I am now, which is a logarithm
> Of other cities. Our landscape
> Is alive with filiations, shuttlings;
> Business is carried on by look, gesture,
> Hearsay. It is another life to the city...

Ashbery declares his readiness, for the first time, to make his peace with today—the world of the present, and to come to terms with his own native city. Ashbery's New York is unique, as is the contemporary moment it inhabits. It is the world's central city, as Ashbery aspires to be the country's central poet. If New York is a "logarithm/ of other cities," past and present, Ashbery perceives himself to be a logarithm of other artists, his central poem ("the sample of everything as it/ may be imagined outside time... all, in the refined, assimilable state") the logarithm of other important artworks, of yesterday, of today. A logarithm is the *exponent* or *power* to which a number must be *raised* to produce a *given* number. The logarithm is a marvelously apt metaphor for illuminating the enigmas of the elusive today, the present, the "nondescript never-to-be-defined daytime," which—to Ashbery's surprise—is now incontestably revealed to be "the secret of where it takes place," both the technical process of drafting our art and the auxiliary process of sifting out of the countless layers of memory and personality that constitute a human self—the seat of identity—at any *given* moment, the materials, quantities, "sawtoothed fragments" of imagination that feed the poem's art. Both processes are found to be indissolubly anchored in today's spotlight, the present moment in history:

> On the surface of it
> There seems no special reason why...
> The city falling with its beautiful suburbs
> Into space always less clear, less defined,

> Should read as the support of its progress,
> The easel upon which the drama unfolded
> To its own satisfaction and to the end
> Of our dreaming, as we had never imagined
> It would end, in worn daylight . . .
> This nondescript, never-to-be-defined daytime is
> The secret of where it takes place.

The upshot of this revelation, this éclaircissement, for Ashbery's radical searching *ars poetica,* is that the poet must achieve a secure footing in the public daytime life, the garish, overexposed here and now, if his work is to achieve full stature, if indeed it is to become an aesthetic slide-rule which may calibrate the correct logarithms for transposing beautiful artworks—momentous historical events, in their age—from the past into the present light of day. The poet, likewise, will undergo metamorphosis into a logarithm, the one correct *exponent* to which an artist of the past—Parmigianino, say—must be *raised* to be resurrected in the present, today's dream-life.

Both the mathematical concept of the logarithm, and the language of today's exact science in which it is couched, signify the startling advances of this poem's art over Ashbery's earlier work in its commitment to "siphon off the life" of contemporary daily actualities, drawing intellectual and linguistic resources directly from the city's workaday world of business and technology. The artist in his studio must make his "lair" in the present, whether he fancies that today's climate welcomes him or not. He cannot function viably today if he is centered in a mythology cut off from contemporary raw materials in a dream-exile, or exiled dream-life. The artist's craft will dessicate, its roots shrivel up and waste away, without periodic fortification from the present light of day, however debased and repellent the current social and cultural milieu to his individual sensibility. For Ashbery, this realization has been perhaps more delayed than a proportionate coming to terms with the present in the work of most other American contemporaries.

*

To implement a stronger bond between poet and community, a new readership must be cultivated, trained by the poet to decipher the marvelous wave of a poem's form as it crests into the present, breaking on the rock of the poem's language:

> They [our dreams] seemed strange because we couldn't actually see
> them.
> And we realize this only at a point where they lapse

Like a wave breaking on a rock, giving up
Its shape in a gesture that expresses that shape.

Disciplined readers, readers with visionary second sight of their own, will be gifted with the perceptivity to decode the accumulated pressure of dreams that fed the wave, rose with it out of the great sea of our sleeping being, and burst, collapsing into the luxuriant shape that became the form of the poem. The good reader, decodifying the dreams reversed in the mirror of the poem's wavelike structure, rescues the dream's shape from the form that expresses it. This reader-writer interchange, a creative process which complements the poet's act of composition, would serve as a conduit for tunneling the stream of dream-associations back into the imaginative life of the community.

All distortions of the poem's style—whether discords of music and rhythm, or exaggerations of pictorial detail—are aspects of caricature fashioned to capture the dream's shape, to translate invisible dream realities into public visible forms:

Sydney Freedberg in his
Parmigianino says of it: "Realism in this portrait
No longer produces an objective truth, but a *bizarria* . . . .
However its distortion does not create
A feeling of disharmony. . . . The forms retain
A strong measure of ideal beauty," because
Fed by our dreams, so inconsequential until one day
We notice the hole they left. Now their importance
If not their meaning is plain. They were to nourish
A dream which includes them all, as they are
Finally reversed in the accumulating mirror.

The poet profoundly trusts the forms—however bizarre or exaggerated—which ideas and images instinctively take in the poem's wavelike structure, since he trusts the serial chain of dream-images, arriving on an "unassigned frequency," to declare their own shapes, to express their own hidden gestures through the patterning and molding of lines. These images, telegraphed as by radar from past to present, are delivered on dream-currents flowing directly from the poet's excursions into the copious flux of personal memory. The poem's form is all surface. Hence, the *surficial* poem—like a seismograph rendering visible on a flattened-out graph invisible tremors, temblors, and earthquakes—graphs oscillations and rumblings of our magical otherness. The poet's fidelity to "secrets of wash and finish" of his craft, therefore, bespeaks his trust that the recurrent waves of the dream's arrival will engrave their distinctive contours upon the lines of his verse and, as they recede, flowing back into the dream-sea, will leave their telegraphed markings imprinted in the forms, everlast-ingly.

For Ashbery, our dreams "have eternal life." How can we sustain belief in the reality that we cannot see? Siphon the dream's perpetual hourglass flow into the poem's unfolding design, and the forms will forever embody the submarine life that inflated them, billowing into their skins, then withdrawing, sucked back beneath the sea.

IV

Today's artist is inescapably wedded to today, often a bad—but unar-guably necessary—marriage of embattled opponents, a symbiotic host/parasite relation in which, as in neurotic marriages between human mates, host and parasite frequently exchange roles. But ironi-cally, both the city and the artist turn their backs on each other today, to their mutual disaster. The modern world hides from itself the reality that art is the secret wellspring, the artist caretaker, of the communal dream-life; while the artist evades the reality that it is his actual life in today, in the present, that supports and perpetuates all that is most beautiful in his art.

Today, would we regard Francesco as being politically aware, much less an activist or revolutionary? No doubt we'd have written him off as a mere hermit, or recluse. And yet, his passion for shaping exact detail endured the constant military threat upon his life, as well as the more difficult total misapprehension, neglect, and finally repudiation by his patrons—he the sole guardian and caretaker of their collective dream-life:

> Francesco
> Was at work during the Sack: his inventions
> Amazed the soldiers who burst in on him;
> They decided to spare his life, but he left soon after. . . .
> Pope Clement and his court were "stupefied"
> By it [the self-portrait], and promised a commission
> That never materialized.

Evidently, the Church felt more threatened by the artist than did the militia. Francesco's staying power, his steadfastness in perfecting the minutiae of his painting, is an index of his fortitude to withstand his age's indifference and opposition, his power to prevail over the com-bined hostile forces of Church and State. The pressure of antagonism to Francesco's work was translated into the intensity of the remarkable details of his art:

> Parmigianino
> Must have realized this as he worked at his
> Life-obstructing task. One is forced to read
> The perfectly plausible accomplishment of a purpose
> Into the smooth, perhaps even bland (but so
> Enigmatic) finish.

In Wallace Stevens' phrase, the "violence within" matches the "violence without." Hence, it is a political force!

Today, we might well suppose that Francesco had simply turned his back on the real world, escaping into a mad, eccentric world of psychotic fantasies, much as today's readership had written off Ashbery as being a willful obscurantist, so far out of the mainstream of fashionable letters as to merit our sheepish disregard. If we felt a bit shaky about our failure to develop the skills of readership needed to accurately diagnose the size of his accomplishment, we disposed of his improbable excellence by consigning him to limbo, that nondescript category of precocious—but inconsequential—rejects and cast-offs. Radical avant-gardist! The one circle in hell which we mask with seraphic veneer, while we secretly pity the misguided divinity, the fallen angel. We banish him from the marketplace, from negotiable currency, then label him exile and outlaw.

Is it essential that we investigate the "small accidents" of domestic living that nourished and perpetuated Parmigianino's—or Ashbery's—creative process? To fully apprehend their self-portraits, must we come into possession of the miscellaneous data of their private lives at the time of composition? Mainly, no. As in Wallace Stevens' aesthetics, we require only enough of this data to assure us that they maintained a "relentless contact" with external phenomena, and drew upon these environmental supports in composing their art. These two artists—poet and painter—are not psychotic, or even phantasmagoric etherealists; rather, they are both obdurate, intractable, and clear-sighted realists. If their life in the world has been enriched by dreams, likewise, their dream-life has been constantly fed by viable contact with surface actualities of the outside world. The precise make-up of the "strewn evidence" is trivial in itself, and may be ignored:

> Long ago
> The strewn evidence meant something,
> The small accidents and pleasures
> Of the day as it moved gracelessly on,
> A housewife doing chores. Impossible now
> To restore those properties in the silver blur that is

The record of what you accomplished by sitting down
"With great art to copy all that you saw in the glass"
So as to perfect and rule out the extraneous
Forever. . . . It doesn't matter
Because these are things as they are today
Before one's shadow ever grew
Out of the field into thoughts of tomorrow.

Constitutionally, Ashbery has preferred—with Stevens and Parmigianino—to found his vision of reality in the shadow-life, the life of the timeless human spirit which transcends the present in "thoughts of tomorrow." In *Self-Portrait,* he dedicates his noblest energies to casting his shadow into the world of the future.

In contemporary America, Francesco Parmigianino's style still lurks in the wind and earth ("the stresses that only seemed to go away"), since no viable new mode has come along which was strong enough to drive it out of currency. The residues of Francesco's technique—though subdued, hidden, ignored by us—are yet strong enough to have great impact on today's landscape. In the timeless geography of Ashbery's vision, scenery in old portraits may rival and overshadow the actual urban scenes of the modern city:

Their reticence has undermined
The urban scenery, made its ambiguities
Look willful and tired, the games of an old man.

The past survives and interacts with the present, whether we recognize the conflict or not. If we ignore the interaction and passively—which is to say, mindlessly—endure it, the past will *undermine* the present, its dying, outmoded identity still more viable, more operative, today than any new art modes we have devised to take its place. The masterworks of the past, defying their incarceration in museums and art books ("where color plates are rare"), will negate the feeble art of today, and beyond this, they may overreach the art world to strike back at the living society that has demeaned them:

The gray glaze of the past attacks all know-how:
Secrets of wash and finish that took a lifetime
To learn are reduced to the status of
Black-and-white illustrations in a book where colorplates
Are rare. That is, all time
Reduces to no special time . . .
Our time gets to be veiled, compromised
By the portrait's will to endure. It hints at
Our own, which we were hoping to keep hidden.
We don't need paintings or

Doggerel written by mature poets, when
The explosion is so precise, so fine.

Today is a no man's land. Neither residues of the past nor fresh sprouts of the present can find a sure rooting in today's landscape of "ambiguities." All is blurred, hazy, out of focus. A new vision is needed to put things back into perspective, and to advance them into a new dynamic relation in which lingerers, hangers-on from the past, may complete themselves, get on with their dyings, while germinal new shoots may sprout, get on with their comings alive, birthings. The seasonal cycles of births and deaths are bypassed, somehow, by the deeper spiritual cycles and art cycles which transcend the natural seasons. Livings and dyings are perceived in a new relation, which is guided and fostered by the interaction of past and present, by the powerful collidings between surviving art masterpieces and new works just coming into being, between the vision of yesterday's best life and the vision of today's.

To all appearances, our own day offers great advantages to the artist. The modern city—New York, in particular—is most propitiously situated for launching bold sweeps into other past eras ("our landscape/ is alive with filiations, shuttlings"). Countless tributaries from the great range of world races and nationalities converge into a mainstream in the city; potentially, it is a great cultural mecca, in which the truly civilized individual may achieve a cosmopolitan diversity of sensibility and intelligence. There is fantastic prodigal wealth of resource hidden in the city today, but one must dig for the musty and forgotten heritage.

In every age, the city has been hostile to the artist, as well as to the dream-life of which he is overseer and caretaker. The modern city is worse. Not only does it try to squelch the artist, and thereby to starve the roots of its own dream-life: it would also ignore the great past—its weapon, total cultural amnesia. The business life, in its obsession with speed and efficiency, muffles the living nuance, the surviving residues—shades, hues, accents, tones—of other best lives that transpired in this topography, and still lurk in the sea of air and light that washes over the surfaces of our living space:

Business is carried on by look, gesture,
Hearsay. It is another life to the city ... It wants
To siphon off the life of the studio, deflate
Its mapped space to enactments, island it.

How can today's artist stave off the city's plot to quarantine him in the marketplace? How can the artist connect with the fecund, buried life of our America, reaching past the commercial nightmare to the living reliquary of ancestral gifts, despite the city's cunning, its bribery, its fraud?

Long sojourns, retreats in the country, the cultivation of leisure—this is felt to be the chief fortification, or embattlement, to preserve the dream-life intact. A return to the slow-paced rhythm of life is felt to be the best defense against the city's hyperactivity, its obsessive reduction of all zones of life within its borders—even "play"—to technologies:

> Certainly the leisure to
> Indulge stately pastimes doesn't [exist],
> Any more . . . "Play" is something else;
> It exists in a society specifically
> Organized as a demonstration of itself.

This society forces all forms of life different from its monolithic technology and business into a clever capsule of the organization. The city sets itself up as mirror to our aspirations—both faces are the same, and the metaphor is murdered:

> We have seen the city; it is the gibbous
> Mirrored eye of an insect. All things happen
> On its balcony and are resumed within,
> But the action is the cold, syrupy flow
> Of a pageant. One feels too confined,
> Sifting the April sunlight for clues,
> In the mere stillness of the ease of its
> Parameter. The hand holds no chalk
> And each part of the whole falls off
> And cannot know it knew, except
> Here and there, in cold pockets
> Of remembrance, whispers out of time.

The city does not notice the dreaming that goes on in each of us—a continuity and progression, a chain of intakes and outflows like the uninterrupted act of our breathing ("whispers out of time"). The dream-life is not recognized to be the indispensable haven of our being. The very reality of our dreaming, the life of imagination, is called into question, nullified, treated as if it does not exist—at best, pushed off on the sidelines, the artist's studio islanded, compartmentalized and encapsulated in a marginal zone, a limbo, falling off into a faceless netherworld, one of the city's countless dying suburbs. Not just artists, caretakers of human imagination, but all citizens are conditioned to demean the free play of mind and spirit in themselves. All forms of human leisure are outlawed, banned. The act of play is named and fitted neatly into the map, since it is assumed that play does not exist until the city has established its legal charter and birth-right, and endowed it with nominal funds and geographical borders, the site of the public playground. Likewise, play will not extend be-yond the city's defined limits.

Ashbery knows the great change is coming, but he vows repeatedly to help the revolution to come about without harming anyone. Though he would spare the city a lethal attack, his defensive posture, in the course of the poem, shifts by gradual shades to an offensive stance—passive and aggressive, at once. Ashbery is somewhat fearful of his own revolutionary impulse, which takes the form of inertia:

> But something new is on the way, a new preciosity
> In the wind. Can you stand it,
> Francesco? Are you strong enough for it?
> This wind brings what it knows not, is
> Self-propelled, blind, has no notion
> Of itself. It is inertia that once
> Acknowledged saps all activity, secret or public . . .

We note the aptness of the nemesis—antidote and punishment—bequeathed to our age on the wings of the blind wind. Ashbery foresees the arrival of this incapacitating nerve gas—tasteless, odorless—that will put us to sleep on our public feet. Inertia, a paralyzing discharge secreted by our atrophied dream glands, will obstruct the hypertrophied glands of city action.

Ashbery finds that he must adopt the stance of a revolutionary if he is to deal with today at all. If ever there has been a moment in history ripe for radical change, Ashbery's *today* is that moment. Today's needed change lurks in a hidden alcove ("in recesses no one knew of"), waiting around one corner or another. Though Ashbery does not ascribe to the poet the Promethean role of "unacknowledged legislator of the world," he makes claims to a prowess in the poet which is a near approach to Shelley's hyperbole. The poet does not beget—or conceive—the great change, but he catches its scent in the wind. The earliest signs of the new spirit are subliminal, below normal thresholds of awareness, the first signals hovering at a level too subtle and refined for ordinary intelligence *or* sense perception. Neverthe-less, the change that is coming, the advent of a new age, registers fully in the poet's prescient grasp of the conditions of existence, and he is ready—as no one else can be—to collaborate with the change, to be its faithful steward, and to facilitate its transmission to the community through the poem's craft and artistry. How does the poet harness the energies of the secret dynamo of change? How does he come into possession of its plasma, and send it pulsing through the poem's ar-teriovascular network?

> But something new is on the way, a new preciosity
> In the wind. . . .

Wind is the vehicle upon which the new modes governed by necessity are borne aloft. It is both a timeless and timely wind. It travels freely, without limits, across vast distances in time and space. Also, it transports into the present vital residues of the past, the surviving durable "white precipitate" of the past's dream life, which, with the help of today's providential artist—as if sent by Providence, a special configuration of the planets orchestrating over Ashbery's birth in the "Holy Land" of western New York State—will prompt and initiate the momentous timely *change*, a change in the mode of artistic expression, as well as in the sensibility of our whole cultural epoch.

In the poem's penultimate movement, battle lines are starkly drawn between the city and the artist's studio. In Ashbery's mythology of nemesis, words are endued with otherworldly forces, a power generated by a retributive source outside of time. A small percentage of the population may read and comprehend the poetry itself, but the words will act by indirection, chiefly, to inaugurate and engineer the needed spiritual change. A pejorative explanation of this aesthetic might attribute it to Ashbery's failure—by mid-career—to connect with a large enough body of readers to support his aspiration to work for the change by direct action solely upon the ears of reader-listeners. But the poet is an underground man, an urban word-guerrilla. The poetry will achieve its effects less by enlightenment, or even sensual awakening, than by fostering a radical change of mood, of tone, of pace and tempo that spreads throughout the air and light—the aura surrounding perception, the rhythm of perception, rather than the contents of thought and feeling. It is not what the words themselves deliver, or even the intelligence they evoke in us, that shall constitute our change. Instead, we shall be transformed, enigmatically, by "whispers out of time,"

> Whispers of the word that can't be understood
> But can be felt, a chill, a blight
> Moving outward along the capes and peninsulas
> Of your nervures and so to the archipelagoes
> And to the bathed, aired secrecy of the open sea.

Whispers of the word, whispers out of time, suggests not a mere fleeting— or evanescent—force, but a tough, omnipresent political agency which can act directly upon the land, as well as in the air and light. It is an unstoppable effluence sweeping outward, carrying over from language to all margins, borders, edges, peripheries of our terrain. Like an invisible gas, refusing confinement to the city's "parameter"—the suburbs, the outer reaches of the city's purlieu—it slowly envelops all boundaries, all perimeters of the natural environment. The *whispers* would revive the dormant spirit of the American outlander in us, that pilgrim explorer impulse that went to sleep after the mythic West had been tamed and domesticated. The wilderness—ostensibly decimated—has merely been driven underground, sunk into dormancy. The whispers would send us back to the buried wilderness, the forgotten—but not obliterated—primeval American heartland which is celebrated and vindicated in the last far outcry of Faulkner's best prose, as in the *Far Field* of Roethke's eloquent last meditations ("Old men should be explorers"). The sleeping pioneers in us are, once again, summoned to colonize new outposts ranging, in Ashbery's new work, from the perimeters of the North American continent ("the capes and peninsulas") to offshore waters of the U.S. mainland ("the archipelagoes . . . the open sea").

V

The author-protagonist, having played a number of roles in succession, is now able to visualize the remarkable last role that may carry him through to the finish. I find that there is more than a trace of Don Quixote tilting at windmills in this prevision of the poem's conclusion, and this is a good moment to be reminded that Ashbery has not lost his sense of humor, despite the profound seriousness of his enterprise. Here, then, are the dramatist's last stage directions and typecasting, the final assigning of roles, as the poem's long finale commences:

> What we need now is this unlikely
> Challenger pounding on the gates of an amazed
> Castle.

A master-artist today may conscript the past masterworks as allies in his struggle to evolve a new mode of mental receptivity, the past collaborating with the present to germinate the new intelligence. In the supreme moments of Ashbery's vision, the castle walls between past and present, between living generations and the great dead, fall away: spirits of other centuries ("whispers out of time") join hands with spirits of today, and a reciprocity of mind—a timeless, communal oversoul—manifests itself:

> . . .the sands are hissing
> As they approach the beginning of the big slide
> Into what happened. This past
> Is now here.

Ashbery is training himself to dwell increasingly in this mental dimension which transcends the seasonal cycles, and is at the heart of high civilization. The "High Renaissance" ideal abides there. The "unlikely challenger" is the artist of today whose craft and vision are strong enough to lift him out of the "slum" of the present into the timeless Elysium. The castle is "amazed" because no poet of our present generation has yet taken up the burden, shouldered the task—none since Yeats perhaps, writing in English. The castle had grown deaf to our claims, turned its back on us.

An artist's life and work are his argument with his age, his lover's quarrel with his world. If he wishes to help implement the great changes, it is best for his mind to be laid "bare for questioning" in his art—then, as the sparks fly, generated by collisions between his work and his age, paramount answers may be "forthcoming." Parmigianino's argument, so far ahead of his moment in history, hung fire for centuries. A work may achieve levels of towering genius, but the vision will grow stale if neglected by its own, or immediately ensuing, generations. Whenever an age faces away from its exemplary major artist's vision, two disasters inevitably result: the age, unmirrored, is deprived of its enlightenment; the artwork itself fails to come fully into its own ripening, since interaction with the age is needed to fertilize the vision. But encounter with a later age may complete the work and send it coursing down the mainstream of the ageless flow of civilization, though the living artist will have lost forever his single-life chance to build upon his own give-and-take battle of healthy, if hostile, exchanges with his milieu, the program of aggressive interchange that Ashbery clearly envisions for his own current and future work:

> Your argument, Francesco,
> Had begun to grow stale as no answer
> Or answers were forthcoming. If it dissolves now
> Into dust, that only means its time had come
> Some time ago, but look now, and listen:
> It may be that another life is stocked there
> In recesses no one knew of; that it,
> Not we, are the change; that we are in fact it
> If we could get back to it, relive some of the way
> It looked, turn our faces to the globe as it sets
> And still be coming out all right:
> Nerves normal, breath normal. Since it is a metaphor
> Made to include us, we are a part of it and
> Can live in it as in fact we have done,
> Only leaving our minds bare for questioning
> We now see will not take place at random
> But in an orderly way that means to menace

> Nobody—the normal way things are done,
> Like the concentric growing up of days
> Around a life: correctly, if you think about it.

Throughout the poem, Ashbery has been feeding upon the special nutrients of the portrait, enriching his own dream life, mediating between past and present; but now he calls for a major shift of stance, a radical pivoting and re-focusing of perspective. Ashbery knows, beyond melioration, the terror of the sizable risk he takes. Prior to this passage, all encounters with the self-portrait involved moderate and safely calculable hazards. If the painting deflected, shifted focus, or failed to match the demands or expectations he fixed upon it; or indeed, if the painting recoiled from his visionary trance altogether, he could safely withdraw, incubate in creative reverie, and resume his engagement with the painting refreshed. But now he must subject the painting to the one irreversible test. This is the pivotal moment. Ashbery is about to cross the great Continental Divide in time. The portrait, held in suspension for centuries, had been embalmed. Its resources for invigorating profound thought—untested and unappropriated—may have grown stale with disuse, or they may have strengthened with aging:

> If it dissolves now
> Into dust, that only means its time had come
> Some time ago...

Ashbery assumes that he is the first heir and fellow-artist to put the portrait to the test. It may be a work that reached its peak accessibility to later artists, or spectators, generations after the death of the painter, but lost its potency at a specified locus that can be pinpointed in time past, the artwork enjoying a life far beyond the mortal term of the artist, but limited—circumscribed in time—all the same. Either the painting still contains a hidden reservoir of intelligence-for-change which can be viably appropriated into Ashbery's improvising of a new mode to surmount today's terrible impasse in consciousness, or Ashbery has sold himself a forgery, and, like an embalmed mummy suddenly exposed to the poisonous oxygen, "it dissolves now/ into dust."

At this moment in the poem, all previous interactions between Parmigianino and Ashbery appear to have been rehearsals, ceremonies of initiation. All legitimate preliminaries have played themselves out. By a succession of raids on past genius, Ashbery has trained himself to mediate between past and present, to build a psychic bridge between them, carrying provisions from one to the other. But now he braces himself for the final exhaustive raid. He senses that the key to the change we need to survive in spirit today dwells in the beautiful whole-mindedness and clear-sightedness of Parmigianino's self-portrait. The message waits there, undisturbed. Parmigianino's argument—a unique cosmos of intelligence, a unique mind-gestalt—had advanced to a mental plateau so far ahead of his time that no one of his contemporaries, his colleagues in the arts, could recognize the profound importance of his futuristic mentality, or build upon his advances in the mastery of craft. Either his "argument . . . had begun to grow stale as no answer/ or answers were forthcoming," or the prime moment in history for its disclosure and application still hadn't arrived. Ashbery gambles his elaborate and labyrinthine vision on the latter explanation in this grand canvas, his most valiant enterprise. He makes his bet with fate on a wild guess, an existentialist hunch guided by blind instinct—how else to make a wager with the invisible world?

The creative mind of our times is blocked. It must be unplugged somehow. Hence, Ashbery's lines, in this crucial section of the poem, evoke the authentic nuance of total risk, total surrender to chance against the odds. The size of possible gains is matched against the magnitude of hazard. So many of the writer's best hours of agonizing growth, search of selfhood, and self-surrender have been invested in fashioning the cornerstone and groundwork of a poetic edifice upon which the superstructure of a revolutionary new art mode for today might be raised. But it is formidably clear that the indispensable catalyst for the whole operation is the strength of reserves stockpiled in Francesco's self-portrait:

> It may be that another life is stocked there
> In recesses no one knew of; that it,
> Not we, are the change.

All of Ashbery's preparatory raids upon the painting's delicious "hues," "curves and edges" have fortified his aspiration, but whether it can now burgeon into the chief bulwark, or rampart, for shoring up his new mode is unforeseeable.

In the course of prolonged communing with the portrait, Ashbery had become an ideally expert receiver of the waves of sensation arriving on an "unassigned frequency" from the artwork, adjusting his mental antennae correctly and swiftly for each new wave. It seemed as though the painting had become his home. Settling down in its chambers in comfort, imbibing its warmth and wealth of niceties, he had *moved in,* and found himself included in the work's life:

> Since it is a metaphor
> Made to include us, we are a part of it and
> Can live in it as in fact we have done . . .

The painting invites all spectators to share in its trance. To *live in* the world of the art work, to be *a part of it,* is far more than an ordinary aesthetic experience—it becomes the chief preoccupation, even obsession, of our mind's activity. But, even so, the essential seat of himself, the very core of Ashbery's being, was secretly withheld. It clung to his own time, his own city, body, face, name! Who he is remained intact.

But now he would be transfigured, changed profoundly in the uttermost depths of himself, by the painting's action upon him. Ashbery was drawn irresistibly to this luminous painting, as I to this one poem, because it contains—in embryo—the change he needs to be reborn in the self, and thus to survive in spirit through his age's hard, chilled time. For a time, it had seemed as though all the cycles of his adventuring in the painting's metaphor were to be an unending refreshment, an incomparably rich entertainment, but, at bottom, no more than a relief from the serious crises of his human life, the problems with his fellow humans, his fate, his death, and finally, his survival— his power to transcend today, his art's "will to endure" in the life of tomorrow. His dwelling in the wonderfully variegated ambience of the painting's vision had grown to seem a perfect escape from these terrible burdens of being a man alive today:

> This could have been our paradise: exotic
> Refuge within an exhausted world, but that wasn't
> In the cards, because it couldn't have been
> The point.

Perhaps the legacy he least expected to unearth in this elegant art-Elysium, when he began work on the poem, was the key to get things right in his mortal life. But now Ashbery finds that he must welcome a different kind of interaction with the painting, one that can never be repeated, a kiss-of-death encounter. It is no longer sufficient to be the ideal recipient of the painting's beauties. He must invite the artwork to inhabit him, the portrait to resume and complete its unfinished life within his psyche:

> It may be that another life is stocked there
> In recesses no one knew of; that it,
> Not we, are the change; that we are in fact it
> If we could get back to it, relive some of the way
> It looked, turn our faces to the globe as it sets
> And still be coming out all right:
> Nerves normal, breath normal.

To *get back* to the painting, to *relive some of the way it looked,* is to breathe the air of the past! It is to glance about at objects, at surfaces, lit by the light of the past. It is to look at the world of the painting with the other past man's eyes. It is the whole miracle of making the past

spring alive in the present, making the past be here now by re-living
the look, taste, touch, and feel of things as they were then, in the great
ago, the yesterday. But he will be witnessing yesterday directly with
today's eyes, with today's second sight. Yesterday will live again,
rounding out the part of its life that couldn't realize itself in its own
age. Its time was not yet, its time still has not come, but its time is very
near. Its time is now!

Ashbery becomes, at last, demonically possessed by the painting.
His identification with Francesco Parmigianino is astonishingly com-
plete. It reaches a terrifying apocalypse in which the poet's "reflec-
tion," his self-image, is abducted by the painter:

> ... you could be fooled for a moment
> Before you realize the reflection
> Isn't yours. You feel then like one of those
> Hofmann characters who have been deprived
> Of a reflection, except that the whole of me
> Is seen to be supplanted by the strict
> Otherness of the painter in his
> Other room ...

It is a painful depersonalization, though purifying, and Ashbery feels
ravaged at first. So vulnerable, so nakedly exposed, all his defenses
freely and unconditionally surrendered to the painter, he has risked
devastation of his unique selfhood by the portrait's interior cosmos.
But his strength of self-curtailment, his willingness to divest his ar-
mor, grows into a fierce continuity of restraint—a power to stand still
and wait out indefinitely the momentous drama that is acting itself out
upon his sensorium, which comes to feel like a holocaust the universe
inflicts upon him to test his mettle. This bravery has been sustained
throughout the poem, and finally it becomes the mode—the
rationale—for Ashbery's turning the tables on Parmigianino, who, at
the last, cannot resist the invitation to reciprocate, to relinquish his
own shield. The poet's self-vanquishment disarms the painter:

> Therefore I beseech you, withdraw that hand,
> Offer it no longer as shield or greeting,
> The shield of a greeting, Francesco:
> There is room for one bullet in the chamber:
> Our looking through the wrong end
> Of the telescope as you fall back at a speed
> Faster than that of light to flatten ultimately
> Among the features of the room ...

The poet was ready to die into the painting and be born again out
of its metaphor, a drowning and miraculous coming back to life from
death. The painter, too, can now welcome, and participate in, his own

final stages of immolation. The relation between poet and painter rises, finally, to a climax in which the spiritual heir—the son—kills the father, a death outside of time for which the mentor-father has yearned across the centuries.

*

> Since it is a metaphor
> Made to include us, we are a part of it and
> Can live in it as in fact we have done,
> Only leaving our minds bare for questioning
> We now see will not take place at random
> But in an orderly way that means to menace
> Nobody—the normal way things are done,
> Like the concentric growing up of days
> Around a life: correctly, if you think about it.

Quite an ambitious agenda for the poem's finale! The compositional process shall be one of both existential discovery and explicit pedagogy, investigative. The mind of the poem shall never stop. At each step of the novel adventure, the mind is to be left "bare for questioning." The continuous rhetoric of learning-on-the-run shall be on display, exposed at every joint, hinge, swivel, juncture of the poet's evolving consciousness. The simultaneous disclosure of enigmas of Ashbery's human identity and his art medium shall be articulated, concurrently, in the verse's utterance. It is a noble and beautiful aspiration to make the composition-in-progress devise an intellectual rhetoric to match, or complement, its experiential rhetoric.

A new species of poetic identity, linking enchanted being with enlightened mentality as they have rarely been joined—wedded—in contemporary poetry: this is the salient new dimension that most impressively abides in *Self-Portrait*. The vivacious grand drama of dawning awarenesses moves into the foreground of this heretofore unexplored art mode: fecundity of ideas, mental excitations, exposed hyperactivity of thought speaking out—for the reader to witness so much power and exercising of mind on exhibition in the broad canvas of this sumptuous masterwork is to be reminded that it is normal and correct, after all, for the poet to be a tirelessly thinking being in the body of the poem. But it required the most irregular and innovative poem by our most radical contemporary verse-technician to restore us readers to the missing dimension—neglected, forgotten, as if absently misplaced—of our normal lives. *Passionate intelligence.* Epiphanies of awareness, increment by increment, build into the corpus of our revelation. Our health of mind must be renewed, replenished periodically, at this wellspring.

Nobody is going to get hurt, neither reader nor writer, neither artist nor his adverse social milieu. The peaceable revolutionary will implement the great change without violence, without terrorism. His creation vows "to menace nobody." It is a relief and a solace to him to learn that radical change may be installed without injury to himself or to others. He has discovered that great disorder and chaos, greatly conceived by the mind of the poem, may be articulated "in an orderly way." Likewise, the revolutionary change in the mass sensibility of an age may be installed without anyone's coming to blows, since the creative process of the artist-iconoclast is plugged into the normal round of domestic life. However much he may transcend his own day in visionary flights, he stays firmly rooted in the garden of normal, caring humankind, and his discoveries, consequently, will nourish—never poison—the community.

Though the author-protagonist has witnessed miracle after miracle, the poise of meditational calm has characterized nearly every phrase of his utterance, but in the final movement the guise of insouciance cannot mask, or shroud, the great wave of passion that is cresting, and finally brims over:

A breeze like the turning of a page
Brings back your face: the moment
Takes such a big bite out of the haze
Of pleasant intuition it comes after.
The locking into place is "death itself,"
As Berg said of a phrase in Mahler's Ninth,
Or, to quote Imogen in *Cymbeline,* "There cannot
Be a pinch in death more sharp than this," for,
Though only exercise or tactic, it carries
The momentum of a conviction that had been building.
Mere forgetfulness cannot remove it
Nor wishing bring it back, as long as it remains
The white precipitate of its dream
In the climate of sighs flung across our world,
A cloth over a birdcage. But it is certain that
What is beautiful seems so only in relation to a specific
Life, experienced or not, channeled into some form
Steeped in the nostalgia of a collective past.
The light sinks today with an enthusiasm
I have known elsewhere, and known why
It seemed meaningful, that others felt this way
Years ago. I go on consulting
This mirror that is no longer mine
For as much brisk vacancy as is to be
My portion this time.

During the moments of high passion, Ashbery's meditational lucidities are admirably kept up. A reader can see, at last, the great leverage that Ashbery now has at his command from having placed a high priority—throughout his career—on the nuances of clear-sightedness. A lesser mind, a less acutely disciplined vision, would have been content to allow the argumentative grasp to sink into abeyance when the grand wave breaks and the poem's foreground is suddenly flooded with human complexities beyond measure, "the fury and the mire of human veins." A conventional Romantic poet would have made a virtue out of letting great passions run off through the fingers of the glove of intelligence like water through a sieve. Yeats and D. H. Lawrence are Ashbery's two chief forebears in mastering the *Spiritual Intellect* to the point that it becomes an unflagging tool for deciphering the great enigmas in our deep passional being, for solving the riddles of the human condition in the heat of action and conflict ("Cast a cold eye/ on life, on death./ Horseman, pass by!"). Ashbery is another who comes upon the radical and irreducible truth of things by a tough-minded and merciless peeling away, layer by layer, of all the false disguises that reality wears, and the truth, or a near approach to it, is what survives this radical reductive process:

> The moment
> Takes such a big bite out of the haze
> Of pleasant intuition it comes after.
> The locking into place is "death itself,"
> As Berg said of a phrase in Mahler's Ninth . . .

There is no suppressing, or ameliorating, this privileged moment, the superhuman moment hailed by Yeats in the Byzantium poems. It is the moment of falling into the narrow abyss that divides mirror opposites, the great antipodes, the one pole becoming indistinguishable from the other. *Death-in-life/Life-in-death. The-past-in-the-present/The-present-in-the-past.*

A thin mist of intuition, slow-building, often delivered with quiet wit of pleasantries, has characterized most of this poem's discourse. It had seemed a medium in which no event could mature and declare itself with undue haste, no shock or surprise could occur swiftly enough to catch us off balance. The key tone of mildness, relaxed, clear-headed inquiry, always prevailed; a decided lassitude and halting pace governed the momentum of revelation. Therefore, for any single moment in time to announce itself abruptly as the instantaneous change in our whole perceptive machinery is a "big bite," to be sure!

All of music's past was summed up, telescoped, in that one compact, super-compressed phrase of Mahler's Ninth Symphony, and what choice had Berg but to collaborate in the birth of music's future, huddled in embryo of the next phrase? The expressive possibilities of harmony and tonality had never before been stretched to such extreme limits, and beyond the snapping point—some threshold, some barrier, would have to make way, some wall be toppled over, as music soared into that beyond. But the music of Mahler's Ninth is incredibly beautiful because the symphony's monumental form is resilient enough to withstand the radical dismantling of music history's most revered canons. The agonized outcries of an anguished soul that knew he would soon have to give up his hold on life matched the music's anguished wails as, with each succeeding phrase, the certainty grew that the art of music in the Western world would soon have to relinquish its grip on the conventions that had fed its finest hours, nourished its best life, throughout its short history. Melody. Harmony. Tonality. The moment of "locking into place." The last unquenchable outcries of a dying species of music are channeled into phrases of a form imperishably alive in its lavish symmetry, in its ordering intelligence—a form prodigal enough to confer immortality both upon its contents, the residuum of dying modes of music, and upon its soon-to-be-dead composer, triumphant in his outraged resignation to death. *The locking into place.* In a single exalted phrase, the past dies into the present, the present is reborn out of the past, and carries forward into the new mode of life and art just coming into being the salvageable remnants of the old, jaded modes, especially those surviving residues which had pointed ahead to the future and had helped to predispose the art medium for the emergence of the new mode. In like manner, the great changes in the music of Berg, Webern, and Schönberg were molded upon changes waiting to be appropriated in the final work of Mahler, who may be viewed as a colossus of modern art, his stance firmly implanted at the great crossroads—one leg in the past, one leg in the future—holding steady in this hybrid anchorage as the violent waves of the present life wash across his forms. Mahler's great forms—both "steeped in the nostalgia of a collective past" and prophetically anticipating the great changes of the future—rival Parmigianino's self-portrait in their unshakable "will to endure."

It was Mahler who—cursed in his music with a fatal gift of prophecy—always forecasted, with flawless prescience, the tragic events of his own life: his daughter's death augured by the song cycle *Kindertotenlieder*; his own terminal heart ailment and death foretold by *Das Lied von der Erde* and the Ninth Symphony. However, the composer's innovatory structures were capacious enough in grand sweep to contain and transfigure into health of spirit massive quantities of

personal and collective dyings. Mahler, then, a heroic model for the
future possibilities of form, is the prototype of the art theory ad-
vanced by this poem in which the art heir, Ashbery, resurrects his
ancestor and spiritual brother, Francesco Parmigianino.

*

How can the mere single phrase in music, the single details in
paintings, single images in poetry, achieve an intensity that simulates
death? The perfected details of an artwork ("secrets of wash and
finish that took a lifetime to learn") are isolated samplings of ideal
beauty of form. But if the artist thinks he works alone (sings only to
himself, the song locked in his own ears), many generations of artists
and master artisans who lived before him—some known to him, oth-
ers not—may partake secretly of his act of creation. His technical
expertise is informed not only by his one lifetime faithfully devoted
to learning those inestimable skills, but centuries of ancestors may
have handed down tips, hints, clues, as well. When his artistry has
achieved a certain level and scale of perfection, those other master
practitioners long dead may return in the magic of his exalted hand's
strokes, gestures, swerves—the ancient voices enter that hand's
moves, and roll through its exquisitely measured craftings:

> Or to quote Imogen in *Cymbeline*, "There cannot
> Be a pinch in death more sharp than this," for,
> Though only exercise or tactic, it carries
> The momentum of a conviction that had been building.

The hand's "momentum" is propelled by a league of helpers, the
unseen guides, "unknown instructors." Thus, an initiated and per-
ceiving beholder of the artwork—reader, listener, spectator—can rec-
ognize the accumulated pressure and intelligence of a build-up of
generations in the "conviction" behind the fastidiously wrought de-
tails. Only a novice witnessing these mere techniques, these man-
nerisms of style, would fail to perceive that they are not simply orna-
mental or decorative embellishments, but that they embody the
cumulative wisdom and sagacity of a legion of forerunners. To dis-
count the elemental importance of surpassingly good technique is to
ignore the root-systems, the true scaffoldings, behind any major art
form. As if "exercise or tactic" were a magician's plaything, rather
than the excruciatingly fostered methodology which, embraced in the
course of a lifetime of hit-or-miss, trial-and-error experimentation,
crystallizes into the artist's unique personal style:

> Mere forgetfulness cannot remove it
> Nor wishing bring it back, as long as it remains

The white precipitate of its dream
In the climate of sighs flung across our world,
A cloth over a birdcage . . .

This "white precipitate" of individual style has incredible staying
power. It is indestructible like the minerals quartz, feldspar. Later
generations can alter its form and change its basic make-up by fusing
it with other ingredients, forming compounds, alloys. But its essential
particularity and individuation perseveres, from century to century.
It is indivisible by any other man's art, but chipped-off flakes of it
may be employed as additive components of another's developing
technique. Neither individual nor collective "forgetfulness" can "re-
move" the embodiment of the artist's unique identity in idiosyncrasies
of style which, like Christ's embodiment in the cross, endures, survives
as a model of the single human identity carried to its uttermost pitch
of fulfillment, even if the chief art masterworks are forgotten or de-
stroyed. That "white precipitate" of each greatly achieved human
dream endures, somehow, in the air and light, in the electricity of
brain waves. This singular mode of feeling and sensual thought
couldn't have come into being, apart from the unrepeatable indi-
vidual life steeped in its own very special context—a relation to both
present and past, also unrepeatable. One timely moment, one
lifetime's moment in the expanse of ages, produced this remarkable
novel combination, this new element in the world's physical make-up,
an aesthetic equivalent of plutonium, uranium, californium. But once
this new substance has been deposited in the planet's earth and air, it
endures in "all time," becoming the indestructible possession of all
future generations.

Ashbery's re-possession and revivification of Francesco Par-
migianino's self-portrait, after so many generations of neglect, is the
proof of this. "Wishing" alone couldn't have achieved this profound
act of rehabilitation. The individual will of the guest artist must be
supported by necessity, acting in concert with his vision, to catalyze
the wedding with the host artist. Ashbery's claims for the marvelously
novel individuation of any great artist's stylistic oddities—non-
duplicable "secrets of wash and finish"—parallels the claims of scien-
tists first discovering the elements, each separate and distinct plant
and animal species, each chemical substance in the laboratory test-
tube. Thus the peculiar couplings in Ashbery's diction yoking to-
gether, in amazing hybrid linkages, words from specialized vocabu-
laries of science and art—"the white precipitate of its dream"— syn-
chronizing the language and imagery of the poem with its network
of ideas. What survives the artist's death is both "precipitate" and
"sighs," a wail of being embodied in a durable, crystalline substance.

The artwork combines, in balanced proportions, the ethereal and the substantial, celestial and corporeal. Ashbery's new style achieves an amazing composite of material and immaterial elements.

In his quarrel with his culture, Ashbery attributes to the world of art many of the virtues, the sagacities, fashionably attributed only to the twin worlds of science and technology: precision, dependable quantities, stable and calculable materials, fixed variables, reliable criteria for distinguishing the authentic from the fake. Such a use of the word "precipitate" also underscores Ashbery's willingness to invest both the factual data and the vocabularies of the exact sciences with preeminent trustworthiness, demonstrating beyond question his own good faith, his attempts to negotiate a healing spirit of good fellowship and mutual high regard between the arts and a culture that consistently demeans artists, relegating the Olympians among them to a status of second-class anomalies, outcasts.

Since the beginning of his career, Ashbery has been obsessed with designing poetic forms capacious enough to embrace all key dimensions of contemporary life. The dazzling new vivacity of Ashbery's style in this major poem may be ascribed to his successful improvising of technical means to bring the poetry's art into closer touch with indigenous commonplace events in his day-to-day life. A reader notes, with surprise, the accelerated flux of sensory excitation in Ashbery's poetic diction. He achieves a broader realism in his language, drawing upon the widest possible range of contemporary, indigenous American resources:

> Today has that special, lapidary
> Todayness that the sunlight reproduces
> Faithfully in casting twig-shadows on blithe
> Sidewalks. No previous day would have been like this.

Nor indeed would any previous Ashbery poem have been like this one, a poem which—in its gorgeously sculpted detail—achieves a dense, lapidary texture. It is a style replete with Asbery's most incisive experimental writing, a language that abounds with lavishly engraved images, pictures, emblems. His language, in its prodigal variety, draws upon an astonishingly broad frame of reference in the specialized vocabularies of the modern fine arts and sciences, implicit evidence that Ashbery is more attuned than ever before to contemporary life, to his own moment in history: "logarithm" (modern mathematics), "programmed" (computer science), "capes ... peninsulas ... archipelagoes" (geography), "skin ... tough as reptile eggs" (zoology), "white precipitate," "deposited in irregular clumps of crystals," "sample ... in a refined assimilable state" (chemistry), "a magma of

interiors" (geology), "flourish like a cabbage-rose" (botany), "ner-
vures . . . the city is the gibbous/ mirrored eye of an insect" (entymol-
ogy), "a globe like ours, resting on a pedestal of vacuum, a ping-pong
ball/ secure on its jet of water" (astronomy and physics), etc.

Major artworks—the world's collective memory—are invested with
their age's very mode of sensory receptivity. History springs alive to
our senses! We come to know the way things looked to the eye of the
past, the way things registered upon the hand that touched them, or
upon the living breath that circulated around them and inhaled them,
in turn, or upon the tongues that gave voice to their shape. We can
resuscitate more of the ambience of the past directly, by engaging art
masterworks, than by any other agency:

> The sample
> One sees is not to be taken as
> Merely that, but as everything as it
> May be imagined outside time—not as a gesture
> But as all, in the refined, assimilable state.

One central artwork of an age, the one epitomizing sample of a cen-
tral artist's style, bequeaths to us not only the beautiful, unique gift of
his vision and sensibility, but also the look and feel of his age grasped
by the finest imagination current, and codified into a form that can
lead us into that age's center of happening and feeling response. The
central artwork renders available to all later generations a "refined,
assimilable" sampling of all the best that was felt, and responsively
reported, about that period, that milieu. What other poet writing
today has made so grand and sweeping a claim for the possibilities—
indeed, the efficaciousness—of his *own* art medium!

VI

In "Self-portrait in a Convex Mirror," John Ashbery breaks new
ground in the archeology of global art. Toward the end of the poem,
Ashbery's great archeological finding surfaces, and gradually it as-
sumes definitive shape for the reader. Not only are all the details of
Francesco Parmigianino's portrait stamped with his unique artist per-
sonality, but his distinctive spiritual handprint—indelibly marking the
wind—also materializes and re-materializes across the centuries. The
lapidary crafting intelligence by which the artist sculpts the formless-
ness, the scattering disarray of the present day all about him, is a
divinity of organizing consciousness which survives hiddenly in the air
and light ("a cloth over a bird-cage"). It is a gestalt of structural ar-
chitectonics that never existed in the universe before, and it survives

as a "white precipitate," possibly for thousands of years! Today's artist may engage this miraculous, indestructible substrate of a past artist's vision by studying the poem or painting which contains it. But beyond this, in the elevation of his own high vision, he may meet the "diagram still sketched on the wind" nakedly and directly, in the form of a visitation from the other world. If this interaction occurs, the ancestor's very style of perception may then utterly transfigure the descendant's sensory apparatus, his mode of witnessings of the natural world. His every glance will enjoy the stamp of his tutor's diagrammatic ordering intelligence, as if the master's actual nervous system has been transplanted—or transferred by deep hypnosis—into the willing recipient-beloved of the visionary wedding. When this miracle of transplantation occurs, we recognize that our choice of mate, as in the mysterious selection of partner in sexual falling in love, was arranged in advance by Providence, by great impersonal forces in the universe:

> Its existence
> Was real, though troubled, and the ache
> Of this waking dream can never drown out
> The diagram still sketched on the wind,
> Chosen, meant for me and materialized
> In the disguising radiance of my room.

Ashbery's otherworldly tone, his ghostly accents in this passage, strikes a reader's ear as a disembodied voice, more the voice of mirage or apparition than of man. The voice traverses a terrible distance. I am accustomed to a similar tone only in the last poems of Yeats and Hardy, the strange, deathly beauty of unstoppable throats the grave had already halfway tenanted:

> I go on consulting
> This mirror that is no longer mine
> For as much brisk vacancy as is to be
> My portion this time.

It is now the moment *after* the supreme moment of coalescence, the wedding of present to past. Ashbery has so exhaustively transported himself into Parmigianino's world, re-lived the look and feel of things there, that he becomes for the time perfectly contemporary with those events, surfaces. But perfect contemporaneity with the past is found to have its drawbacks. The past ceases to be the past, and can no longer act as a mirror—it has become too transparent, a window directly into the self. Ashbery's mirror has lost its convexity.

In the poem's final pages, Ashbery awakens to the shortcomings of his habitation in the painting's cosmos, a universe complete in itself. Neither the aesthetic it espoused nor the styles of perception it tutored will suffice to prepare today's artist to come to terms with today, to make his own peace with the contemporary moment. When Ashbery's adventuring in the world of the past has run its course, he finds that the canons—or conventions—of the past must be relinquished:

> Aping naturalness may be the first step
> Toward achieving an inner calm
> But it is the first step only, and often
> Remains a frozen gesture of welcome etched
> On the air materializing behind it,
> A convention. And we have really
> No time for these, except to use them
> For kindling. The sooner they are burnt up
> The better for the roles we have to play.

To have shared the vision of Francesco's portrait, for a time, has been sufficient reward and fulfillment, in itself; but occupancy in the mentor's surviving masterpiece—though it provided fecund kindling to Ashbery's dream-life, sending him exotica of sensations on recurring waves of arrival—is recognized, finally, to have been a default of identity. Any exile or refuge from the present is found to be, at best, temporary. However alien and inimical the city of today to the world of dreams, the voyage into the dream is launched from today, and, by whatever oblique, circuitous route, ends in today:

> Each person
> Has one big theory to explain the universe
> But it doesn't tell the whole story
> And in the end it is what is outside him
> That matters, to him and especially to us
> Who have been given no help whatever
> In decoding our own man-size quotient and must rely
> On second-hand knowledge. Yet I know
> That no one else's taste is going to be
> Any help, and might as well be ignored.

No other artist—past or present—can prepare each contemporary to decipher the possibilities and limitations today of his own gift. Ultimately, in dealing with our own unique moment in history, each absolutely different day of the present we keep *cresting* back into, no one can help us. As in facing death, in coming to terms with each special context of present experience the artist is fundamentally alone, a pioneer-existentialist, a pilgrim staking claims in the foreign country of the newly hatched today. Each today is a genuine original, a novel, unique webbing—a "special lapidary todayness" of "sunlight casting twig-shadows"—to be identified in its complexity, its wonderfully stark and cleanly delineated precision of details. Each today is a rebirth, each sunrise spawning a novel interplay of lights and shadows. How hard the poet must work to trace the outlines of this unfamiliar and strange terrain that unfolds one new face after another! The elusive today.

As Ashbery returns to the present for the last time, witnessing Parmigianino's "globe as it sets," *the change* inhabits him and is carried forward into our own day. The author-protagonist, a first inter-epoch astronaut traveling through the time-machine of the painting, has accomplished this miraculous adventure of being transported bodily into the past time-zone without injury, and makes the return trip unharmed ("nerves normal, breath normal"). It is the normal, ordinary man, in good health, in full command of his faculties, who has returned unimpaired. No avant-gardist freak, no madman, no rarefied obscurantist-elitist, he is an ordinary skilled laboring man of our own day (one who works harder than most, perhaps, at skillful dreaming), as surprised by his hard-bought acquisition of simple normality, his charter and passport to a humble domestic life in the present, as we can ever be. His unconditional voyaging into the cosmos of the great past, leaving behind no human part—body and soul, both irreducibly transported—is at last revealed to have been the fixed ransom qualifying him to embrace, as if for the first time, his full "man-size quotient" of an artist-livelihood in the world of today.

THE AMERICAN POETRY REVIEW, 1977

A. R. Ammons

OF MIND AND WORLD

Northfield Poems

Not the least of A. R. Ammons' virtues is that he is an original philosopher in his poetry, though often he parades in the guise of poet-as-anti-philosopher, much as Plato wore the guise of philosopher-as-anti-poet. In "Uh, Philosophy," he cuts deeper into the subject the more he pretends, with graceful offhandedness, to dismiss its importance:

> I understand
>   reading the modern philosophers
> that truth is so much a method
>   it's perfectly all
> right for me to believe whatever
>   I like or if I like,
> nothing:
>   I do not know that I care to be set that free:

He comes at each idea a little from the side, obliquely, with a chuckle of ridicule in the voice of the poem every time the meandering river of the speaker's mind inclines to become trapped by any one idea or perspective, or threatens to take ideas in and of themselves as having supreme consequence:

> philosophy is
> a pry pole, materialization,
>   useful as a snowshovel when it snows;
> something solid to knock people down with
>   or back people up with:
> I do not know that I care to be backed up in just that way:
>   the philosophy gives clubs to
> everyone, and I prefer disarmament:

The irony masterfully saves the poem, always reminding the reader that ideas are so many disinterestedly linked events in the circuitous drama of the poem's argument, which ends exactly where it began:

Northfield Poems, by A. R. Ammons. (Cornell University Press, 1967.)

what are facts if I can't line them up
    anyway I please
and have the freedom
    I refused I think in the beginning?

The poem's secret, which is revealed subtly and implicitly in its movement, is that the mind finds truth, is truest to itself, when it is released into the self-discovering rhythms of a good poem. To be true to the voice and line of the poem, an ever-changing field of play, always captures the speaker's first allegiance, never the ideas themselves. Most ideas would remain inert if not for the vivid life the poem's artistry imparts to them.

Ammons' knack for self-mockery saves the studiedly philosophical poems from self-conscious straining, as in "Zone," in which matter-of-fact remarks about the time of day, and such, interrupt the flow of formal scientific discourse. Ideas, in the poems, are quantities of form, shape, design; they are not vehicles for conveying logic, truth, validity. Ideas have texture, color, size, weight. To Ammons, they have the quality of physical objects:

A symmetry of thought
is a metal object:
is to spirit
a rock of individual shape . . .
a crystal, precipitate

Ammons treats ideas as so many jointed bodies colliding with each other, and with observed natural phenomena, interchangeably. Conversely, actual objects may be decomposed into substanceless vapors by the intense play of the mind. The interchange of form between ideas that have grown solid and objects that have turned gaseous, or bodiless, may have been suggested to Ammons by Einstein's formula $E = mc^2$, demonstrating the relation between energy and matter. (Ammons, indeed, has been schooled in the sciences, and this background broadened the scope of his poetic imagination from the start.) Whatever the source of his idea/thing inversion, one may more profitably inquire into the use he makes of it, the way he fits it to his unique sensibility. I see it as a particularly apt formula for embodying Ammons' original view of the relation between mind and world, between inner and outer reality. Though ideas and things may exist separately, they can have no importance or vitality, for Ammons, unless they disturb each other, interact. When this interaction is carried to the point of total engagement, the poet achieves his vision, a state in which elements of thought and elements of nature mix freely, and exchange identities, in a kind of ecstatic flux of poetic imagination, as in "Peak" (I quote the poem entire):

> Everything begins at the tip-end, the dying-out,
>   of mind:
> the dazed eyes set and light
> dissolves actual trees:
>   the world beyond: tongueless,
> unexampled
> burns dimension out of shape,
> opacity out of stone:
> come: though the world ends and cannot
> end,
>   the apple falls sharp
> to the heart starved with time.

The peak experience is defined and demonstrated. Mind stretched to its utmost limits (the "tip-end" of consciousness), after acute concentration on particulars of concrete experience ("actual trees"), casts into "the world beyond." Paradoxically, a scrupulous attention to the thing itself, its precise identity, begets a mental state in which the most solid things lose their form, become dimensionless, apparitional ghosts in the poet's vision (trees dissolve, stone loses its opacity). Ammons' genius is most evident in the transition into the final stanza: "come, though the world ends and cannot/ end." Invitation to the reader to take the final step, to throw himself fully into the world of the poem without holding anything back, is a frequent device; in this poem, it is perfectly timed and has the disarming simplicity of a handshake. The reader was at the point of recoiling from the experience, since the poem had shown that mind's peak is a sort of mindlessness in which the lovely things of this world fade away into shadows of themselves, but Ammons now assures us that we shall return from the "peak" (as Frost swings back on his birches) to find a world of things more solid for having undergone his visionary dissolution: "the apple falls sharp." One must be willing to sacrifice the world completely, in faith, if one is to get it back whole, regain it to the peak of mind's embrace.

Ammons, the craftsman, often declares that he will risk everything, technically, to avoid the temptation to take refuge in the safety of pre-given forms; and, from time to time, he discards methods, devices of his own, that have proven successful, as in "Muse":

> . . . how many
> times must I be broken and reassembled!
> anguish of becoming,

>   pain of moulting,
>   descent! before the unending moment of vision:

In learning to write all over again, he stumbles, gropingly, the lines of the poem "inching rootlike into the dark." Since he must slog through many failed poems "to find materials/ for the new house of my sight," he takes his place beside D. H. Lawrence and Whitman in the Anglo-American free verse tradition of blessedly "uneven" poets. Probably that sort of unevenness will always be the sacred trademark of the most gifted and revolutionary poets, since most of our good writers seem satisfied, if not compulsively driven, to maintain a constant of external polish in everything they write.

Ammons is pursuing a theory of poetry that radically departs from the theory advanced by the poetry of Yeats and the criticism of Ezra Pound. Ezra occurs as an advocate to be resisted or revolted against in a number of poems in this book and in the previous collection:

>   I coughed
>   and the wind said
>   Ezra will live
>   to see your last
>   sun come up again . . .
>   the wind went off
>   carving
>   monuments through a field of stone
>   monuments whose shape
>   wind cannot arrest but
>   taking hold on
>   changes
>   (from "The Wind Coming Down From")

If Ezra is a monument of stone, Ammons chooses to identify with the lowly weed. If Ezra advocates the poem of permanence, the indestructible art-object, Ammons prefers the poem as a way of being, of being in touch. While Ezra affirms what is most tough and enduring in man, the ruthless will to immortality of the conventional major poet, Ammons reveres a delicate, sensitive transitoriness of being. The best of Ammons' poems point, finally, away from themselves, back to the most evanescent motions and vicissitudes of wind, leaf, stream, which first enchanted the poet and finally stole his heart away. The gentlest motions of things touch him most deeply, speak to him with a sort of ultimate, if non-human, intimacy. He is vulnerable, nakedly exposed, receptive to the touch of feather, pebble, birdsong—in fact, these phenomena have such command over him as to leave him looking helplessly struck (or struck dumb), as by indecent or obscenely overpowering forces:

> I turned (as I will) to weeds and . . .
> weedroots of my low-feeding shiver

So far is Ammons from forcing or contriving his vision, his awakening, in the best poems—in "The Constant" he struggles to resist, even to suppress, the *onset* of revelation, with the air of a man who has been used overmuch, exploited, by his admittedly favorite mistress:

> When leaving the primrose, bayberry dunes, seaward
> I discovered the universe this morning,
>   I was in no
> mood
> for wonder,
>   the naked mass of so much miracle
> already beyond the vision
> of my grasp:

If formerly the mistress of experience (of miracle) consented to be a passive, supine guest to his advances, in "The Constant" she has become the aggressor: the poet, helpless and reluctant, allows himself to be overpowered by her mastery.

In a number of poems, Ammons unleashes surprising resources of power in himself by a sort of feminine submission to experience. In "Kind," "Height," and "The Wind Coming Down From" there is a fierce insistence on lowliness and passivity ("preference sends me stooping/ seeking/ the least"). This is his answer, his refusal, to the male challenge addressed to him by the massive antagonist in each poem—the giant redwood, the mountain, the wind; in each case, he recoils. Like St. Francis (and unlike Ezra!), he savors the strength of weakness. Strangely, all three poems seem facile, the dialectic merely clever and fanciful, perhaps archly whimsical. The poems are all statement, all philosophy, despite the illusion they try to advance of drama and dialectic. I don't believe the wind or redwood as antagonists because their *being* in the poems lacks the solidity of a felt presence. They exist only as foils to the persona, and the poems never extend beyond direct emission of "message." They desperately need extension into the world of substance and event.

The weakest poems in the book suffer from over-writing. "Sphere," like "Discoverer," is all writing: the subject—a voyage through the dark waters of the womb—recedes, as the dense filigree of language drives it underground. The subject is so self-limiting, the language so overtaxed, a reader has no sense of traveling any distance across its sinuous contour. Only the agility of Ammons' rhythms can induce a reader to proceed from one end of the poem to the other. A succession of weighty phrases, strung like clothes on a line, smothers the poem's life-breath: "... amniotic infinity ... boundless in circularity ... consistency of motion arising—annihilated ... infinite multiplicity, in the deepening, filtering earthen womb...."

"The Constant" succeeds precisely where the other poems fail because the poet's experience of the world, even though felt to be a "drab constant," is so intense it forcibly invades the poet's mind and takes possession of the landscape of the poem. Though the opening and closing lines (quoted above) are clung to by the speaker's intellection, those lines are the feeble, defeated cries of a lover ravished by his mistress, who inhabits the dominant central section of the poem's battlefield. The war between mind and world, though a losing battle for mind, yields fantastic life to the poem. The mind's defeat is the poem's victory. And yet, the speaker's dissatisfaction of mind, resentment even, at the end of the poem, is a valid redirection in itself. In "Corson's Inlet" and "World," poems of the previous volume, Ammons had already fully mastered the plateau of experience successfully revisited in "The Constant": the apocalyptic stroll along the dunes, the Blakean discovery of an entire universe in a clamshell-enclosed "Lake," the sense of totality and self-containment balanced by the sense of fragility and temporariness, likening the clamshell universe to the poem:

> ... a gull's toe could spill the universe:
> two more hours of sun could dry it up:
> a higher wind could rock it out:
>
> the tide will rise, engulf it, wash it loose:
> utterly:

Perhaps the only distinctly new element in "The Constant" is the recognition that the poet has been here before and is anxious to break out of the enclosure of old experience, to escape into a fresh territory. I suspect there is a hushed cry of frustration at the heart of *Northfield Poems*. The author senses that most of the good work in the book is a repetition of past success.

Some of the very short poems indicate a remarkable new direction in Ammons' work. At first reading, there is no clue to a significance beyond the purely pictorial and imagistic. Suddenly, one word or line will touch off an astonishing number of overtones. In "Trap," one is at first merely enticed by the visual clarity of the mating butterflies:

> ... they
> spin, two orbits
> of an

invisible center:
rise
over the roof

and caught on
currents
rise higher

than trees and
higher and up
out of sight,

swifter in
ascent than they
can fly or fall.

The poem's surprising force comes from the last lines. The spareness, cleanness, sharpness—the absence of ambiguity or overtones—all contribute to the astonishing impact of the finish, which transforms the entire poem, at a single stroke, into symbol. The reader is left stunned: where did all the hidden propulsion spring from? The restraint with which most of the poem is rendered allows the body of the piece to serve as a perfect conductor of the charge that travels between the two poles—title and last lines—as swiftly as lightning takes the tree.

The most impressive poem in the volume is a long one which achieves a new scope emerging unexpectedly in the familiar setting of the best former poems: the shore. In "One: Many," after the slightly stilted and heavy-handed philosophy of the opening lines, Ammons resumes his favorite technique of cataloging brilliant ephemera along the creek bank: "When I tried to summarize/ a moment's events along the creek...." Following a delicious summary, the sentence concludes: "I was released into a power beyond my easy failures." At this point, the mind leaps into a new dimension of world, as the catalog extends suddenly from the familiar imagery of shore to the free-ranging geography of the American continent. Ammons finds himself, for the first time, in the company of Whitman's wayfaring and wandering, or that of Roethke's last North American meditations. But the imagery is uniquely Ammons'; it has been revived and re-tuned to his most sinuous lines and rhythms:

I think of California's towns and ranges,
    deserts and oil fields;
and of Maine's
    unpainted seahouses
    way out on the tips of fingerlands,
lobster traps and pots,

freshwater lakes; of Chicago,
    hung like an eggsac on the leaf of lake
Michigan, with
its
Art Museum, Prudential Building, Knickerbocker Hotel
(where Cummings stayed);
of North Carolina's
    sounds, banks, and shoals,
    telephone wire loads of swallows,
of Columbus County
        where fresh-dug peanuts
        are boiled
            in iron pots, salt filtering
in through the boiled-clean shells (a delicacy
true
as artichokes or Jersey
asparagus): and on through villages,
along dirt roads, ditchbanks, by gravel pits and on
    to the homes,
inventions, longings:

He started in his own back yard, and fumbled into the impossibly
new ground, into "unattainable reality itself." At his best, Ammons is
willing to stake everything on the full health of the single imagination,
cut loose from history and the genius that labored the language into
monuments, to begin poetic art afresh.

THE HUDSON REVIEW, 1967

Selected Poems

I have spoken at some length of the originality of A. R. Ammons'
verse technique in other reviews, but in all my attentiveness to the
ingenuities of his line, I seem to have missed—or just barely touched
on—the more abiding quality of his language that transcends all ques-
tions of style or prosody:

    I raid
        a bloom,
    spread the hung petals out,
        and surprised he's not
    a bloom-part, find
        a moth inside, the exact color,
    the bloom his daylight port or cove . . .

Selected Poems, by A. R. Ammons. (Cornell University Press, 1968.)

So many of A. R. Ammons' poems are such raids, his lines fingers and tongues harmlessly loosening the fallen leaf, the petals of the flower, to surprise the hidden yucca moth, who is secretly "lifting temples/ of bloom." The words, like those intricately delicate moth-wings, would "go in to heal" our days. They have a spiritualizing power. The poetry glides with a lingering, light-fingered savoriness over the shades, tones, and hues of sensory experience. Ammons' language, disciplined by attending to the minutest motions in nature with the intensest caring for the "lowliest" forms of life, exhibits a precision and a quality of quiet spiritual rejoicing that carries over from his eye to his verbal ear. He has won his way through to an imperishable quiet at the heart of words, and he has infused more of this quality, this quietness—this one of the available essences of all language—into his poetry than is to be found in the work of any other poet now writing.

The spirit Ammons embodies in his poems is "the mode of motion," a mischievous imp that clothes itself in objects—or words of a poem—only to divest itself at whim, disposing of all forms, racing spryly from one incarnation to another. Its favorite condition is to sidle at the threshold between matter and non-matter, and to tease its faithful servant the poet by exercising its impulse for sheer caprice:

> I change shape,
> turn easily into the shapes you make
>   and even you
>   in moving
> I leave, betray.

Ammons' absorption in ephemera of nature is so enticing in itself, it is doubly rewarding to find, as we do in most of the poems, a veiled metaphor for the poetic process running through the description. The central drama of Ammons' poetry is the quest of the Ariel-self to escape the enclosure of materials. But these words are too heavy, for they miss the gaiety and lightness and buoyancy of spirits shaking off the bonds—the chains—of matter. This drama complements the struggle in Ammons' line to free itself from any formal pattern, any stricture of form exterior to the immediate line-by-line determinant. The poem aspires to remain open-ended, resisting closural devices at either extremity. It is a poetry dead set against the tendency to close off thought or language, the tendency to lock up a chain of ideas *or* words: "I have reached no conclusions, have erected no boundaries ... so I am willing to stake off no beginnings or ends, establish/ no walls."

The anti-closural gesture is one of the central impulses of art in our time, and Ammons' best poems ("Corson's Inlet," "Strait," "Expressions of Sea Level") do not simply participate in the pursuit of a freer poetics, but afford a definition of free verse which goes beyond the art of poetry to render more intelligible, more conscious, more *visible*, a mode of craft that partakes of the confluence of all the contemporary arts. Ammons carries on the adventure of aesthetic formulizing inside the body of the poem itself, and usually without self-consciousness. What his poetry demonstrates for us all is that the highest degree of critical self-awareness—a total consciousness of the possibilities and limits of medium articulating itself explicitly in the poem—is not incompatible with a total art.

POETRY, 1969

Briefings

"Always I hear wings." "He described his trip very well." You may recall these lines of *poetry* from the Peanuts comic strip one Sunday last summer. Charlie Brown has been watching (and overhearing!) the flight of a butterfly. The first line appears in the first frame, the last in the last frame, and in between all the saying is left to those fluttering wings.

The short, delicate flights of A. R. Ammons' new poems resemble those buoyant, nearly weightless butterfly wings. The book's abiding spirit is one of humor, ease, lighthearted and lightheaded playfulness—partly for the sheer pleasure of it, partly for the discipline of staying loose, open, fluid, responsive, available. As in "Square," Ammons refuses to square off or round out his perceptions, or his poetic forms:

> I thread the
> outskirts of mandate,
> near enough
> to be knowingly away &
> far enough away to
> wind and snap through
> riddling underbrush.

In this new collection of eighty-odd *Briefings*, most of the poems and the perceptions they articulate are partial and fragmentary by design, since the lucky moments of grasped spiritual wholeness that informs them spring from a self held lightly and uneasily in balance; subject to momentary fits of change: wakings, dyings, clarities, opacities— waveriness is espoused as a way to findings, allowed failures and fumblings as a way passively to court renewals.

Briefings: Poems, Small and Easy, by A. R. Ammons. (W. W. Norton, 1971.)

To be constantly on the watch for possibilities in nature for being struck into awe and wonder is a very exacting discipline, and Ammons' fourscore of "small and easy" poems suggest clearly that to maintain this discipline—to keep its gears well-oiled—requires daily practice in tuning up, to be constantly in training. The eye, rivaling a high-powered telescopic rifle, must train for perfect marksmanship ("My eyes' concision shoots to kill"), and the imagination must train to stay available for enchantments, to be ready always to respond with wonder, to be lifted by such beauties as that sniper the eye has picked off:

> pick a perch—
> apple branch for example in bloom—
> tune up
> and
>
> drill imagination right through necessity:

In a good many of the short-shorts of this book, either the sniper fire has flown wide of the mark or the imagination picked too high or low a perch, but nearly every poem contains some moments—flashes of loveliness—that ricochet from arrested points of fire in nature to the eye, from eye to verbal ear—and from there, why deny it?—straight to the heart. And in the best poems, the whole delivery bursts forth with the surety and ease of a supreme word acrobat who can juggle the beautiful simplicities of the natural heart as though such artistry were mere play.

Ammons' pleasures, like his vision in this book, are all—by predilection—tenuous, fragile, temporary; mortal, not mystical or otherworldly: life is an affair of abrupt reversals. "Briefings," if they stay on their graceful, imagistic toes, can dance in step with life's ups and downs—they might even get good enough or lucky enough to stay one step ahead ("only above the level of most/ perception"), lazily lofted on the liftoffs, riding easy on the splashdowns. Ammons is content just to keep in pace with the natural event most of the time, and oh how grateful—tickled, even—now and again, to come out on top! Even to break even, or perhaps to fall a little behind, to be *under* the weather—his mind's or the world's—is secretly to stay ahead, since "uncertainty, labor, fear" are "the rewards of my mortality," and he bids a kindly, but mistaken, Providence *not* to take them away, his weaknesses, his failures: *not* to grant him comforts, or fame, or faith, or mission, or belief in a poem of heroic denials ("This Black Rich Country") as profoundly moving and authentically radical in its negations of the transcendental tradition in nature poetry, of which Ammons himself is the most distinguished living exponent, as was

Shakespeare's sonnet "My Mistress' Eyes Are Nothing Like the Sun"
in its deflations of the hackneyed images of romantic love poetry:

> grant me no mission: let my
> mystical talents be beasts
> in dark trees: thin the wire
>
> I limp in space, melt it
> with quick heat, let me walk
> or fall alone: fail
>
> me in all comforts . . .

If I'm often a little suspicious that Ammons, out taking his nature
walks, is just a bit too deliberate about pouncing on any and every
instance or insect or incident (as if words and bugs and events are,
finally, just various equally assimilable species of poem parts) as occa-
sion for reconceiving and saying out his aesthetic theory, the good
poems always correct me: *theory* is too theoretical a notion for ideas in
poems which transfigure idea-making from a formal enterprise into a
primitive natural process. Words never merely talk about or sym-
bolize nature: bugs, ticks, mites, weeds, leaf/stem/root—all are reborn
as words in Ammons' poems. The words are so sticky, musky, sodden
with smirch and soilures, we forget the poems are made of language
at all.

After laying aside this book, we wonder: is it that we are left feeling
that the pricklings from thorn and briar have infiltrated and contami-
nated the words, or is it rather than we would find words fallen like so
much loose change and clinging to stem and creeper in the fields of
the "City Limits" of Ithaca where "the radiance . . . does not withhold/
itself but pours its abundance without selection," and where Ammons
has wastefully strolled away his time, spilling the coin of his ardent
gabble through forever patchless and unpatchable holes in his literary
trousers' pockets? We wonder, and wander, and when we take up the
book again and begin to read, we know we have taken both walks.

James Dickey

THE WORLDLY MYSTIC

The persona in James Dickey's new poems, those that appear in the final section ("Falling") of his new book, is a unique human personality. He is a wordly mystic. On the one hand, a joyous, expansive personality—all candor, laughter, and charm—in love with his fully conscious gestures, the grace and surety of moves of his body. An outgoing man. An extrovert. On the other hand, a chosen man. A man who has been picked by some mysterious, intelligent agent in the universe to act out a secret destiny:

> ... something was given a life-
> mission to say to me hungrily over
>
> And over and over *your moves are exactly right*
> *For a few things in this world: we know you*
> *When you come, Green Eyes, Green Eyes.*
>   (from "Encounter in the Cage Country")

How does a man re-connect with common, unchosen humanity when he has just returned from the abyss of non-human, chosen otherness? That is the chief problem to which the final volume addresses itself. How to be a man who feels perfectly at home, and at his ease, in both worlds—the inner and outer. A man who can make of himself and his art a medium, a perfect conductor, through which the opposed worlds—both charged with intensity—can meet and connect, flow into each other. The worldly mystic. It is the vision of a man who for years has been just as committed to developing his potential for creative existence as for creative art. All discoveries and earnings, spiritual or worldly, must carry over from one universe to the other.

In the best poems of the previous volume, *Buckdancer's Choice,* the self is frustrated, paralyzed, helplessly unable to establish liberating connections with the world. The chief obstacle to self-liberation is a sense of moral guilt. In "The Firebombing," "The Fiend," and "Slave Quarters," the self is pitilessly subjected to encounters with life that induce feelings of criminality. Clearly, the writer has deliberately trapped the persona in predicaments of contemporary American life that automatically create an aura of grave moral jeopardy. In all three

Poems, 1957-67, by James Dickey. (Wesleyan University Press, 1967.)

poems, the conflict between the worldly-mindedness of modern life and the inner life of the spirit is dramatized. Materialism, of a kind that blocks the persona in its struggle to connect with the world, is embodied in the indulgences of suburban middle-class home life of "The Firebombing"; in the businesslike exterior of "The Fiend," his guise of normalcy and ordinariness; and in the catalog of inferior occupational stereotypes, earmarked for Negroes by our society, in "Slave Quarters."

Wherever being is trapped in oneself or in others, the existential self must work, either through art or directly in life, to make life-saving connections—all those connections which create the free interchange of spirit between being and being. The word *connect* is the central one in Dickey's new poetry. His spirit must connect with the world, with "all worlds the growing encounters." In the best poems, all the connections are good. "I am a man who turns on," and when he turns on, all worlds he connects with turn on, since wherever he connects, he creates personal intimacy, injects intensity: "People are calling each other   weeping with a hundred thousand/ Volts."

The one poem that perfectly reconciles the contradictions between worldliness and the inner life of the spirit is "Power and Light." The happiness of power and light heals all broken connections, "even the one/ With my wife." For the artist, the hardest connections to "turn good" may be the home connections, the ones thorny with daily ritual and sameness: "Thorns! Thorns! I am bursting/ Into the kitchen, into the sad way station/ Of my home. . . ." But if the connections are good, all worlds flow into each other, the good healing, cleansing the bad. There is woe in the worldly side of marriage, but it is good in its spiritual and sexual dimensions, in the "deep sway of underground."

"Power and Light" dramatizes the secret life of a pole-climber, a technician who works for the power company. Through the disguise of the persona, Dickey explores symbolically the ideal relationship between the artist and his audience, the poet and his readers:

> . . . I feel the wires running
> Like the life-force along the limed rafters   and all connections
> With poles   with the tarred naked belly-buckled black
> Trees I hook to my heels   with the shrill phone calls leaping
> Long distance   long distances through my hands   all connections
> Even the one
> With my wife, turn good . . . Never think I don't know my profession
> Will lift me: why, all over hell the lights burn in your eyes,
> People are calling each other   weeping with a hundred thousand
> Volts   making deals   pleading   laughing like fate,
> Far off, invulnerable   or with the right word pierced

To the heart
By wires I held, shooting off their ghostly mouths,
In my gloves.

The pole-climber's spirit raises the spirits of the dead and damned from Hell—marriage, too, being a kind of hell. The "ghostly mouths" of the spirits can all re-connect through the power lines—lines of the poem—and save themselves. The poet is blessed with such an access, a surplus, of lifesaving joy, that he can afford to let it—the flood of power and light—overflow into the grave, into Hell. He doesn't so much give life to the damned as open them up to hidden resources of life, newly accessible in themselves, by making connections. "Long distance," an eerie experience to begin with, becomes more haunting still when Dickey extends it to include connections between living and dead spirits.

Dickey proceeds in his vision to a point "far under the grass of my grave." No matter how deep he travels, even to Hell, in the fuller mastery of his art he is confident that "my profession/ Will lift me," and in lifting him, it will lift thousands of others from Hell, his readers all over the world, symbolically making long-distance phone calls all night, connecting, all the connections good. He feels the same power, whether in the basement of his home, "or flung up on towers walking/ Over mountains   my charged hair standing on end." The spirit which pervades and dominates this poem, finally, can be identified as the spirit of laughter, a laughter closely akin to that of Malachi the stiltjack in Yeats's "High Talk," or the mad dancer of "A Drunken Man's Praise of Sobriety." Like these poems, "Power and Light" verges on self-parody in its hyperbolic imagery and rhetoric: "And I laugh/ Like my own fate watching over me night and day."

The comic spirit of "Power and Light" recovers the ground lost by the tragic spirit in the moral dilemmas of "The Firebombing" and "Slave Quarters." If modern man feels helpless before the massive political nightmare of his time, he finds he can retreat into "pure fires of the Self" for spiritual sustenance. This is the artist's escape and salvation. If he can't connect with the tragic people of this world's hell in daylight, by direct political action, he must reach them in "the dark,/ deep sway of underground." The artist's night is the "night before Resurrection Day." He will resurrect the imagination, the spiritual life, of his age. He performs these wonders, ironically, drunk in his suburban basement. A general in disguise. An unacknowledged legislator of the world. Regrettably, the philosophy *if I turn on everyone turns on with me* may offer small comfort in the political world.

If the worldly mystic spends a good portion of his day-to-day existence reconnecting with the world, at other times we find him searching for the pure moment in solitude, waiting to receive messages from the unseen beyond, and to answer the call. If he is receptive enough, he may pick up clues to learning his being from a wide range of sources: a rattlesnake, a blind old woman, a caged leopard. In all such poems Dickey himself would seem to be the protagonist, the poem being a kind of reportage of an event from the author's life, in contrast with poems like "Power and Light" and "Falling," in which the persona and the author are completely separate, on the surface level.

"The Flash" is a weak poem, hardly more than a fragment of verse, but it gives the key to understanding the revelatory moments in the other poems in the group:

> Something far off   buried deep and free
> In the country   can always strike you dead
> Center of the brain. There is never anything
> It could be   but you go dazzled . . .

You can't explain the flash logically, or fasten hold of it with your senses, but what is felt when "you go dazzled" is instantly recognizable, and can be distinguished, unerringly, from other events of the spirit. The flash is a spiritual fact that registers in the poet's intelligence with the same cold, tough certainty as snakebite. It is a guarantee of the inner life, but also insists on the inner life of the Other, of others "far off   buried deep and free."

In "Snakebite," the encounter with the Other seems fated. "The one chosen" finds "there is no way not/ To be me." There is no way out, or through the experience, except saving oneself:

>   . . . It is the role
> I have been cast in;
>
>   It calls for blood.
>
> Act it out before the wind
> Blows: unspilt blood
>
> Will kill you. Open
> The new-footed tingling. Cut.
> Cut deep, as a brother would.
> Cut to save it. Me.

One must act out the roles that are thrust upon one by the Other, inescapably, as by the rattlesnake's poison. Art must invade those moments in life when failure to perform the correct self-saving gesture is to die. Art is a strange kind of intimacy, a blood brotherhood, between the artist and himself. The poem must be an act of bloodletting. In saving the poem, as in saving one's life from snakebite, a man must be his own brother. No one else can help.

Midway in the action, the speaker shifts from the mortal necessity of lancing the wound to a moment of comic staging. At this point in Dickey's art, it seems appropriate and convincing for the comic spirit to interrupt the most serious human act of self-preservation. The laughter of self-dramatization parallels similar moments in "Encounter in the Cage Country," in which comic relief enhances the seriousness of the exchange between man and leopard:

> ... at one brilliant move
>
> I made as though drawing a gun from my hip-
> bone, the bite-sized children broke
> Up changing their concept of laughter,
>
> But none of this changed his eyes, or changed
> My green glasses. Alert, attentive,
> He waited for what I could give him;
>
> My moves my throat my wildest love,
> The eyes behind my eyes.

In "False Youth II," the blind grandmother's message, like the word of an oracle, is delivered with absolute certitude: "You must laugh a lot/ Or be in the sun." Her advice strikes a reader as being a deeply personal and literal truth in the author's life at the time he wrote the poem, and this hunch is borne out by the relevance her words have to many of the best poems of the new volume. A comic spirit pervades poems like "Power and Light," "Encounter in the Cage Country," and "Sun" that one had not met or foreseen in Dickey's earlier work.

Dickey presents an experience from life—in "False Youth II"— which taught him to see deeply into the shifting sands of his own personality as he slid, imperceptibly, from youth into middle age. Youth is a "lifetime search" for the human role, or roles, which, when acted out, will serve as a spiritual passport of entry into middle age. The necessary role may take the form of a physical gesture that perfectly corresponds to deep moves of the spirit: "My face froze... in a smile/ That has never left me since my thirty-eighth year."

The old blind woman unknowingly assumes the role of a fortune-teller. She has developed a superhumanly receptive sense of touch. Her life is contracted intensely into her hands, her fingertips having grown fantastically sensitive and alive. As she runs her fingers over his eyes and forehead, the poetic images envision a scientific and quasi-scientific composite of data linking electromagnetism, fingerpainting, astronomy, genetics, and fortune-telling:

> ... I closed my eyes as she put her fingertips lightly
> On them and saw, behind sight something in me fire
> Swirl in a great shape like a fingerprint like none other
> In the history of the earth looping holding its wild lines

> Of human force. Her forefinger   then her keen nail
> Went all the way along the deep middle line of my brow
>   Not guessing but knowing   quivering   deepening
> Whatever I showed by it.

The wisdom of the old woman has a primeval quality about it. Her acutely sharpened instincts and sense of touch precede the scientific age and surpass recorded modern science in a revelation of human personality that draws on the learning of many sciences, but goes beyond each in its ability to *connect* them all: which is not to say this literally happens in life. It happens, rather, in the images of the poem's vision.

She leads him to discover that he has come to a crossroads in his life and art. He must learn his life, as his art, and each stage of existence—in both worlds—concludes with a search for the blueprint to the next stage. The blueprint cannot simply be willed into existence. It is contained as a deeply true, hidden map of possibility within his developing self. If there are alternative paths latent and waiting to be journeyed in the self at any particular spiritual crossroads (as in Frost's poem "The Road Not Taken"), there is one best route available at each crucial juncture. It is discoverable, and once discovered, it has an unmistakable ring of truth: "Not guessing but knowing   quivering   deepening." Though the answer waits inside him to be released, he cannot find his way to it by himself. He arrives in himself through a deep conjunction with another being, in faith, "some kind of song may have passed/ Between our closed mouths as I headed   into the ice." There must be communion with the Other. Connection.

If one of the major new themes in Dickey's fifth volume is comic dramatization of his own personality, another is sexual realism. In both, he parallels the later Yeats. If we compare the vision in "The Fiend" with that in "Falling" and "The Sheep Child," we can get an idea of how far Dickey's art has traveled between the first major poem dealing with the theme of sexual realism and the last. In "The Fiend," the free-flowing form and the split line are fully exploited. This technique is well suited to sustained psychological realism. Also, the fiend is a thoroughly convincing persona. The encounter between him and life experience, though voyeuristic and "abnormal," is presented as final, incisive, fulfilling.

But somehow, the center of the poem's vision is too far from tragedy and believable danger: the poem lacks risk, the emotional pitch of a cosmos of love/beauty stretching to contain and transform a brutal agony of being. The sexual transcendence the persona unknowingly achieves is almost too evident, pre-ordained. Equipoise is

not felt to be the outcome of a fierce yoking together of oppositely
charged beings, as in the act of coitus between the farm boy and the
mother ewe of "The Sheep Child":

> ... *It was something like love*
> *From another world that seized her*
> *From behind, and she gave, not lifting her head*
> *Out of dew, without ever looking, her best*
> *Self to that great need....*

The stench of evil in "The Fiend" is smothered under the catalogs of
domestic inanities. There is no trace of the searing terror of "The
Sheep Child," the terror of our settled scheme of things being ripped
apart. It is too easy to dismiss the fiend as a genial saint—spiritually, if
not bodily, harmless. "The Sheep Child" and "Falling" threaten us
with glimpses into a world of becoming that is grimly near to us, a
mere hand's-reach away from those extensions of being into the be-
yond that we all easily attain in moments of emotional intensity. And
yet, that farther reach somehow eludes us, staying just out of our ken.
The secret of uncompromised being is just a spiritual stone's-throw
away, but we are cut off. These poems soar into that further beyond
with a sense of effortlessness and inevitability.

"The Fiend" was a breakthrough into the hinterland of sexual tran-
scendence, but what begins as a reader's sympathetic identification
ends as a comfortably removed appreciation of the poem's novelties.
"The Sheep Child" and "Falling" trap the reader in a haunting, if
inexpressible, certainty that a much larger, grander, demonic
world—compounded of Heaven and Hell—lies just the other side of
the limits of his known, calculable existence. And it waits, like the
dead, for him to step inside:

> *I woke, dying,*
>
> *In the summer sun of the hillside, with my eyes*
> *Far more than human. I saw for a blazing moment*
> *The great grassy world from both sides,*
> *Man and beast in the round of their need,*
> *And the hill wind stirred in my wool,*
> *My hoof and my hand clasped each other,*
> *I ate my one meal*
> *Of milk, and died*
> *Staring...*

The reader must be willing to drown, fly, burn with a flame that sets
all dreams on fire, and be the fire.

From "The Fiend" to "Falling," Dickey has been trying to find a
medium that would enable him to *use* the maximum of his creative

intelligence in poetry. To this end, he has chosen in "Falling" exactly the right subject and form. Both are moving toward a rhythm of experience that can sweep away all obstacles to realizing the fullest human potential: "*One cannot just fall   just tumble screaming all that time   one must use/ It.*" When a woman's life-space has suddenly contracted into a few seconds, the necessity to conquer mental waste, to salvage every hidden but discoverable shred of mental possibility, becomes absolute.

The opening sections of the poem stress the extent to which the girl's will, intention, participates in her experience. Her body and mind are both forced initially into reactions of powerful self-protective resistance, a mere reflex response to shock. But her will and creative imagination take on a larger and larger quotient of control. The female style of control is mixed with passivity, but the dynamic passivity of girding the body, sensually, as she "waits for something great to take/ Control of her." The beauty of healthy fulfilled physical life is Dickey's momentary stay against the chaos of the poem's life-crushing void. Within a moment of perfectly fulfilled physical being, her spirit lives an eternity.

The girl is strangely mated to air. The first half of her long, erotic air-embrace is a turning inward. She is learning how to be, to be "in her/ Self." She masters "one after another of all the positions for love/ Making," and each position corresponds to a new tone or motion of being. The second half of her adventure is a going outward. She is no longer waiting to be taken hold of, but now *she* is the aggressor, who "must take up her body/ And fly." The shifts in her body-cycle—falling, floating, flying, falling—stand for consecutive stages in a being-cycle, rising, as she falls to her death, to a pinnacle of total self-realization. It is a movement from extreme self-love to extreme beyond-self love, a movement from being to becoming, from becoming to going beyond. Though her fall concludes with an auto-erotic orgasm, she connects, at the moment of climax, with the spirits of farm boys and girls below—there is a profound flow of being between them. This unobstructable river of feeling between the self and the world is the life process to which Dickey ascribes ultimacy in his vision.

If ideas of rebirth and reincarnation are among the most compelling and pervasive in Dickey's art, the idea of resurrection by air—not water, earth, or fire—is the one that rises, finally, into apocalypse. A cursory glance at Dickey's biography might well support my hypothesis that, since the gravest spiritual losses to his manhood were incurred in air—via the incineration of women and children in the napalm bombings of Japan—he could be expected to seek compensatory gains to redeem himself, paradoxically, through that medium. In fact, he does achieve his most sustaining spiritual and poetic gains through the vision of air genesis. It is my hope that in the years to come Dickey will return to the perplexing questions of war and race dealt with in "The Firebombing" and "Slave Quarters," and bring to his renewed treatment of those themes—surely the most troubling specters of our day—the larger generosity of spirit we find in the vision of "Falling" and "Power and Light." If there is a passion today that can counterbalance all the hell in us, it is the ardor that fills these poems.

THE HUDSON REVIEW, 1967

James Dickey

THE DEEPENING OF BEING

The poetic vision in James Dickey's fifth volume of poems, *Falling*, contains so much joy that it is incapable of self-pity or self-defeat. There is a profound inwardness in the poems, the inner self always celebrating its strange joy in solitude, or pouring outward, overflowing into the world. No matter how much suffering the poet envisions, the sensibility that informs and animates him is joy in the sheer pleasure of being.

The condition of joy works remarkable transformations, in literature as in life, often converting the tragic condition into a saving buoyancy. This power to transform is typical of the best poems in the Romantic tradition. It derives from a special conjunction of the intelligence with the poetic imagination. The transforming joy in Yeats's poetry works its way into the antithetical spheres of private and public life. One measure of the greatness of Yeats's achievement is the expansion in the scope of his vision to include, with equal rigor and authority, personal disasters of the self and global catastrophes such as the Irish Revolution and World War I. The joyful vision of Theodore Roethke, the American poet for whom Dickey feels the strongest spiritual affinity, rarely extends into the political arena; instead, it journeys forever inward, probing darker and more perilous recesses of the interior self. The more tragic emotion—suffering, bitterness, despair—art can absorb and transmute into joyousness of being, the healthier it is. Dickey's vision aspires, above all, to that kind of supernal healthiness, but it moves uneasily into larger sociopolitical issues of war and race. His joyousness is generous to a fault, uncontrollable—thus working to disadvantage in a few of his most ambitious poems. In "The Firebombing" and "Slave Quarters," for example, the moments of ecstasy threaten to overbalance the moments of agony.

In the four volumes prior to *Falling*, Dickey seems to vacillate, as did Yeats, between two spiritual poles: stoicism and romantic passion. The problem of facing death without fear elicits by turns, now one, now the other, as in "The Ice Skin":

> Not knowing whether
> I will break before I can feel,

Poems, 1957–67, by James Dickey. (Wesleyan University Press, 1967.)

> Before I can give up my powers,
> Or whether the ice light
> In my eyes will ever snap off
> Before I die.

The ice light, a heroic "masterly shining," is a dispassionate state, a calm radiance of the spirit learned through a series of existential encounters with "the dying" and the "just born." The prevailing spirit of the poem is the power to endure suffering and meet death quietly, with steadiness and poise—a stoical transcendence over death by intellect.

However, Dickey's vision is far more sustaining when he achieves transcendence over death by passion, intensity of self, deepening of being, as in "The Performance," an early war poem that, with "The Jewel," initiates a sequence of war poetry culminating in a poem of the first importance, "The Firebombing."

In making an assessment of Dickey's war poetry we must ask, Does the sum total of the author's writings on the subject of war move us to respond humanely to the massive political crisis of our generation—that is, to respond with the human, or superhuman, compassion and commitment necessary to redress the wrongs, first, in our individual souls, and last, in the soul of our age?

In "The Performance," the Japanese executioner will have to carry the scars of Donald Armstrong's death in his soul, since, miraculously, Armstrong's ritual performance has converted the mechanical, inhuman relation between executioner and victim into a personal and inescapably spiritual—an existential—encounter:

> . . . the headsman broke down
> In a blaze of tears, in that light
> Of the thin, long human frame
> Upside down in its own strange joy,
> And, if some other one had not told him,
> Would have cut off the feet
>
> Instead of the head . . .

The fatally impersonal relation between man and man is a central dilemma of our time, occurring in its ultimate form in war. In "The Firebombing," Dickey conceives the dilemma of impersonality as being insoluble. The protagonist, however hard he tries, cannot connect spiritually with his victims below. Conversely, in "The Performance," the ritual acrobatic stunts create personal being, restore the I-thou, so that even the headsman, though powerless to disobey his superiors and follow his impulse to spare Armstrong's life, finds a kind of spiritual absolution during the killing. Armstrong's acrobatics transform the killing relation between them into a saving relation, a forgiving relation. Both souls are saved.

If many veterans are content to claim the depersonalization of their acts and the beings from which they sprang—in wartime—as grounds for absolving themselves of personal responsibility for their crimes, James Dickey is not. Witness his mercilessly uncompromising self-judgment in "The Jewel." Recalling his years as a fighter pilot, not only does he impute personal involvement to his flying missions, but he remembers feeling the sort of joyful fascination for his life in the cockpit that men ordinarily feel for precious gems. He is a passive lover—mated to his plane—who allows himself to be abducted by the overpowering beauty of the machinery, "being the first to give in/ To the matched priceless glow of the engines." He sees himself lovingly enclosed in the jewel-cockpit, as in the warmth of a womb. Now, years later, in the warmth of the family tent during a holiday, he recalls the pleasure he received from the enclosure of the plane. The old joy floods into the present, mocking his present security, leaving him feeling, once again, more than ever alone in his soul's late night.

"The Jewel" is one of Dickey's earliest attempts to identify and cope with the residue of guilt left by his role in the war. In the poem, the poet sees himself more as a paroled or pardoned criminal than as a survivor. But can he pardon himself? Does he qualify as a spiritual parolee? "The Jewel" is a predecessor of "The Firebombing" in a way the other war poems are not. In "The Performance" and "Drinking from a Helmet," he allows himself to feel the innocence and compassion of the detached bystander, a stance that conveniently removes the persona from his guilt, so the horror of war may be treated as a subject in itself, apart from whatever moral responsibility he may himself feel for perpetrating evil of his own making or perpetuating evil set in motion by the state.

In "Drinking from a Helmet," a new form—employing short, self-contained numbered sections in place of the usual stanza units—facilitates a rapid, to and fro fluctuation between inner experience and external action. It moves almost effortlessly between controlled hallucination and stark realism, a remarkably apt strategy for a poem that sets out to present extraordinary spiritual events in a setting of extreme dehumanization. Written in a tradition of war poetry, running from Wilfred Owen to Randall Jarrell, in which spiritual uplift in the midst of carnage of battle would be unthinkable, Dickey's poem provides uplift as much because of the soul's depravity as in spite of it.

In the opening sections of "Drinking from a Helmet," the level of awareness of the speaker keeps shifting, refocusing. He is possessed by two beings, recognizably separate early in the poem. Who is speaking, I or ultra-I?

> In the middle of combat, a graveyard
> Was advancing after the troops . . .
> A green water-truck stalled out.
> I moved up on it, behind
> The hill that cut off the firing. . . .
>
> I swayed, as if kissed in the brain.

One being perceives everything with a casual directness, a down-to-earthness necessary to mental self-preservation ("A green water-truck stalled out"); the other registers profound ultra-events ("I swayed, as if kissed in the brain"). The two zigzag, at irregular intervals, through the voice of the speaker, without any noticeable jarring of tone. The voice provides a continuum that can contain both irreducible beings, and gradually the two converge and interpenetrate in the vision of the poem's action:

> I threw my old helmet down
> And put the wet one on.
> Warmed water ran over my face.
> My last thought changed, and I knew
> I inherited one of the dead.

The speaker has imbibed and mystically reincarnated the spirit of the dead soldier in his own living spirit by drinking water from the man's helmet.

In the closing sections, as he envisions a plan to transport the dead man's spirit to his brother's home in California, incredible life bursts into the poem:

> I would survive and go there,
> Stepping off the train in a helmet
> That held a man's last thought . . .
> I would ride through all
> California upon two wheels . . .
> Hoping to meet his blond brother,
> And to walk with him into the wood
> Until we were lost,
> Then take off the helmet
> And tell him where I had stood,
> What poured, what spilled, what swallowed:
>
> And tell him I was the man.

The poem creates the illusion, finally, of being a prayer girding the speaker for a move back into life. The poem is like a launching pad to an actual experience; simultaneously, it contains within itself that future experience and opens into the event-to-be. The barrier between poem and lived act is swept away, just as the threshold between the living and dead soldiers was dissolved earlier in the poem.

In "The Firebombing," also, two beings function simultaneously but separately. In "Helmet," the two beings are coincident in time but move on different psychic levels. In "The Firebombing," present being collides with past being. Both seem to be hopelessly blocked, ineligible for entry into the full import of the experience—one lost in time, the other in moral stupor. Will the collision between the two lost selves, in the dream-dance of flight, result in a clarity of mind within which the unified self may seek absolution through a true confrontation with its crimes? This question comprises the central strategy of "The Firebombing."

At the finish, Dickey explicitly admits his failure to achieve his intended end: to assuage the moral guilt for past crimes by experiencing again the events in the imagination. He tried, through the medium—and mediation—of the poem, to feel some of the human horror and shame that his moral conscience tells him he should have felt twenty years before, and thereby to achieve moral expiation through art—the fire in the poem would cleanse the author's soul, purify it, burn away the sense of sin. But he finds, in the most piercingly honest revelation the poem affords, that art itself is an unclean instrument in his hands. The feelings of guilt and horror stirred by the experience of the poem cannot effect catharsis because they are hampered by the remembered sense of beauty and joy felt during the act of murder, "this detachment,/ The honored aesthetic evil,/ The greatest sense of power in one's life."

Early in the poem, it becomes evident to the reader that the moral jeopardy of the present is just as insuperable as that of the past. Self-purification must occur in the world of the suburban present, but the handicap of present prosperity and excess spreads across the poem in a Whitmanesque catalog of luxuries that quickly accumulate into an insurmountable obstacle to the self's redemption. There are many self-scalding images that take the speaker partway through the complex initiation ceremonies his redemption requires:

> It [the blazing napalm] consumes them in a hot
> Body-flash, old age or menopause
> Of children, clings and burns ...

If such images don't contain seeds of expiation, how can ideas or slogans, or even direct prayer, redeem him?

Dickey finds himself in much the same position as Claudius, who fails in the sincere attempt to repent of the murder of the elder Hamlet because he still possesses the spoils of the crime, queen and kingdom, and knows he is too weak to give them up. Likewise, not only is Dickey still blessed, or cursed, with the luxuries of the American suburban middle class, but he persists in being as "American as I am, and proud of it." Further, Dickey's incapacity "to get down there or see/ What really happened" can be attributed to other factors. First, the only way you can know exactly what it feels like to see your own child (or your neighbor's) walk through a door "With its ears crackling off/ Like powdery leaves" is to see it actually happen. Second, in writing the poem, Dickey places himself once again in the "blue light" of the "glass treasure-hole," deep in the same "aesthetic contemplation" he felt as he flew over "The *heart* of the fire." His spirit is perplexed by his joy in the act of writing, trapped in the tools of his art.

The poet senses that the experience of the actual firebombing gave birth in his soul to his deepest aesthetic instincts and talents, which he has never before more directly exploited than in the writing of "The Firebombing." Ironically, the poem seems better even for his having interrupted its flow of experience at the finish to comment on its inevitable failure to achieve its main goal:

> Absolution? Sentence? No matter;
> The thing itself is in that.

Perhaps this is a sort of ironic punishment: the poem gets better as the author backs away from it, refuses to exult over its beauties, insists that the purely human act of salvation from this massive sin is too great a burden for this poem, or indeed any poem, to carry.

How, then, do we account for the success of the poem, not only as art, but as a human (politically human, even) document? How account for the success of a major poem which unconditionally fails to achieve what the author explicitly intended it to achieve? Simply by acknowledging that whatever is not contained in "the thing itself"—the dramatic confrontation between self and its guilt, its crimes, in the action of the poem—cannot be stated parenthetically at the end as an afterthought, a dissipated message. To state it so would be to falsify the poem's central concern and mode of delivery. The writer has attempted the impossible, and he admits it. He is not ready for self-forgiveness yet, because he is not yet able to feel a guilt commensurate with his crimes. Perhaps he never will be ready. These are grave truths, but they are fully realized truths nonetheless, however lacking they may be in the kind of heroism fashionable at peace rallies in the sixties.

Moreover, if the poem admits its own failure to feel what must be felt, it carries the reader a step closer to having the feelings necessary to spiritual survival, and carries the instrument of language a step closer to meeting the ultimate life-challenge art faces in our time. If we read this poem—and, indeed, all Dickey's best work—with the brain in our eyes, with the intelligence to see that we call a *vision*, we find it to be poetry that constantly sends *us* back from the printed page to the gravest life-challenges.

As a survivor of two wars, Dickey feels spiritually hunted by disinherited beings (pursued by the "downed dead," as in "Pursuit from Under"), who silently accuse him of usurping their birthright to existence, leaving him with intimations of spiritual illegitimacy:

> Out of grief, I was myself
> Conceived, and brought to life
> To replace the incredible child . . .
> *Dead before I was born.*
>   ("The String")

In a number of war poems—"The Firebombing" particularly—Dickey feels like a cosmic criminal who, by luck or trickery, has miraculously escaped punishment and walks in freedom while innocent souls rot in purgatorial confinement, serving an eternal sentence for another's, his, crimes. He finds most harrowing the thought that he has been personally responsible for the death of many Japanese women and children, and in some poems he tries desperately to make his peace with the phantoms from death's dream kingdom.

Another source of these psychic misgivings is the stories he was often told by his parents about the brother who was "dead before I was born," stories antedating his war years by long enough to have been buried deeply in his memory, ready to be disinterred years later. The stories became indelibly, if invisibly, stamped on his impressionable young mind, and they haunted his early childhood, when he often felt as if he were possessed by a disembodied alter-self, living "within another's life." This long-forgotten obsession revisits him in his early poems, and he shapes it into a unique personal myth or legend. It is the first in a chain of mystiques that embody Dickey's developing logos of being.

To assuage his inexplicable guilt, the poet seeks devices for the revival of dead beings. In "The String," the dying brother's string tricks, such as "foot of a crow," are conceived of as the ritual magic that can guarantee his eternal return in living beings. The performance can be imitated by the living and used as a way of entering the dead child's being or of taking his being into oneself. The ritual performance with the string converted the brother's dying into an act of love. But it was purely self-love. There was no hint of the child's reaching out to others—parents or friends—through the string game. Contrarily, the speaker's performance with the string is a love act that engages the other being deeply. It connects him with the dead brother, and he aspires to use it to connect the living parents to the brother, but fails: "I believe in my father and mother/ Finding no hope in these lines."

A comparison between "The String" and the later "Power and Light" can be used to illustrate the remarkable distance Dickey's art has traveled between his first book and *Falling*. In "The String" he connects his own being to the Other, the spirits of the dead, but cannot, or will not, mediate between others as a neutral, but fiercely charged, spiritual conductor, as in "Power and Light":

> and I feel the wires running
> Like the life-force along the limed rafters   and all connections
> With poles   with the tarred naked belly-buckled black
> Trees I hook to my heels   with the shrill phone calls leaping
> Long distance   long distances through my hands   all connections
>
> Even the one
> With my wife, turn good . . . Never think I don't know my profession
> Will lift me: why, all over hell the lights burn in your eyes,
> People are calling each other   weeping with a hundred thousand
> Volts   making deals   pleading   laughing like fate,
> Far off, invulnerable   or with the right word pierced
>
> To the heart
> By wires I held, shooting off their ghostly mouths,
> In my gloves.

The power lines of this poem exceed the string by the same vast margin as "Power and Light" surpasses "The String" in spiritual intensity.

In "The String," as in most poems in *Into the Stone*, ritual hangs back from the reader in an ephemeral landscape of dream-memory. The reader is enticed by the strangeness of images, and if he feels somehow left outside the speaker's experience—a charmed, but displaced, onlooker—he is persuaded mentally by the ingenuity of the poem's argument:

> My eyes go from me, and down
> Through my bound, spread hands
> To the dead, from the kin of the dead . . .

In a number of the earlier poems, however, the gap between the reader's life experience and the poem's drama is too large. In an attempt to bridge the gap, the mind's activity, in the form of willed images or willed ideas, dominates the poem. The reader recoils from the tone of intellectual stridency as the poem's ever-extended machinery quavers like a house of cards.

In contrast, in many lines of "In the Tree House at Night," a later poem that revives the dead brother's spirit, there *is* something of the lightness of air—one can almost hear inbreathing sounds, a wind-sucking voice:

> The floor and walls wave me slowly...
> In the arm-slender forks of our dwelling
>
> I breathe my live brother's light hair.

It is perhaps no accident that in the early poems we find the inexplicable beginnings of a vision of genesis in air that eventually develops into the fulfilled air-birth of Dickey's most achieved vision, in "Falling." Unlike the play dwellings of "The String," the hypnotic lyricism of "Tree House" creates a castle in air that takes the reader's heaviness away and converts him into a being afloat, a just-lighter-than-air self. The poem's drama instills the sense of flying, of a soul set free in its body:

> When may I fall strangely to earth,
>
> Who am nailed to this branch by a spirit?

In "Tree House," atmospheric elements of scene, setting, time of day—all become dynamically enmeshed in the poem's drama. As in a movie, these elements create the illusion of action taking place *now*. The ritual magic of the poem's movement pulls the reader, irresistibly, into its happenings. He is himself one of the actors, sharing the tree house of the poem's ritual flight with "My brothers and I, one dead,/ The other asleep from much living,/ In mid-air huddled beside me."

In "Tree House," as in the other best poems of the second volume, *Drowning with Others,* Dickey evolves a mode of experiencing a double vision that seems ideally suited to his poetic imagination, thereby anticipating the more complex dualism of later poems like "Drinking from a Helmet" and "Firebombing." Two separate, but interdependent, dramas occur simultaneously in "Tree House." A familiar scene or event is presented directly, and an equally clear and sharp experience of the spirit is envisioned through it. Usually, in the best poems, the two dramas, outer and inner, are nearly evenly balanced. Neither dominates the poem. The poem can be read with equal interest at either level, but it is experienced, ideally, at both.

A lifeguard trying to forgive himself for letting a child drown, two brothers striving to oppose the real world with the fantasy world of their tree house—both are familiar experiences and hence create immediate and intensified human interest, but they become unfamiliar, beautiful, and strange as a unique spiritual experience is filtered through them. The familiar story seems, of necessity, to call up from the inner depths a strangely new spiritual history to explain it. At the same time, the spirit half-creates the illusion of being the reflection or mirror image of the story half—the familiar leading effortlessly into the unfamiliar, and back again. If the spirit half dominates many of the best early poems, the story half dominates Dickey's best later poems—"Shark's Parlor," "The Sheep Child," "Falling"—in which the poet is bent on exploring novel, rather than ordinary, experience, to stir up strangely new spiritual overtones, and to extend the resources of his art.

In "Tree House" and "The Lifeguard," a familiar experience is turned inside out. As the poems proceed, the focus of the drama shifts from the outer world of story to the inner world of magic. What begins as a tale of two boys playing house in a tree changes into a mystical vision in which the speaker experiences a transmigration of three beings—his own, his dead brother's, and his sleeping brother's—through the medium of the tree. The state of spirits in flux is expertly dramatized by lines that enter the inexplicable thresholds between brother and brother, alive and dead, asleep and awake:

> I stir
> Within another's life. Whose life?
> Who is dead? Whose presence is living? . . .
> Can two bodies make up a third?

The lifeguard returns to the scene of his defeat and recounts his failed attempt to save the drowned child's life in details that suggest the pain of self-mutilation:

> And my fingertips turned into stone
> From clutching immovable blackness.

His ritual suffering, in memory, summons the dead child's spirit to his aid. Though he is still "thinking of how I may be/ The savior of one/ Who has already died in my care," paradoxically, the relation between saver and saved is reversed through the medium of water as the dead child's spirit rises to free the living, helpless man from his guilt.

Both poems awaken the reader to the unexpected realization that a profound spiritual life lies hidden just below the surface of most routine experiences, and that perhaps this inner life of being is inherent in all experience, waiting to be released by the healthy imagination. This inner life erupts with the intensity of hallucination and pervades our being with the strangeness of the supernatural, yet it is, at all times, available to the normal mind. It is a richer totality of being than we are accustomed to enjoying in our daily lives. It seems to be delivered to the conscious self as from an inexhaustible source. At a moment's notice, it can transform grief into boundless joy. It is a state in which each one's being is both alone in a self-contained peace and indissolubly connected, in love, to other beings, living and dead, as in the beautiful closing lines of "Tree House":

> To sing, must I feel the world's light?
> My green, graceful bones fill the air
> With sleeping birds. Alone, alone
> And with them I move gently.
> I move at the heart of the world.

Never again in his poems about children does Dickey achieve such a full expression of the way he perceives the strange beauty—the otherness—of children's fantasy vision as he does in "The Lifeguard" and "Tree House." Yet in neither of these poems do we find purely a child's vision; rather, they offer a vision inaccessible to children, possible only to a man childlike in his freedom from incapacitating rigidities of mind and in his absolute faith in the saving power of imagination. The lifeguard's vision contains, in addition, the belief that a powerful healing forgiveness dwells in the souls of small children: a forgiveness strong enough to balance a man's guilt for taking the place of the brother "dead before I was born," and a healing power soothing enough to close temporarily the wound sustained by his spirit when he poured fire-death on the children of Japan. The evidence of thematic development strongly suggests that the guilt that is partly assuaged through the persona of the lifeguard is only temporarily forestalled, while the poet gradually fortifies his craft to deal with the larger challenge of a direct encounter, in art, with the events of the war which planted in his heart seeds of guilt that can never be entirely purged or expunged. The searing, insurmountable guilt is presented in raw form in many lines and images in "The Firebombing," and, again, in the final passage of "Slave Quarters," in which the southern white father meditates on the face of his choice possession, an illegitimate mulatto son:

> ... There is no hatred
> Like love in the eyes
> Of a wholly owned face? When you think of what
> It would be like   what it has been

What it is to look once a day
Into an only
Son's brown, waiting, wholly possessed
Amazing eyes, and not
Acknowledge, but own?

Dickey's imagination is obsessed with a man's responsibility—human and mystical—for the lives of children, especially those entrusted to his care. It is one of the very few themes that have engaged him deeply at each stage of his development, the problem having its own self-defined limits, peculiarity, and obsessive strangeness. Dickey is always at his best when he tackles a subject that entirely engrosses and excites his imagination, such as the most basic challenges to his manhood—befriending, fathering, husbanding.

One of Dickey's most sustaining and pervasive faiths is his absolute belief that the human imagination can save us from anything. No human disaster or tragedy is too large for the imagination to encompass or too crushing for imagination to convert it into life-savingness. This credo reaches its culmination, and its apotheosis, in the poem "Falling." Who would have guessed that a woman's falling to her death from a plane could be converted by Dickey's imagination into a symbol of fantastic affirmation of life? The thought of his being responsible for the death of a child fills Dickey's heart with extreme terror, a terror that arouses an instantaneous sympathy and recognition in most readers. Every parent harbors a secret voice in his soul repeating over and over—consciously or unconsciously—that if harm or injury comes to his child through his neglect, he'll never forgive himself. That *never* is a powerful and terrifying idea, and Dickey's imagination obstinately refuses to submit to never. Some of his best poems, such as "The Lifeguard" and "The Firebombing," are desperate attempts to forgive himself, spiritually, for what he recognizes to be humanly unforgivable.

The development of Dickey's treatment of the theme of human/animal relations is central to his art. Moreover, since this theme is unhampered by the overwhelming moral guilt of much of the war poetry and the poems about children, it can be used to demonstrate an evolving logos of being.

Dickey's engagement with the animal world was never cultivated simply as equipment for his poetry. He is intent on exploring the animal's dimensions of being. His experience of hunting, like that of soldiering, antedates his career in poetry by many years. As in the war poetry, the passion he feels for hunted animals is so intense that it enables him to put out of his mind the tradition of nature poetry in

English—D. H. Lawrence's excepted—and induce a literary amnesia, allowing him the latitude of imagination necessary to do justice to a series of strangely unique human/animal encounters.

The stages of relationship he depicts closely resemble those of a love affair between man and woman, especially in the way the poet's mind explores possibilities—limits—of relationship in search of a truer sense of identity. Dickey's realization of personal identity is always sought through a deep conjunction with the Other, whether the Other happens to take the form of animals, children, man, or woman. Consider, for example, "The Heaven of Animals":

> Here they are. The soft eyes open.
> If they have lived in a wood
> It is a wood.
> If they have lived on plains
> It is grass rolling
> Under their feet forever.
>
> Having no souls, they have come,
> Anyway, beyond their knowing.
> Their instincts wholly bloom
> And they rise.
> The soft eyes open.
>
> To match them, the landscape flowers,
> Outdoing, desperately
> Outdoing what is required:
> The richest wood,
> The deepest field.
>
> For some of these,
> It could not be the place
> It is, without blood.
> These hunt, as they have done,
> But with claws and teeth grown perfect,
>
> More deadly than they can believe.
> They stalk more silently,
> And crouch on the limbs of trees,
> And their descent
> Upon the bright backs of their prey
>
> May take years
> In a sovereign floating of joy.
> And those that are hunted
> Know this as their life,
> Their reward: to walk
>
> Under such trees in full knowledge
> Of what is in glory above them,

And to feel no fear,
But acceptance, compliance.
Fulfilling themselves without pain

At the cycle's center,
They tremble, they walk
Under the tree,
They fall, they are torn,
They rise, they walk again.

"The Heaven of Animals" is a classically pure statement. It pictures the animals in an utterly unpeopled landscape that recalls D. H. Lawrence's wistful misanthropic vision in *Women in Love* of a world "all grass and a hare standing up." Dickey conceives of the animals as being ideally beautiful and innocent, incapable of evil. All violence, or bloodshed, is performed with "claws and teeth grown perfect." The spilling of blood is a necessary condition of this idyllic state that "could not be the place/ It is, without blood." If the animals' "soft eyes open," they are capable of ferocity, as well as of gentleness, "More deadly than they can believe." But the victims are spared both fear and pain since hunter and hunted alike flourish in a "sovereign floating of joy." "At the cycle's center," killing and being killed comprise a total love-relation, a fulfillment of animal life, since all beings are instantly reincarnated and reborn: "They fall, they are torn,/ They rise, they walk again."

At times, Dickey's unqualified adulation for animals, like his glorification of the healthy-mindedness of children, verges on absurd romanticism. The vision in "The Heaven of Animals," however, as in most of Dickey's poems, works two ways. It suggests that man is the only corrupt animal. If he were removed from earth, beatitude would automatically transpire, just as it must have prevailed before his coming. The vision also anticipates later poems, beginning with "Fog Envelops the Animals," in which man the hunter tries to qualify for re-entry into the animal heaven from which he has been excluded. To do so, he must purify himself, divest himself of all those aspects of humanness that unfit him for animal beatitude. The fog is the medium of purification: "Soundlessly whiteness is eating/ My visible self alive./ I shall enter this world like the dead." As the visible self is eaten away, the fear and guilt of man the hunter are dissolved. Despite the fact that he kills, he can feel innocent.

In the earlier poems, the action is symbolic ritual; in "Springer Mountain," the action is realistic narrative interrupted by the advent of miracle—a plunge into the mystical beyond. If the earlier poems offered symbolic justification of the master-slave relation between hunter and hunted, "Springer Mountain" converts that relation into

an erotic encounter between two equal, but qualitatively distinct, be-
ings. The man spontaneously strips off his clothes and runs joyously
in the woods with the deer. The hunter expresses his love for the
animal-being in a more direct intimacy than ever before. He ap-
proaches the deer on a strictly human level, expressing the ardor and
laughter of exuberant human affection. In contrast, in "Fog Envelops
the Animals," he entered the animal's life-sphere by giving up his
human qualities entirely to the transforming symbolic fog. The gains
for entry into the foreign element were balanced, or canceled, by
losses of realism and human identity. There is a kind of emotional
dishonesty in glorifying the animal's otherness and integrity of being
while debasing one's own human otherness, as though it can be taken
off and put back on with one's clothes. Thus in "Springer Mountain" a
deeper honesty is exhibited than in earlier poems. Though the hunter
has become farcical in his excessive attempt to assume the identity of
the deer-beloved, he has retained his human personality, and even
though he ludicrously overshoots his human limitations in trying to
identify with the deer, he salvages a sizable reward:

> For a few steps deep in the dance
> Of what I most am and should be
> And can be only once in this life.

The ultimate lesson Dickey brings back from his poems would seem to
be wisdom of being. The poems teach him how to be, and we may
suppose he learns as much from blundered tries for impossible being
as from the successes.

As a poem, "Springer Mountain" is less successful than "The
Heaven of Animals," because it is less compact and less technically
achieved. As the poem searches for a new experience, a further reach
of vision, the rhythms fall into a decadent sing-song and the experi-
ence is diffused, not intensified. Also, the laughter in the poem occurs
at the extremity, rather than at the center, of its experience. It does
not become a controlling point of view, as does the comic spirit in later
poems like "Power and Light" and "Encounter in the Cage Country,"
but the poem winds up a chapter in Dickey's art. Once he has loved a
deer with personal intimacy, he can never return to the master-
slave relation again. He has hunted "Deer for the first and last time."
He is a man who has learned, irrecoverably, that a deep give-and-
take exchange is possible between man and animal, an exchange that
maintains the identity in separateness of each being. He is now ready
to bring to the final and fulfilled meetings of "The Sheep Child"
and "Encounter in the Cage Country" a full quotient of human per-
sonality.

But first, it remains for the speaker of the poems to stretch beyond human limits in another extreme direction. In "Reincarnation 2," man literally becomes a bird, not merely evolving certain birdlike characteristics as in earlier poems. Kafka has captured the horror of man's turning into an animal in "Metamorphosis"; Dickey evokes the beatitude of man reborn as animal. Gradually, in Dickey's vision, man has qualified for complete entry into animal heaven. In "Reincarnation 2," entry, following elaborate ritual initiation, is irreversible. Man reborn as a bird can never change back into man again, as he can in myths and fairy stories of human/animal interchange. Early in the poem, the man senses that he has been transformed into a bird, and that he must learn to live with it. He still has human feelings and ideas, so they must either become annexed to the new bird-instincts, bird-senses, and bird-spirit, or give place to them. On one level, the man gradually divests himself of all aspects of humanness as he learns his new life, wears his new bird-identity. On another, the entire experience is perceived through the human awareness of the author. So man-spirit and bird-spirit are wedded in the bird's body, much as owl-spirit and blind child's spirit had become wedded in the father's dream song in "The Owl King."

Somehow, the conception of "Reincarnation 2" seems too settled in advance, and the experience seems contrived. In "The Sheep Child," terror and sexual mystery achieve the focus and compression of experience the other poem lacks. Too much of "Reincarnation 2" is diffused in the bloodless void of philosophical abstraction, but one really believes the sheep child's vision because its identity is so palpable, so uniquely realized in language of passionate intensity:

> I am here, in my father's house.
> I who am half of your world, came deeply
> To my mother in the long grass
> Of the west pasture, where she stood like moonlight
> Listening for foxes. It was something like love
> From another world that seized her
> From behind, and she gave, not lifting her head
> Out of dew, without ever looking, her best
> Self to that great need. Turned loose, she dipped her face
> Farther into the chill of the earth, and in a sound
> Of sobbing   of something stumbling
> Away, began, as she must do,
> To carry me.

"The Sheep Child" develops in two movements spoken by two separate personae, the narrator and the sheep child, a method that recalls the method of "The Owl King," in which each of three speakers views an experience from a different angle of vision. The sheep child is a vastly better poet than the narrator, exceeding him as the superhuman exceeds the human. The narrator's introductory remarks are delivered with the maundering stammer of a southern yokel spinning a ghostly yarn. In his soliloquy (above), the sheep child maintains that the farm boy regarded his sheep-mate as a thing without being, selfless, defenseless, caught unawares. To couple with the sheep would be a mere extension of the act of masturbation, like coupling "with soft-wooded trees/ With mounds of earth." Shrewdly, the sheep complies with this falsification of her role to trap the boy into completing the act of bestiality. The boy mistakes the female sheep's absorbed passiveness for indifference, for *"she gave, not lifting her head/ Out of dew, without ever looking, her best/ Self to that great need."* The ewe experiences a perfect fulfillment of being; the farm boy, "stumbling away," is sobbing, haunted, driven wildly afraid by the profundity of her experience. His fear is mixed with guilt for having committed the forbidden act.

The ewe takes her place alongside "Crazy Jane" in the gallery of mindless sexual heroines in modern poetry in English. The farm boy's amazement and terror at her unexpected passion dramatize, in an original and unpredictable way, the mystery and depth of female sexuality. Yeats provided religious-erotic motifs that anticipate this poem in "Leda and the Swan" and "The Second Coming." But while Yeats molds the poem around myths taken from Bible, folklore, or literary tradition, Dickey draws on legends concocted by nonliterate, superstitious people to curb the wildness of the young. The poem combines the supernatural otherness of nightmare with Ripleyesque shock effects, but the vision is so powerfully conceived that it escapes sensationalism.

If "The Sheep Child" opens up new possibilities for deepening man's sexual identity, "Encounter in the Cage Country" explores opportunities for deepening his spiritual identity in a worldly setting (in this poem, the zoo). "Encounter" succeeds because the fabulous experience occurs unexpectedly, in a completely mundane context. The astonishing recognition and exchange between the narrator and the leopard unmistakably carries the ring of truth. Mystical events very likely do seem to invade the author's worldly life, leaping into his experience where he least expects to find them. They strike him, and those witnesses who happen to be present and looking on, with crushing reality:

> Among the crowd, he found me
> Out   and dropped his bloody snack

And came to the perilous edge
Of the cage, where the great bars tremble
Like wire. All Sunday ambling stopped,

The curved cells tightened around
Us all   as we saw he was watching only
Me.

"Encounter" is a celebration of individual uniqueness. As in "Snake-bite," the protagonist pictures himself as the *one chosen,* chosen by some mysterious intelligent agent in the universe who

was given a life-
mission to say to me hungrily over

And over and over   *your moves are exactly right*
For a few things in this world: we know you
When you come, Green Eyes, Green Eyes.

Most of the poems that employ the theme of human/animal rela-tions try to maintain a balance between emotional extremes of joy and terror. In "The Heaven of Animals" and "Springer Mountain," the terror is felt to be too easily contained, or counterbalanced, by the joy. An irrepressible terror is unleashed in "The Sheep Child." Finally, a truer balance between deepened emotions is achieved in the vision of "Encounter in the Cage Country," in which the comic spirit becomes a center of focus:

... at one brilliant move

I made as though drawing a gun from my hip-
bone, the bite-sized children broke
Up   changing their concept of laughter,

But none of this changed his eyes, or changed
My green glasses. Alert, attentive,
He waited for what I could give him:

My moves   my throat   my wildest love,
The eyes behind my eyes.

While the humor enhances the seriousness of the exchange between man and beast, it also balances the terror as the poem rises to a peak of spiritual transcendence.

In the earlier poems, Dickey supposed he could give up his human self to the animal realm. The human/animal encounter in the last poem of the series, "Encounter in the Cage Country," has become a medium through which his human limitations can be transcended, but in going beyond his human condition, he no longer transforms into a new, wholly other being; instead, he intensifies and deepens the human self by adding animal powers to it. He becomes more truly human by realizing and releasing animistic powers recognized to have been inherent in him all along but not available until the fulfilled vision of the later poems. It is a vision which places the living man before us, a man whose daily experience may, at any moment, speak to him in the profound otherworldly language of dreams, a man who is instantly recognized by his spiritual kin among the animal kingdom, a man whose days are lit with wonders that never cease to amaze both himself and witnesses standing by, when they occur: "the crowd/ Quailed from me   I was inside and out/ Of myself."

THE ACHIEVEMENT OF JAMES DICKEY, 1968

Notes on James Dickey's Style

In *The Suspect in Poetry,* a first collection of James Dickey's criticism, he eliminates from his canon of taste, one by one, those writers of reputation he finds suspect. Similarly, the development of his art, from book to book, is a conscious stripping away of those techniques of style and mental strategies which have grown suspect after repeated use. In the poems themselves he may leave the explicit record of steps in a willed metamorphosis of style; moreover, each conversion of manner bolsters a corresponding conversion of imagination.

To begin with, Dickey's handling of figurative language suggests a basic distrust of the remoteness from human experience of traditional figures of speech. In the early war poem, "The Performance," the speech figures are so closely wedded, annexed, to the human events that it would be a mistake to think of them as being metaphors—or figurative—at all, in the usual sense. They are elements of style and expression which are an extension of meaning that is felt to have been already inherent in the experience itself, waiting to be released, or to emerge from the living receptacle as a photo emerges from a negative. The phrases have all the mystery and suggestiveness of metaphor, but reduce decorative and artificial qualities to a minimum: "blood turned his face inside out," "he toppled his head off," "the head rolled over upon its wide-eyed face," "sun poured up from the sea." Style takes the reader deeply into the experience, intensifying the being in the poem without literary self-consciousness. The poet is telling a story, and if the way he tells the story is as remarkable as the story itself, the *way* of telling remains dutifully subordinate to *what* is told—imparts urgency and intensity to the story.

In the later war poem "Drinking from a Helmet," as in "The Performance," metaphor and personification are so well anchored to harrowing sense impressions that they heighten physical realism:

(1)   I climbed out, tired of waiting
       For my foxhole to turn in the earth
       On its side or its back for a grave.

(2)   In the middle of combat, a graveyard
       Was advancing after the troops . . .

(3)   Where somebody else may have come
       Loose from the steel of his head.

(4)   Keeping the foxhole doubled
       In my body and begging . . .

(5)   I drew water out of the truckside
       As if dreaming the helmet full.

So far are these images from creating the usual remove, the abstracting from literal experience which we expect from figures of speech, that these figures seem to carry us into a more intense and immediate literalness than literal description could possibly afford. The figures suggest a mind stretching its natural limits of perception to assimilate experience of pain and anguish that can only be apprehended accurately through hallucination. Excruciating mental experience is translated into exact physical correlatives. There is no question of a straining after clever or original images—rather, these queer transpositions of qualities between beings and things are the mind's last resort to keep a hold on its sanity, to stay in touch with its physical environs.

Dickey's use of symbolism is as innovatory as his language. Quite often the least fully realized poems reveal, in a raw lucidness, ideas and symbols that become the subtly hidden mainstay in the best poems. He draws on the arcane system of thought and symbology in these poems, much as Yeats drew on *A Vision,* in crystallizing the structure of ideas in his most achieved art. We can turn to these poems, as to a skeleton key, for clues that can often be found nowhere else.

Perhaps the first poem of this type is "Dust." In Whitman's vision of reincarnation, traditional worms feed on corpses and bring them back to life through the soil and grassroots. In *Helmets,* Dickey's third volume of poems, his vision is largely confined to that view. However, in "Dust"—a poem in the fourth volume, *Buckdancer's Choice*—he moves toward a new vision of reincarnation through wormlike dust motes, "spirochetes boring into the very body of light," a rebirth through sunlight and air. He conceives dust as a middle condition, a mediating form between organic and inorganic matter, life and death, much as scientists conceive the virus as a sort of intermediate limbo—a twilight zone—between plant and animal life. Dust motes seem to embody a partial being, or intelligence, as they wait in air and sunlight for spirits just arisen from the newly dead to whirl through them, changing them into "forms of fire," into "incandescent worms," and finally amassing them into a shape, "a cone of sunlight." That shape of dust is pervaded by being, and becomes a human. The leftovers, "extra motes," are unable to get into a human form at this time, but ready. They wait.

In "Dust," as in many poems of the later volume *Falling*, Dickey seems to be formulating his symbology into a coherent system of thought, a metaphysics of being. A formal theosophy begins to take shape, if these poems are read conjointly. Subsequently, to trace the development of these symbols in Dickey's cosmos is to find that he has been consistent and scrupulous in carrying them through successive stages of his art. Though particular symbols deepen in meaning and intensity in poems which treat them as primary subjects—"Dust," "The Flash," "Snakebite," "Sun"—their basic identity is consistent with their meanings in other poems. Dickey seems to have deliberately extracted recurring components of his art for specialized treatment, each in a separate poem. Partly, he seems to be trying to find out for the first time why each of these symbols, or symbolic events, has such a powerful hold over his poetic imagination. Also, he is codifying the symbols into a systematized philosophy.

To turn from symbolism to a discussion of the management of line and form: in Dickey's early work the long sentence, often extended over several stanzas, is the chief unit of measure. This type of verse movement served Dickey well for three volumes of work, though in some poems the line falls into artificiality and rhythmic straining when the technique becomes self-imitative and lacks complete absorption in the subject ("The Island" and "The Scratch").

In "Drinking from a Helmet," Dickey breaks away from the line and stanza units he has grown so attached to. But he stays confined to many of the old sentence rhythms until he begins to evolve the split line of *Buckdancer's Choice*. The form in "Drinking from a Helmet" operates like a film strip. Each frame/stanza focuses on an event, physical or spiritual, separate in time from the others. The movement is that of a film strip, rather than a motion picture, since the pauses or silences between frames are as functional in the poem's rhythmic structure as are the stanzas themselves. This form is an extremely important development for Dickey, since it readily achieves effects exactly opposite to the unbroken flow and rhythmic sweep of most of the previous work. Any such innovation in Dickey's form is accompanied by equivalent modifications in the handling of line and pacing of action.

In the poems of *Buckdancer's Choice* and *Falling,* the chief unit of measure is the phrase, a breath unit (or breathing unit), as opposed to a grammatical unit. The sentence, as a unit of measure, is all but lost, though occasionally a sentence beginning or ending does seem to punctuate a larger compartment of verse, and more important, a reader usually keeps the illusion that he is moving within the extremities of a rather free-floating sentence (an illusion that is completely lost, say, in parts of the stream-of-consciousness flow of Joyce and Faulkner). This form adapts perfectly to a welter of experience in flux. The rhetoric keeps drawing more and more live matter into the poem, as from a boundless supply. The entire poem maintains a single, unbroken flow of motion. In this respect, the medium owes more to the moving picture, to film technique, than to other poetry. The verse paragraph break is never a true interruption to the rhythmic sweep of the phrase chain. It merely suggests a shift in perspective, a slowing down and speeding up of the unstoppable momentum, an occasional amplification of the breath spaces that already separate every phrase from phrase.

Dickey's new form, incorporating the split line, is most successfully managed in the poem "Falling." The triumph of the split line technique in "Falling" is principally the net result of the ingenious variety of effects Dickey is able to achieve by playing off the phrase unit against the hexameter line unit. The length of the breath phrases ranges from a single word to a couple of lines. A single line frequently affords as many as five separate phrases:

> Do something with water   fly to it   fall in it
> drink it   rise
> From it   but there is none left upon earth   the clouds have
> drunk it back
> The plants have sucked it down   there are standing
> toward her only
> The common fields of death   she comes back from
> flying to falling

The enjambments between lines are nearly always consciously functional, whether they interrupt a single breath unit and break up the phrase, or connect breath units:

> ... My God it is good
> And evil   lying in one after another
> of all the positions for love
> Making   dancing   sleeping ...

The astonishing variety of rhythms is mainly induced by balancing caesuras within the line, and varying the patterns of balance in successive lines:

> She is watching her country lose its evoked master shape
> watching it lose
> And gain   get back its houses and peoples   watching
> it bring up
> Its local lights   single homes   lamps on barn roofs
> if she fell
> Into the water she might live   like a diver   cleaving
> perfect   plunge
> Into another   heavy silver   unbreathable   slowing
> saving
> Element: there is water   there is time to perfect
> all the fine
> Points of diving . . .

The new form makes available to Dickey avenues of sensibility and resources of language and subject that were not accessible in earlier poems. For the poet, what it is possible to say is mainly a matter of versatility of technique. In many of the best poems of Dickey's most recent collection, he is moving toward a more direct engagement with life experience than ever before. In "Power and Light" and "Encounter in the Cage Country," the art is less in the writing than in the uniquely comic personality of the persona, who treats his life as a medium for realizing hidden possibilities for creative existence. There is a strange new departure here in Dickey's work. The poems hardly seem like literature. "Encounter" is perhaps the most personally explicit of all his poems. Usually Dickey's poems reporting true personal experience combine explicit concrete reportage with a revelation of meaning, as in "The Hospital Window" and "Cherrylog Road." A reader senses that the poem's discovery is a dimension of the experience that came to the poet as an imagined afterthought, even though the symbolic language and imagery of the poem suggest the experience and the meaning that informs it occurred simultaneously in life. But then, it is the business of poetic art to create that illusion.

"Encounter in the Cage Country" drops the usual barriers between Dickey's life and art. It is as though the writer has reached that stage of his life when the skills of his artistry—comic staging, search for identity, haunting intensification of being—must spill over into his life experience:

> . . . I knew the stage was set, and I began
>
> To perform   first saunt'ring   then stalking

> Back and forth like a sentry faked
> As if to run...

Life itself becomes the instrument for creative becoming. It is no longer necessary for the poem to add the dimension of mystery to the experience through consciously willed art, since the personal event itself contains more magic, a sharper ring of truth, than the most subtly imagined poems can afford. The poem creates the illusion, if illusion it is, of being merely a sort of heightened reportage, and it may well stand in the same relation to Dickey's poetic art as *The Sacred Fount* assumes in the canon of Henry James's fictive art. It is a poem that will probably be examined by critics as a key to understanding the fascinating relation between Dickey's art and life. In "Encounter in the Cage Country," Dickey holds up a mirror to himself.

THE FAR POINT, 1969

Jean Garrigue

THE BODY OF THE DREAM

New and Selected Poems

Jean Garrigue is endowed with a metaphysical temper of mind. Her characteristic fragility is a super-sensitiveness to physical experience of the world. In many of her early poems, the obsessive need of her spirit to keep the upper hand over sensory experience defeats her ear and her eye, while the vigorous sensuosity of her language at its best is dispersed in trance, giving way to the language of dreamy essences. But her later development, from book to book, indicates a steady and valiant strengthening of those elements in her art which can secure a foothold, a vital anchorage, in the world of living forms.

"A Dream," an ambitious new poem, journeys into an ultra-real awakeness *within* the dream: a deepening trance in which fantasy is slowly divested of its dim outlines, and all that is vague and abstract in our mutual dream-life is pared and peeled away, layer by layer, like so many skins. Suddenly, we are inside the "tent of cloud or snow/ Not unlike a sailing silk," inside the body of the dream looking out, flowing, unable to pinpoint the exact moment when the delicate osmosis of entry drew us irresistibly into the circulatory life of the poem's deep vessels. Whatever seemed blurred, out of focus, in the vision—at the poem's outset—has grown, through a chain of subtle transformations, to be supernaturally clear, luminous, at the finish.

A brash new underground personality emerges in several of Miss Garrigue's new poems: the catlike, groveling saboteur of "Police of the Dead Day" ("Ignorant of all but my skin, I may be skinned—/ And it is possible for the sake of the pelt, alive—"); the homeless and despoiled mongrel of "Proem" ("I turn/ And cur-like snarl at what I'd once cherished"); and the owlish solitary of "Nth Invitation." In these poems, there is a hoarse, rasping defiance, with no loss of Garrigue's accustomed feminine grace, that results in a toughening of voice. The most impressive incarnation of her new identity is the guerrilla infighter of a number of successful political poems, most notably "Written in London after a Protest Parade."

Miss Garrigue is perhaps more skilled than any other poet writing today with the power to dramatize emotional thresholds between

New and Selected Poems, by Jean Garrigue. (Macmillan, 1968.)

jeopardy and renewal. She has a genius for returning to life's viable starting points following defeats, disappointments, hovering over the twin craters of frustrated love and failed art, owning up to the bleakest shortcomings in the self. In poem after poem, her subject is the failure of events in daily life ever to measure up to her spirit's aesthetic craving for perfectability. In "The Flux of Autumn," the poem that ends the book, her art is conceived as a religion which takes the fierce impact of natural beauty on the senses as a first step in the strenuous discipline of achieving her sensibility. The process involves a series of selective denials of the heart's pleasure, yielding to the higher demands of the dream: "The shadow of a bird has crossed my heart/ That we are these, these living things, enough!" She relentlessly subjects her keenest life-experiences to the refining "restless eye" of her dream-life. It is because she is able to enjoy all living beauties so much, strictly for themselves, that one is assured of the tragic heroism of her deprivations, of the demands her theology imposes on her responsive being. Her triumph is one of restraint, a succession of inured resistances to all pleasures easy of access, delaying and fore-stalling her natural gift for spiritual uplift until she has reached the supreme moment in which we are able to "think all things are full of gods." She will settle for nothing short of that arrival, and if she has had to sacrifice the more fashionable virtues of poetry in our time— expressiveness and immediacy—to evolve a middle range, a plateau, of vision (halfway between the language of feelings particularized and the language of elusive dream-states), we can only be as grateful for the qualities her art withholds as for those it affords, for there are rewards to be secured in reading her best poems of a kind that can be found in no other body of work.

POETRY, 1968

Studies for an Actress and Other Poems

"Studies for an Actress," the title poem of Jean Garrigue's last volume completed shortly before her tragic death in December and published posthumously, is an anthology of studies, improvisations, five-finger exercises in the theory of poetry, dramatized as a case study or case history of crises—upheavals, triumphs, collapses, ecstasies—in the life and career of a famous actress, the persona: the poem was evidently inspired by, and perhaps modeled after, the actual performances on stage of Galina Vishnevskaya in Dubrovnik. On another level, the

Studies for an Actress and Other Poems, by Jean Garrigue. (Macmillan, 1973.)

poem is a disguised chronology of stages in Jean Garrigue's own career in poetry; some parts are backward-looking and autobiographical, others are a survey of her poetic resources and devices. The author, who had reached a crossroads in her art, was undertaking a strenuous, aesthetic search, and mobilizing the implements in her poetic tool kit from which to select the best set of components for a new poetic strategy. Most of the aesthetic theory in the poem is a seesawing between poles, "The dialogue of self with soul, the quarrel of self with world," which she cited in 1969 (in a commentary on her own work published in *Contemporary Poets of the English Language*, St. James Press, London) as her favorite subject, during the transition between her last book—an expertly stripped-down, but comprehensive, selection from five earlier volumes plus some new poems—and the current volume.

With the rebirth of her art in this final work, a more energetic, various, and personally expressive collection than any published before it, she won an undoubted victory over the brutal, impersonal muse that, for some time, had paralyzed her creative impulse, as recounted beautifully in the title poem:

> She flees all action now, she has gone in
> Upon a demi-day that sinks towards night
> Under instruction from the strangest powers
> She would appease and cannot, who reveal
> In the most obscure and sinking down of ways
> This that they want which will fulfill
> This that she does not know, which she must do.
> Can she turn back? The path is overgrown.
> Ahead,
> Roads like lines in the palms of the dead
> Now fade.

Increasingly, in later career, Jean Garrigue evidently felt haunted by forces beyond herself that informed her art, as they had in the past— forces which she could seek or implore to come to her aid, but which she couldn't invoke at will, or fully control, once they came into play; but now, they often seemed to bind her in servitude to an anonymous lord outside herself whom she felt helpless to satisfy ("Under instruction from the strangest powers/ She would appease and cannot"), often leaving her in a state of bewildering cosmic frustration and, finally, spiritual exhaustion:

> And so she falls half out of life,
> Out of the net of things into the dark,
> Who has no strength now for that bright-in-dark,
> That second life those emblemed figures knit.

> Blind fit. Nothing to hold her back from this descent
> Into a void, opaque, unlit.

These conflicts are enacted in her poem by the actress-protagonist's endless vacillation between the masks, disguises, roles she performs in the theater and her own human identity, a chameleon—a shifting multiplicity of selves—in its own right.

Again, in her poem dealing with the characters in Chekhov's play *The Seagull*—a favorite drama she felt compelled to see performed again and again—she finds another stunning correlative in the theater for her inward struggle with the merciless gods, those strange powers. Though her artist-will was strong enough, in time, to break the grip on her spirit of the antihuman demonic forces in the universe that would contract us as will-less hirelings, puppets in their service, the Chekhovian sufferers are helpless to break the spell they are under, since the savage muse who governs their lives by an iron hand of fatalistic emotional determinism is the muse of the truth:

> The boy is all wrung, unstrung,
> For his mother has laughed at the wrong time.
> Were he other than he, he would leave,
> But the truth of her laughter is, and he knows it . . .
> He knows and knows no better
> That clue to the tears she can shake him down to,
> Treading on all his prides
> So obscurely linked to his fears.
> How can he solve himself! . . .
> And you see how in the interests of truth,
> The anonymous truth that respects no one,
> Whether it was intended or not,
> His purpose in life was to be broken.

She is allured both by the tragic beauty of their fidelity to the "anonymous truth" of their spirits, the invisible world within, and, more consequentially, by the mirror they hold up to her own divided psyche in its struggle to reconcile the rivalry between the actress and the live sufferer in her own poetics. It is as if the Chekhov players fool us twice: first, his characters achieve perfect verisimilitude, true-to-life credibility; but second, by the oddest inversion of convention on the stage, the lifestyle projected by the play's hypnotic mimesis is one in which all the flesh-and-blood subjects behave as if life were a theater, in which the necessity to brilliantly act out every sensation and extremity of feeling with the utmost intensity seems more important than breathing. Life must be *performed* to be life ("as if it were very life performing her"), and performed "at breakneck speed of remorse" if it is to keep up with the very timetable of survival. At this pace, the mind will be driven by the heart until the mind snaps, which accounts for the poem's title, "Why the Heart Has Dreams Is Why the Mind Goes Mad."

The very short poem with the long title, "Movie Actors Scribbling Letters Very Fast in Crucial Scenes," is a more comprehensive, though exquisitely compact, illustration of the schism of the poet-actress in whom the mask and the face, the role and the person, the disguise and the guise it veils become indissolubly fused, or blended, in moments of crisis:

> The velocity with which they write—
> Don't you know it? It's from the heart!
> They are acting the whole part out.
> Love! has taken them up—
> Like writing to god in the night.
> Meet me! I'm dying! Come at once!
> The crisis is on them, the shock
> Drives from the nerve to the pen,
> Pours from the blood into ink.

The humorous overtones of this piece give it enough buoyancy and lightness to deliver without strain a complex set of equations, or parallels, between the actor-audience contract and the reader-writer contract. All boundaries between art and life—whether on stage, on screen, or in the poet's verses—are swept away, extinguished, in the illuminations born of shock.

Miss Garrigue's engagement in politics emerged as an important theme in a few poems of her previous book. In *Studies,* her political interests move to the forefront of her concerns, and in the new political poems she codifies an original and enlightening set of guidelines for the relation between poetry and politics in our age. In "Resistance Meeting: Boston Common," she discovers the viable roles that her own ceremonial and emblematic art may play in the theater of the politics of resistance without violating the integrity of her unfashionable elegance: she would restore to our vision of ourselves something of the lost glory of the classic portrait virtuoso's skill in apotheosizing the most noble and beautiful elements in the handful of sublime models among us of a man of parts, a woman of parts, in the active life of politics; she would revive the lost art of celebrating and defining, for our unique age and moment in history, "the dream of fair men and women":

April in the Public Garden.
The boys who will be drafted are here,
some bearded like disciples,
others with the large dark eyes of *The Volunteers of 1792*
as painted by Thomas Couture,
horsemen-like as a painter might see them,
stilling, instilling their fire
of so much being to be praised by the future.

No point in going on about handsome people
with their thick hair glittering in the wind
about which we have had much comment from ads
so that we are less free to think of Titian's *Man with a Glove*
or a Degas portrait of some olive-skinned pride,
the élan of the painter and subject met at the point of imagination
where the magnificent being
garbed in the full dress of his civilization
completes in himself by his beauty
the rose of every expectancy.

For those lounging and lolling here,
what painter will arrest them in their gear,
at their height of time?
Not hardened yet or tarnished.

A veteran of several decades of distinguished work in the poetry of romantic lyricism, the rich embroidery of mythic scenes and emblematic figures, she is now able to import the expertise formerly ascribing grandeur to classic works of sculpture, tapestries, great cathedrals, to contemporary heroes—her friends and colleagues in the resistance movement. They achieve stature and mythic grandeur in her portraits. Moreover, this poet, whose phantasmagoric otherworldly bent would seem too rarefied for an active role in politics, perceiving that the concepts of *power* and *order* have become equated in our country's ad-mind-set (which passes for imagination in most quarters) with the proliferating armories of nuclear missiles and moon rockets, vows to make her art assume the full burden of guardianship and caretaking of the language of the inner order and the power of the mind's soul-life. She would mobilize a counter-arsenal of life-giving words, an artillery of vocables of resistance, to fend off the new faceless vocabulary from the ballistics' pantheon of demigods, an invasion of our language that subtly undermines us by poisoning the roots of common speech:

Now we need not go mad on abstractions
about Power, Fire Power, Garrison, Arsenal
Fire Power, Power, Poseidons
(giving a "multiple warhead Navy Missile" the name of a god)!

Her political poems lose their authority and verve when they subscribe to explicit virulent judgments attacking the State, her language, at times, sinking to a propagandist journalese with accents embarrassingly akin to the political jargon she abhors:

Escape artists, fed on swill,
Wanting more and more, forever more.
Not one "improvement" will we let go by,
Still cuddling picture postcards of the ideal....
But who will judge the victor? Might's still right
In this our swollen pigsfoot of a state.

The poems in the political mode are most arresting when she dramatizes the inner struggle of noble individuals—solitaries—caught, willingly or unwillingly, in the pythonic coils of the political juggernaut, recalling Yeats's emblematic portraits of Irish revolutionaries. "For Such a Bird He Had No Convenient Cage" is the record of a spiritual rape:

Her dreameries had been raided.
To the utmost rag and bone they had been hauled
Over the coals and up the flagpole for inspection,
To their limits they had been exposed
And all but sneeringly investigated.

This woman had achieved a rare triumph of exalted being, her whole sensibility trained to a scale of refinement that could never be measured by the brutal calipers of the political mentality. ("Hers was not of the same case.... It was less erect and more elect than that.") Not that the devastation of this woman's elevated consciousness by government committee is, in and of itself, more tragic, or more unforgivable, than countless other crimes by the State against innocents. But the poem transfigures her into a heroic, mythic emblem. She had given all of herself to the life of the Yeatsian spiritual intellect and had grown to exist wholly in a state of purer mind. Hence, she embodies in her own person the sector of the inner secret life of all intelligent beings that must be irreparably poisoned by the blunt instrument of the committee. Since her whole mental life is a reduction to the secret working mind of her creative reverie, a phantasmagoria of images and living forms curiously akin to Garrigue's own interior landscape, "her dreameries had been raided" is a post-mortem statement, the poem an epitaph to a crucifixion. She is emblematic of the solitary, mysterious inwardness in each of us, which is losing ground with each passing hour to the political machine.

Throughout her bountifully productive career, Jean Garrigue consistently adhered to and deepened a poetics in which the invisible or unseen world of the self and soul—a world apparitional, mythical, and palpable to supersensory, by turns—figured as the mainstay of her faith, as against her distrust of "the strange untrue of the real":

> You believed in a world that has never come
> With or without hope of this one
> And therefore you would say
> "I believe in what I do not see."

In fairness, she was always eager to give the unsatisfactory, incomplete material world its due, and in times of intense human experience, she was not unwilling to allow her faith in the pre-eminence of the visionary world to be tested, or challenged, by the visible world; and characteristically she adopts a posture, or stance, poised midway between the two superpowers, "assailed by knowledge of a plenitude/ the dense, packed world refutes in paining ways," inviting the poem's field of interplay to act as a forum for peaceful or embattled negotiations between them, as in the title poem of this volume. Never before, however, has she subjected her visionary reality to so harrowing a test as the massive frontal assault upon it by the "brute Sublime" beauties of the Grand Canyon, and never has her bravery in risking her unmasked sensibility to bombardment by the world of nature led to art of such magnitude, a panoramic sweep of vision rare in American poetry. "The Grand Canyon" is the outstanding masterwork of her career, a triumph of an order that could not have been foreseen from her usual nature encounters. The work explores a fantastic inundation from the outside world that becomes mysteriously and helplessly transformed into a metaphor for the world of the psyche, with no loss of the geological marvel's exact multitudinous particularity of detail.

In the title poem, she had explained her aesthetic crisis in late career, and her slackening of creative energies, as a temporary loss of the "binding element," the power to make swift leaps, associative jumps, connections between distant corners of the psyche:

> And she has lost the thread that let
> Those emblems forth, that rich connecting
> Between their powers and broad awaking . . .

In "The Grand Canyon," she has restored her genius for "that rich connecting," the power to mediate between inner and external worlds. The key to her best life and best love, then, as poet-actress, was neither the open expression of personality nor the effacement of personality to become a perfectly empty medium, or vessel, into which any role could be poured, though she grew to be equally adept in this last book both at projecting her own personal voice directly and at playing the ventriloquist for other voices—whether mythical or realis-

tic *dramatis personae*. She came more and more toward the last to iden-
tify or characterize the *real* of herself, her most enduring best gift, as
the Ariel-sprite, the elf of the spirit that could balance on the high wire
between mind and matter, moving swiftly and decisively between ma-
terials and the immaterial—the power to become bodied and disem-
bodied, by turns, never to be trapped for long in this statue, that
painting, the natural scene or locale, the human character, but like
"the gold of the light nervously darting" up and down the eight
strictly delineated and distinct geological layers of the Grand Canyon,
or "the eye . . . a long-legged insect on a windowpane" which "slithers
and shudders up and down" the canyon walls, or like "the violet-green
swallow stitching its leaps and arcs/ over the gliding raven,/ over the
camber of columns, tawny rotundas of ruins . . .": she would *be* the
light, the eye, the swallow; she would be a voyaging essence, contained
and uncontainable, hitching a ride—a cosmic hitchhiker—on forms,
animate or inanimate, which would allow her to travel in buoyancy
and pure freedom of weightlessness, to span vast chasms in time and
space, the noble distances, in a single instant: to be swept along on the
currents of "a large, impersonal strength/ beyond herself and bor-
rowed from the race."

THE YALE REVIEW, 1973

Richard Howard

THE ARCHEOLOGIST POET

The Damages

In Richard Howard's new book, *The Damages*, nearly every poem achieves a level of excellence not far below the peak moments in the best poems—the book is characterized by evenness of performance. If we can depend upon Howard never to fall short of a rigorous competency in any poem, we can also rely on him to be more predictable—to surprise and uplift us less with moments of genius—than an apocalyptic poet like W. S. Merwin. I hope that these remarks will not be misconstrued as a way of patronizing the artistic dependability of the solid craftsman, or of disparaging him by damning with faint praise. A few thoroughgoing technicians like Richard Howard are desperately needed to provide an aesthetic backbone for any generation of poets. No poet writing in America today is a more exquisite—a more fastidiously deliberate—aesthetician than Howard. His poetry is always lavishly textured, though the components of texture vary extensively from poem to poem. He is never without stylistic finesse, measure, proportion; however, in reading many of his poems at once, I find myself wishing, occasionally, to be outraged by an unseemly disproportion—an idea, or image, that in its crudity or excess may overpower its context. If only he were less determined to be flawless, and more willing to take risks. Howard is perhaps the only contemporary poet in whom unfailing artistic tastefulness may seem to become, at times, a vice.

The most abiding quality of Howard's new poetry is surface brilliance. Though most of the poems are without what is called psychological depth, they contain extraordinary quantities of topographical depth. If we can regard depth in art—unlike philosophy—as being a by-product of denseness and intensity of sensory data, then depth in Howard's poetry is to be sought less in the quality of the author's thought than in the superior elegance of his form. The best poems in *The Damages* are fortresses of poetic structure. The massive architecture of "The Encounter," "The Author of 'Christine,'" and "Bonnard: A Novel"—to my mind, the three most distinguished

The Damages, by Richard Howard. (Wesleyan University Press, 1967.)

poems Howard has written—seems to be capable of sustaining limit-
less amplification without losing the essential rhythm of experience
that is set in motion at the start of each poem. Above all, this is a
poetry of architectonics. Every line is consciously structured, and is
felt to be an integral unit in the superstructure of the poem's surface.

If, at first reading, structure appears to dominate subject in these
poems, repeated readings may reveal that the true subject of this
poetry is the structure itself; each poem being an adventure in which
the structure is a persona, if you will, in the act of discovering and
evolving itself; all the components of structure, then—the phrases,
images, ideas, story—by a peculiar reversal of the usual priorities, may
be viewed as vehicles for the enlargement of structure. It is no acci-
dent that the most successful poems are the ones in which structure is
all of a piece, rather than being deployed as a sequence of stanzas. To
illustrate, let us consider the function of one element of structure—
ideas—in the poem "Bonnard: A Novel." I will excise a random chunk
of the poem for inspection:

> Sophie, damp, dashes in
> dishevelled from the forest, dumping out a great bag of morels
> on the table: the white
> cloth will surely be spoiled,
> but the mushrooms look iridescent, like newly opened oysters
> in the raindark air, blue
> by this light. Calling it
> accidental is only declaring that it exists. Then tea
> downstairs, Jean opening
> the round pantry window:
> the smell of wet soil and strawberries with our cinnamon toast: all
> perception is a kind
> of sorting out, one green
> from another, parting leaf from leaf, but in the afternoon rain
> signs and shadows only,
> the separate life renounced,
> until that resignation comes, in which all selfhood surrenders.
> Upstairs, more Scriabin
> and the perfect gestures
> of Sophie and Jean playing ball with the dog. All the cats are deaf.

Characteristically, this passage presents ideas as sensuous materials,
fragments flowing in and out of the narration, with no more logic of
arrangement than the logic of emotional associations—those intuitive
stopgaps that connect colors in a painting, musical notes in a chord
harmony. Not that the ideas are chosen arbitrarily or inconsequen-
tially, but ideas are consequential in a new way: they act as just one of
many portions in the sensuous amalgam of the poem's dazzling sur-

face. Significantly, the ideas do not function autonomously, nor do they occur on a separate level of mind—or of the poetic medium—from elements of description, or events of narration. A reader unfamiliar with Howard's aesthetics may suspect him of intellectual frivolity—why, one wonders, are the ideas in the poem not held more seriously in the mind of the poet? To fully apprehend Howard's technique, we must acquaint ourselves with a new posture of seriousness in the handling of ideas in art.

THE YALE REVIEW, 1968

Findings

Speaking of the prehistoric cliff-dwellers who inhabited the "cliff fissures"—the Catalan ruins—above the site of the modern Spanish city of Tarragona, Richard Howard discovers an unforeseen kinship:

> Like me they had no ... words? left nothing
>   for history but middens
> which contained red pottery, antlers
>   used as picks, ox-blade shovels,
> a few bushels of shells, the bones of
>   wild boar and goat, of roe-deer,
> fox and badger; of three kinds of birds
>   and seven kinds of fishes.

These mounds of refuse are their sole bequest to us, an art treasure which we insulate from our real lives—a kind of quarantining—by calling it archeology. And indeed Howard has emerged in his two latest books, *Untitled Subjects* and *Findings,* as perhaps our first consummate archeologist poet. He, too, would leave for history not words, but findings. Findings unearthed in that literary archeology of scholarship and translated into a language of invisibility. A language divested of all surface glitter, style reborn as a pure instrument for transmittings, sacrificing all glamor of performance for functional rigor. An unimpeding, uninterfering, unmediated natural language of pure function best suited for the roles, the masks, of mediumship. Findings wrestled into the heaped-up mounds of poems, abandoned by the mound builder at last, leavings yielded to us and our progeny.

These are the poems of a man who has stood squarely at the crossroads between self-demolition and self-reconstruction ("Waiting, doctor, for that/ old visitation,/ the unreconstructed self, to take revenge/ for a wrecked interior/ decoration"), and, in taking unflinchingly the longest single stride across that chasm of lost identity of any con-

Findings, by Richard Howard. (Wesleyan University Press, 1971.)

temporary, he has imported into his remodelings of the self resources
that no American poet before him had guessed could be sponsored
by a thoroughly initiated modern intelligence. Howard has discovered
a mode for mating a heterodox creative scholarship with the art of
poetic composition. His method is a form of impulsive treasure-
hunting and sleuthing that recalls Virginia Woolf's ingenious skirm-
ishes—widening the scope of the familiar essay—in her *Common
Readers*. Howard's free-ranging eye, like hers, in choosing finds,
sources, magical touchstones in the writings of other authors to be
assimilated into his own voice, seems to have been guided alternatively
by idle curiosity, heart's impulse, and a high bold sense of pioneer
adventuring. Staking new claims in old, unsettled territories, How-
ard's re-emerging self claims for its own passages of anecdote, gossip,
worship, devotion, confession, armchair philosophizing.

Nearly always he is alert for the hidden, subconscious metaphors
that come into play in the most relaxed and informal ruminations of
his speakers' fantasy lives. Their most revealing remarks—the ones
that give away the deep mainspring quirks of their natures—are un-
guarded slips, offhand disclosures. Howard dexterously fashions his
speakers' dialectics to unmask their most telling peculiarities when
they fancy they drift off into irrelevant digressions, to betray most
when they think to say least. The accidental metaphors provide a
rationale that integrates for the reader the many apparently chaotic
and disordered tag ends of the drift of the speaker's "free" associa-
tion. Howard is cultivating in the art of the dramatic monologue, I
feel, a Jamesian power to reveal the dream-metaphors lurking just
under the crust of conscious personality, the reality of grasped
wholeness of self rarely supposed by the groping self-willed con-
sciousness. And through these half-masked linkages Howard is able to
create an extraordinary doubling of voice in which the poet and pro-
tagonist mingle identities, "share utterance." It is this artist's great
good luck *to find*, with astonishing regularity, that the crosscurrents of
his speaker's inner life and those of his own feed mysteriously out of a
single parent stream of self-illumination.

Perhaps the history of Howard's metamorphosis into an ar-
cheologist poet may best be traced in the last poem in *Findings*, enti-
tled "Demonstration." The poem recounts a historic fishing expedi-
tion in which a group of men, "Richard Gagne and his brothers,"
while trying to dredge for some lost lobster pots, accidentally (which is
to say, following supernaturally correct instincts) hooked into a sea
colossus with a grappling iron:

> Gagne chose his mooring
> "As if the chart were given"—

And may have been, for the first grapnel struck, held, and
the winch
Wound up the catch:
First of what would be seven
Pieces, sticky, green and hard...
... *Which in the tayl bears a sting*
Hard as any horn, and all
The body over
Set with spines, so that being alive still, it is not handled
Without danger. Whose aspect
Is very fierce and grim, for
Whenever they move, their eyes give a sound from their
eyelids
Much like unto
The tinkling of Brasse.

How do you make yourself available to blunder into great monster
finds like the giant squid of this poem? You follow the "weird hunch,"
while looking for lost gear, lost known equipment, tools for capture
("a dozen lobster pots"), and blindly pursuing the missing traps on a
day all drab greys, you fumble upon the stupendous lucky catch. Like
a plane flying in a fog—trusting to electrical instruments, radar, a
mysterious inner eye to guide the safe landing—the artist knows he is
on the right track when he feels most exiled from his inner self,
starting from lostness, "false starts/ From premises/ Known to be un-
reliable, groundless, without a clue/ To what was coming or had/
Come already."

When he came to write the poems of *Untitled Subjects,* Howard had
reached the point in his career when all the safe, comfortable trap-
pings of his craft—the proven styles and strategies which had grown
familiar with use, adroit with earned mastery—fell away from the
body of his vision like tattered garments. He found himself unac-
countably ("There was no warning,/ No warrant") dispossessed of the
substance of memory and personality, the ready-to-hand accoutre-
ments of the self locked in its private moment of history, its birthright
of time and place. He was dispossessed of the cache of memory that
had seemed inexhaustible whenever he had gone rummaging for
anecdote, exemplum, epistolary. The *life* he had always unequivocally
assumed was his own, the family and childhood chronicle that he felt
to be his chief belonging and which he drew on lavishly in writing the
poems of his first two volumes, lost its savor and grew elusive. When
his home demon banished him, he went promptly into exile, foraging
in journals and diaries of the last century, hunting for provisions to
build new nests for the famished self, that near-starved fledgling.

Home droughts. Home famines. And as he slowly plowed down into the buried secrecies of forgotten lives, burrowing into the dream-reveries of men of letters and artists, he came into surprised possession of their life riddles. As he let himself be emptied of the phantasmagoria of modern life—the present—his voice became invaded by the tongues of his disinterred cast of characters. Overnight, he grew to be the perfect medium, though his years of translating more than one hundred French novels into English, and his monumental critical study of forty-one contemporary American poets, *Alone with America,* were surely a prodigious apprenticeship for the rigorous and exacting art of the dramatic monologue in which Howard aspires, as he tells us in the prefatory note to *Untitled Subjects,* to approach the ideal of Robert Browning, "the great poet of otherness . . . who said, as I should like to say, 'I'll tell my state as though 'twere none of mine.'"

Roughly half of the poems in *Findings* are dramatic monologues in the mode of *Untitled Subjects,* but the longest, and much the best poem he has written to date, is "November, 1889," in which the speaker is Browning himself on the last day of his life. The showpiece is aptly placed in the center of the book, since Browning is the magisterial ancestor who presides over the host of Howard's tutelary mentors. It would be impossible, in the limited space of this review, to do more than hint at this poem's stunning vision of divestitures. Its denouement is a peeling away of all masks, all veils, all disguises, except that last guise of genius arrived: the vision of all life as illusion—a mere beautiful spell—which fades to a shroud of doubts in death.

Another unforgettable finding is "The Snake-Swallower," based on an authentic account of the rare "occupation" reported in Mayhew's *London Labour & the London Poor* (1851). This poem is, by any reckoning, one of the sexiest poems of our time. It combines an august tone with diabolical humor in a stylistic blend that recalls Chaucer's most scandalous tales. May everyone read it who doubts the power of poetry of the American language today to lend itself to the uses of a sufficiently stiff dose of prurience to make a reader gag on the words. No one, I trust, will insult this poem's intelligence by calling it mere pornography, nor by indulging in the frivolous charade of attributing "redeeming social value" to the wonderful sacrilegious joke at the end. In a word, the poem is deliciously—which is to say, criminally—obscene.

THE YALE REVIEW, 1971

W. S. Merwin

THE CHURCH OF ASH

The hard edge of W. S. Merwin's scrupulous negativity is the fiercest poetic discipline around. Readers can hardly fail to assimilate into their ears the violence of vacancy—the exacerbating vacuum—produced by shorn parings of our excesses he leaves behind him, littered on the path following his poems. In the ten years since the publication of *The Moving Target*, the first of four volumes developing his radical new aesthetics, Merwin's artistry has steadily deepened in the anger of an uncompromising honesty that pares away falsities, layer by layer, always leaving him in a condition of final exposure, vulnerability, nakedness. As in his style of writing, so in his style of spiritualizing—an utter divesting of defenses, the risk of more and more perfect defenselessness. He would denude himself of all possessions, all conceivable forms or modes of ownership, even stripping away the charter to his name, his face, since to own anything is to be enchained, shackled, to be owned in turn.

The soldiers have burned down all our churches of wood, whether our names were carved on the doors or written in the humble black of the charcoal floors. The only church left *standing* is made of ash; nobody owns it, and beautiful nameless spirits worship in its pews:

> we have a church where the others stood
> it's made of ash
> no roof no doors
>
> nothing on earth
> says it's ours
>
> > (from "Ash")

Merwin would found the church of the poem, then, from imperishable materials, words of ash. It is to be a poetry of no signatures, no possessorship, a stamp of impersonality on the timbers of every line and stanza. Once complete, the poem is set free from the hand of its maker, its word-carpenter, to be owned by no one, by no place, by no time; thus, like the free nomad-spirit that breathed luminous, unconditional life into the art, the works will be indestructible, and inexhaustible in their power to nourish free spirits of countless readers who partake of their bounty.

Writings to an Unfinished Accompaniment, by W. S. Merwin. (Atheneum, 1973.)

Merwin's aspiration is to become an empty nobody, an impersonal, expertly trained thing—a tool, an instrument, a pure vehicle for the "one truth," the vision that suddenly fills the fertile, incubating emptiness: the state in which the spirit has completely freed itself from comforts, needs, habits, freed from a human personality, freed from the body's claims, freed from the demands of other beings, freed from the brand marks of colleagues, family, country:

> If it's invented it will be used
>
> maybe not for some time
>
> then all at once
> a hammer rises from under a lid
> and shakes off its cold family
>
> its one truth is stirring in its head
> order order saying . . .
>
> (from "Tool")

This is the state of uttermost self-purification, disaffiliation, dispossession that Merwin has cultivated with unwavering tenacity in his last four volumes of original poetry, and throughout his prodigious career as this country's foremost living translator of verse from other languages. It is a condition of maximum plasticity and availability, a priming and predisposing of the receptive ear to become a psychic medium for the poetry of foreign tongues, as well as for deep images springing from the subconscious mind, or from the racial preconscious: images germinating in the visionary dream-life which have the authority and unshakable finality about them of last basic necessities; images which are as indispensable to survival in worlds of the spirit stretching to its outer limits, on the verge of breaking into new uncharted territory, as the barest physical necessities—a little water, roots, scant body-covering—are crucial to survival in the desert.

Regrettably, he cannot sustain this level of peak accessibility, since the habits of our cumbersome sensory apparatus operate in most of our routine daily living at levels of imprecision and inefficiency far less sensitive, less in touch with the hidden spirit in words, images, or objects than is necessary to support the scrupulous fidelity to quantities, nuances, shades, hues, lusters—quieter brilliancies, faded grays, softer delicate radiances—that Merwin's spirit of aspiring perfectibility demands for his art. Hence, the disturbing perplexity, approaching a cosmic vertigo, of psychic states in which we have fallen hopelessly out of touch with the spirit centers, registered in poems like "Habits," "Something I've Not Done." Suddenly, we may feel alienated, or dissociated, from our own delicate—if unwieldy—senses: our eyes, our ears, our tongues, our hands, our lungs—yes, even the

most intimately undeliberated act of our breathing itself, every breath
we take, or give back, may seem to work against us, to be at war with
our wills, or to operate in a dimension so far removed from our
conscious awareness, we may feel as if our sense organs have been
invaded by alien identities, beings, presences:

> Even in the middle of the night
> they go on handing me around ...
>
> even when I'm asleep they take
> one or two of my eyes for their sockets ...
>
> when I wake and can feel the black lungs
> flying deeper into the century
> carrying me
> even then they borrow
> most of my tongues to tell me
> that they're me
> and they lend me most of my ears to hear them
>   (from "Habits")

This state of the psyche seems linked to the immense frustration, born
of a relentless perfectionism, in "Something I've Not Done":

> Something I've not done
> is following me
> I haven't done it again and again
> so it has many footsteps
> like a drumstick that's grown old and never been used
>
> In late afternoon I hear it come closer
> at times it climbs out of a sea
> onto my shoulders
> and I shrug it off
> losing one more chance ...

To be always obsessed with doing, making, crafting—as is this in-
exhaustibly prolific writer—is to be perennially haunted by the ghosts
of the "not done," to be possessed by the demons of the one failure,
the one forgetting, the one loss amidst a horde of gains: it is an
aesthetic of tirelessness, forbidding rest or ease of spirit, much less
gaiety, exuberance, or comic ebullience.

Behind all our words and acts, behind each very signing of names,
lurk absences, vacancies, emptinesses. Active, not passive, voids.
Dynamic silences. Alert negative spaces. This mysterious sector of our
mental life, usually hidden from us, is vivified with astonishing poi-
gnancy in a dozen-odd impressive short poems of a strikingly new
species in Merwin's proliferating canon. They are stark, direct in de-
livery, coolly remote and stingingly intimate at once, like daggers of

hot ice: raw, naked, brutally overexposed—in the sense of a photo
with too much glare drowning the outlines of things, but so hypnotic
in their quiet chanting that we cannot look away, or even a little to the
side to shield our eyes, and we can't keep our gloveless, perishable
hands off of them. The missing things embraced behind the lines of
the poem exert an immense negative pull working invisibly upon the
reader's ear. If we examine the few words and lines that are present,
with much white space surrounding them on the page, we can hardly
locate the source of the great suction that freezes a reader's ear to the
poem, invisible like the lines of force of a powerful electromagnet.

The remarkable artistry in this cluster of poems is no idle exercise
or mere exhibition of verbal legerdemain—the poems make an un-
mistakable impact on the conscience of our unique American genera-
tion. In the peculiar way they make moral designs upon us, I have
never read anything like them. They would shock readers into illumi-
nation of the slow, irreversible dyings of the true spirit within us,
within animals, within things: the slow retreat of the mysterious inner
beauty of each thing and being which *is* its life, its identity, its sole
reality; the slow withdrawal from us of the spirit because of our ne-
glect, our innocent blindness to all the inner secret life that we fail to
recognize, and which enacts its slow judgment upon us by simply
turning away forever, turning its back on us, as in "The Place of
Backs":

> When what has helped us has helped us enough
> it moves off and sits down
> not looking our way
>
> after that every time we call it
> it takes away one of the answers it had given us,

or by staying hidden, locked inside our helpless waiting pencils, as in
"The Unwritten":

> Inside this pencil
> crouch words that have never been written
> never been spoken
> never been taught
>
> they're hiding
>
> they're awake in there
> dark in the dark
> hearing us
> but they won't come out
> not for love not for time not for fire,

or, again, as in "Something I've Not Done," "Every morning/ it's
drunk up part of my breath for the day," and the spirit is eaten up

from within us, and eats ourselves up, bit by bit, during all our most unnoticed, ostensibly harmless, daily routines:

> while we sign our names
> more of us
> lets go
> and will never answer

In the consistent moral vision that informs these poems, a prophecy builds: Merwin foresees the total desertion, or secession, of the spirit from our inner life-space; not that the spirit will cease to exist on the planet we'll soon have depopulated of every animal species but our own—the spirit will simply take up its residence in exclusively non-mortal dwellings, and quite happily flourish without our feeble collaboration:

> While we talk
> thousands of languages are listening
> saying nothing

In another cluster of poems—"The Current," "Surf-Casting," "The Chase," "The Way Ahead"—the metaphysical keystone is the dissection and anatomizing of our age's cosmic greed, our measureless possessiveness and need for conquest. In these poems of the most bitter moral and political indignation since the antiwar poems of *The Lice*, Merwin translates the international politics of grasping into a personal, spiritual condition which can be satisfied by nothing short of the dream of total acquisitiveness: a vast, illimitable gluttony that seeks to swallow everything alive, that would empty the sea of all forms of life in one or two great gulps; and the swindle is all a disguised projection of our human identity onto the extrahuman world, at bottom, the most devastating self-betrayal that can be imagined, in a barren attempt to fill the void in the self left by the spirit's mutiny.

We are "surf-casting," having "practised a long time/ with the last moments of fish." We employ our own irreplaceable toes for bait ("you have ten chances"). Our quarry is "the great Foot." The utter futility of the quest blinds us to the obvious barren terms: it is the vain, blundering attempt to repossess willingly amputated parts of our very being, squandered segments of the body of the self. Having depleted all of the available game in the world, we continue the obsolete charade of the hunt, our own foot for prey, which we do not recognize as a projected hunk of ourselves any more than we have recognized for centuries that all the animal legions we have decimated and all but exterminated were of the one spirit with our flesh, sharing our life, an extension and continuation of our own bodies, like our limbs. The current that surrounds the fish and also partakes of their body fluids is continuous in spirit with the blood currents that flow in our arteries and veins, though "for a long time" we've been "forgetting that we are water." Our blindness to our closest familial kin in the animal kingdom—flesh of our flesh, blood of our blood, of the one family—has progressed to the bizarre extremity of the terms of the last hunt. It must be the last, since we fish for our own "great Foot" using our toes as bait, and we will win, we know it, we'll always win:

> if only the great Foot is running
>
> if only it will strike
> and you can bring it to shore
>
> in two strides it will take you
> to the emperor's palace
> stamp stamp the gates will open
> he will present you with half of his kingdom
> and his only daughter
>
> and the next night you will come back
> to fish for the Hand

There are bewildering ambiguities of tone in "Surf-Casting," as in "The Way Ahead." The process that unfolds in the poem resembles, in many of its particulars, the spare, exacting discipline of Merwin's own most advanced aesthetic of the poem: the painstaking rituals practiced in pursuit of the perfecting of skill, mastery of both the mechanics of a craft and the profound, intimate awareness of the best conditions, the most suitable climate for its flourishing, are, it would seem, set forth sympathetically, and ironically, at once:

> It has to be the end of the day
> the hour of one star
> the beach has to be a naked slab
>
> and you have to have practised a long time
> with the last moments of fish
> sending them to look for the middle of the sea
> until your fingers
> can play back whole voyages . . .

The prophecy of "Surf-Casting" foresees the next stage in "The Way Ahead," envisioning a time in the near future when all non-human creatures will have been removed by us, but in our demented fantasy lives a hierarchy of larger and smaller creatures, an entire undiminished encyclopedic animal kingdom, will continue to flourish and populate our dreamscape:

> A winter is to come
> when smaller creatures
> will hibernate inside the bones

of larger creatures
and we will be the largest of all
and the smallest . . .

"The Way Ahead" is an agonizing oracular performance—all prophecies, all riddles, seemingly optimistic on the surface, but ringing hollow at the center. The poem has Orwellian overtones, true to the tenor of our American present historical moment. What is so disturbingly powerful in the poem is the way its visionary apparatus—the exquisite images, the authentic oracular tone persuading the ear by hypnosis, incantation, persuading the imagination with genuine fabling, mythologizing, riddle-making—all these immaculate skills flawlessly participate in the sellout that hangs us, an aesthetic soft-sell matching the political machinations of our day. The poem's power is enhanced, I feel, because Merwin dares to let his own instrument, his visionary medium at its most heightened pitch of clarity and revelation, fall under the grimmest judgment:

A Monday is to come
    when some who had not known
    what hands were for
    will be lifted and shaken
    and broken and stroked and blessed
    and made

The poet spares neither himself nor his most exalted art from the ferocity of his denunciation. The poem's valiant risk is in resisting the temptation to take comfort in the aloofness of an aesthetic remove from the crimes of innocence, of allowing ourselves to be violated, brutalized, mutilated, our spirits butchered, as we absentmindedly hasten the progress toward our own genocide, and Merwin invites the poem's craft to illustrate how our profoundest visionary myths and arts may be twisted to serve the fatal ends:

Feet are already marching there
fields of green corn and black corn are already
throwing up their hands
all the weeds know and leap up from the ditches
every egg presses on toward those ends
for this the clouds sleep with the mountains
for this in the almanacs of the unborn
terrible flowers appear
one after the other
giving new light
    A light is to come

How much rage is contained in the parody of political optimism in this passage, closing the poem. All living things left—the few survivors of each diminishing species—are fooled by the Nixonian cant of the propaganda machine preaching better times in "The Way Ahead," advocating escape from the pain of the present into the future. All flora and fauna, then, are tricked into hurrying into the premature void of extinction, mistaking their doom, their "first day of ruin," for a "new light" that "is to come."

Our misdeciphering the tragic events of our time goes hand in hand with our misreading, or mishearing, of the words:

> When the pain of the world finds words
> they sound like joy
> and often we follow them
> with our feet of earth
> and learn them by heart
> but when the joy of the world finds words
> they are painful
> and often we turn away
> with our hands of water

Merwin instills a profound belief, here, that everything depends on our learning to find our way back into touch with the true spirit behind the life of words. Our tragedy is our hopeless disaffiliation from the saving, healing powers of our own native tongue, and what could be more desolately mistaken than misreading joy for pain, pain for joy?

However, I find Merwin's new voice most attractive when the quality of intellectual rage, the impulse to scathing moral judgment, is transmuted into a drama of the lone spirit battling with itself, the full intensity of judgment turned inward which, for all its censuring of failures to measure up to standards set by its highest aspirations, is tempered by a compassionate acceptance. In "Division," an austere myth resonating with overtones from American Indian folklore, a dominant saving quality of whimsy, caprice, archness invests the vision with a fortification of human warmth that is, I feel, the most welcome new emotional undertone in a handful of the best new poems in this book—a quality of tempering mercy and self-forgiveness, a willingness to fail:

> People are divided
> because the finger god
> named One
> was lonely
> so he made for himself a brother like him
> named Other One

then they were both lonely

so each made for himself four others
all twins

then they were afraid
that they would lose each other
and be lonely

so they made for themselves two hands
to hold them together

but the hands drifted apart...

There are surges here of the human light of feeling radiating from
humility before weakness exposed, indeed, weakness exalted beyond
all spite that mistakes its whimpers for meagerness of soul. What
abides in these lines is the refreshing quality of quiet ardor, a gentle
self-mockery, with all mere human negativity purged out of the
judgment, that assures me that this poem could utterly charm the
shrewd ears of children, whose infallible capacity to detect some va-
rieties of fraudulence has never been adequately explained or ac-
knowledged. I can only hope that this emergent quality of gaiety and
buoyancy, which approaches ecstatic generosity of spirit in the beauti-
ful new poem which ends the book, "Gift," consummate in its serenity
and happiness of earned spiritual independence, is the forerunner to
the next major rebirth in the work of this poet of many radical self-
restylings, this prince of alchemists:

I have to trust what was given to me
if I am to trust anything
it led the stars over the shadowless mountain
what does it not remember in its night and silence
what does it not hope knowing itself no child of time...

I call to it Nameless One O Invisible
Untouchable Free
I am nameless I am divided
I am invisible I am untouchable
and empty
nomad live with me
be my eyes
my tongue and my hands
my sleep and my rising
out of chaos
come and be given

Still another remarkable new development in many poems of this
volume is the power with which ordinary inanimate objects—a wharf,
a house, a room, a hammer and nail, a door hauled on someone's

shoulders, a burning plank of wood—are endowed with supernatural presence, or haunted being:

O venerable plank burning
and your pegs with you
the hordes of flame gaining
in the marks of the adze
each mark seven times older than I am
each furthermore shaped like a tongue
you that contain
of several lives now only a dust
inside the surfaces that were once cuts
but no memory no tree
even your sparks dust
toward the last some of your old pitch
boils up through you
many children running
into a shining forest

The objects are pictured—or silhouetted, rather, so few the details selected—with hallucinatory clarity and maximum suggestiveness at once. I'm reminded of the drawings of Matisse, in which a single curved line of subtly varied sharpness and intensity suggests intricately not only the shape and position of the model's neck, arch of back, buttock, calf, and a possible gesture, or swerve, of movement; but hints enigmatically the exact mass and density and texture of the missing precincts of flesh—flank, loin, shoulder. By a secret power, by invisible craft, the few lines and dots and fleck-marks hint—but to hint with precision and exactitude is to inescapably command the viewer's eye—the larger, weightier, missing quantities of the figure which blossom in the vacancy, the eye's masterfully controlled hallucinated versions of forms filling in the blank white space, the explosive negative areas, which comprise immeasurably more of the canvas than the *positives,* the areas literally filled with pencilings.

As the draftsman the eye, so does the impresario-poet command the reader's ear. To a degree surpassing every other poet of my acquaintance, writing in English or whatever language, W. S. Merwin has developed with increasing mastery in his last four volumes of verse a Matisse-like notation, a fantastic linguistic shorthand, in which the few irreducible lines and images chosen (or has he mastered, rather, the power of perfect submission, passivity, in allowing the inevitable lines and images to choose *him,* the translator's genius?) guide the reader's ear by unerringly exact bridges across the very hinges—invisible overlaps and interlockings—between the words to the silences behind, or surrounding, the spoken utterances. This wizardry is accomplished by chains of sound and echoes, the echoes of echoes, the tones and overtones—all matings that tie or bind sound to silence, tongue to its dumbness, voice to its muteness; and always, in Merwin's art at its best, that which is given, or revealed nakedly, releases by invisible art those quantities which are withheld, buried, concealed, but *contained* in the silence, and therefore inescapably picked up by the reader's ear, and poignantly heard, leading the reader into the heart of a vision of quietly gathering intensity, balanced halfway between sound and silence. Or rather, not vision—the scores of eyes and eye-images in this book are always closing, or going blind—but *audition,* an integrated totality of incantatory chantings, the insistently felt and intensely heard presences of sound building cumulatively in the silences, the apparent voids of voice, as orchestration builds into a central awakening and reverberation within a listener's ear, resonating wholenesses of the heard and ultra-heard. But no, Wallace Stevens anticipated me by exactly fifty years in the search for an alternate word, beyond *vision,* to take account of an utterly new music in the poetic art of our American language: a *harmonium.*

THE YALE REVIEW, 1973

Howard Moss

BITTER AND SWEET, DREAD AND DESIRE

Finding Them Lost and Other Poems

In *Finding Them Lost,* by Howard Moss, the shorter descriptive poems with plants, animals, or natural settings at their center have much power to charm the reader. It is not a coincidence that a weed is the subject of one of the strongest poems, "The Snow Weed," since Moss seems deliberately and characteristically to avoid choosing subjects that have evident and ornate beauties. Unlike the imagists, who rely on *the thing itself* to generate its own distinctive aura in the poem (the poem tries to become a passive transmitter: it must keep hands off the object and let it speak for itself—a crying out of pure identity or is-ness), Moss selects things that are provisionally drab and vague—a wave, a cricket, a weed—then with the free play of his imagination (*and,* let me add, a keen attention to fact) he discovers the unexpected resources inherent in the ordinary.

The uplift of "The Snow Weed" is achieved slowly ("I let it hatch"). The poet gently leads us through a sequence of images that have the effect of unfolding, oddly, as successive layers of snow fall upon the weed:

> A fan-shaped skeleton, or wide whisk broom,
> A peacock tail but colorless.

The poem rises, finally, to a quiet epiphany:

> It swayed upon its root, remaining firm,
> And bore a second blossoming of storm.

The snow weed is a generic image that typifies a central strategem of Moss's art. In many of the poems in this volume, a scene or image is filtered through his imagination and is revealed sequentially through a series of shifts in perspective which translate the subject; similarly, each layer of snow falling upon the weed delivers, or liberates, *its* peculiar life. This method may owe something to the poet's keen interest in film techniques, which is evident in the long poem, "Movies for the Home."

Finding Them Lost and Other Poems, by Howard Moss. (Scribner's, 1965.)

Moss is at his best when he relates the spirit's struggle to cope with loss, as his book's title, *Finding Them Lost,* suggests. As he broods over his friend's death in "Water Island," grimly baffled by the look of the drowned man's face, his strong feeling for the man is somehow numbed by the raw confrontation with this "body like a log the wind rolled up to shore." His reverie becomes sidetracked by the spectral images of three animals: a horseshoe crab, an "endemic gull," and a heron. The animals emerge as lovely sacred beings in their own right, as they, accidentally, it would seem, release the full volume of emotion felt for the dead friend:

> Going across
> That night, too fast, too dark, no one will know,
> Maybe you heard, the last you'll ever hear,
> The cry of the savage and endemic gull
> Which shakes the blood and always brings to mind
> The thought that death, the scavenger, is blind,
> Blunders and is stupid, and the end
> Comes with ironies so fine . . .

In the poems mentioned earlier, animals and plants are a world in and of themselves. They, and the poems they inhabit, emit splendor, but they lack the amplitude that can impart the fullest sense of life. In "Water Island," the poet is stymied by the helplessness of loss initially. But at last the animals serve as mediators between the speaker and his profound experience; they contribute a vital life-enhancing dimension to the poem.

In the other deeply personal poems, "The Silences" and "The Fall," much power is achieved through restraint of emotion. In writing about himself (or a persona closely akin to himself), Moss resists the current trend toward garish self-exposure. "The Silences," a poem in six parts, is a voyage of the self through the purgatory of estrangement from a loved one. Like the animals in "Water Island," elements—air, frost, rain, moonlight, branches, lake water—become conveyors of the poet's longings. Despite its length, the poem instills a breathless quality, like a drop of water clinging to a tip of leaf.

"The Fall," another poem depicting loss, is a delicate performance. It evokes a completely absorptive trance that deepens with each re-reading. I think it is Howard Moss's finest poem; in its masterful control of repetitions and in the play of mystical refrain against piercingly direct plain statement it bears comparison with Roethke's "Waking" and Thomas' "Do Not Go Gentle into That Good Night." The snow of the refrain eerily transforms from a static ingredient of the setting, in the first stanza, to a hauntingly personified being, a protagonist in the human drama of the poem, at the end:

Did I ever tell you what I meant to say?
Or was I silent as this snowfall? Was I?
How can I take your sudden darkness lightly?
Heavily snow is coming down slowly.

The world is being shut away now. Surely
You felt what I felt. Lately, early
In the morning you rise up from the earth. Unearthly,
Heavenly snow is coming down slowly.

Selected Poems

Reading through "all of the poems Howard Moss wishes to preserve from his six previously published books," and seven new poems, I am struck by how well-pruned a collection this is. In his sagacity of self-criticism, Moss has trimmed back old work in the light of advancing craft and widening vision, and the sustained process of self-winnowing, with each succeeding book, has had a liberating effect on his new work. Prior to the radical second birth of his last full collection, his careful nurturing of assured virtues and weeding out of mannerisms of over-refinement—borrowings from Robinson, Stevens, Yeats—had led to not so much a development of talents as a gradual fulfillment of promise evident from the beginning.

The most commanding and accomplished poems in his three early books are the longer works—"A Swimmer in the Air," "A Winter Come"—in which a mellow calm quietly and slowly builds behind the elaborate structure and peaks in a final organ music, a beautiful sereneness, that is an unmistakable tonality of the earned purer mind:

Who reads by starlight knows what fire is,
The end of words, and how its mysteries
Go running in the flame too quick to see,
As language has a light too bright to be
Mere fact or fiction. By ambiguity
We make of flame a word that flame can burn,
And of love a stillness, though the world can turn
On its moment, and be still. Or turn and turn.

But a reader is left, all the same, with a dissatisfied aftertaste at the finish. The most vivid passages in these poems are those in which the image is anchored to a contemplative, meditating witness, an allured listener; in other passages, abstract thought tends to pull the image

Selected Poems, by Howard Moss. (Atheneum, 1971.)

away from the stream of the poet's life-flow. The poet-overseer, the impresario whose higher mind inheres in the spacious forms, lacks the unifying aroma of a single living human personality: the full presence of the person—the person *in* the presence—an articulating one man's naked human voice such as has arrived lately in full sweep and informs Moss's recent work. In the best poems of this period, we miss that spiritedness of a self speaking out. We feel that perhaps the author withdraws too far behind his performance, standing off from his creations and looking the other way, if secretly pleased with their high finish. However, these poems written in the late forties and fifties were nourished by a thriving genteel tradition that had found its highest expression in the masterful, austere sonority of Wallace Stevens' last poems. Perhaps it is unfair to judge Moss's very substantial poems of that period by subjecting them to standards that derive from his newest work.

In the next two volumes, I'm especially shaken at this reading by three excellent parables—"King Midas," "The Dumb Show," and "Finding Them Lost"—which, viewed again in a perspective modified by the newer directions in Moss's art, signal a search for an identity inside the poem which will be a truer extension and transfiguration of the author's speaking voice in the world, "Oh, then, I might say something close to speech." "The Dumb Show," I feel, registers Moss's growing uneasiness with the masks and endless succession of disguises his "ghostly busybodies" are forced into "putting on or taking off," rushing in to fill the void in things from which true self has departed, trying to repersonate those terrible absences with borrowed synthetic presences, "Each trembling on the fact that is its name . . . Each thinking: What I thought I was I'm not." In "The Dumb Show," Moss yearns to bring the art of the poem closer to experience, to narrow the distance of the poem's self-contained improvisations from the lived act, the alive moment.

"Finding Them Lost" is a rehearsal of amnesias, mental erasures. In its discovery of bankruptcies in the self, the poem resonates with a power akin to the short masterpiece of James's later career, "The Beast in the Jungle":

> Thinking of words that would save him, slanting
> Off in the air, some cracked, some bent;
> Finding them lost, he started saying
> Some other words he never meant.

While the speaker has missed his last chance to recover selfhood ("And what the mirror gave back was him/ Finally tired and very old./ 'My life, begin . . .' But it didn't, wouldn't"), the poet, who shares his

recitation, is providing for another life in this poem of last foreclo-
sures on the mortgage of the house of his formal poised stanzas, his
symmetrical balanced forms.

With the publication of *Second Nature* in 1968, as that book's title
correctly foretells, we witness the arrival of a second wind of the poet's
own human nature, allowing him at last "to say something close to
speech" of the natural live breathing man, not the ill-fated discourse
of a King Midas, his words helplessly turning to little syllabled ingots
of gold bullion by the time they reach the page. Certainly Moss hasn't
found it necessary to turn his back on any of his early accom-
plishments in the mastery of craft. But in the style of his new poems,
an austerity of avoidances is felt in the spareness and disciplined
accents of the lines. The pressure of fierce realities held in check
roughens the deceptively light rhythms and mild tones of the poetry's
music. It is a poetry with toughness at the core, and has nothing in
common with light verse, which a hasty reading could easily mistake it
for, but surface charms: transparency of clean statements, ease and
grace of manner, an elegant and scrupulously selective—but never
artificially or narrowly *select*—language. Moss has an inborn and ines-
capable ear for symmetries of style. "The rational derangements" of
his newer work suggest the taking of larger and larger risks in draw-
ing life's harrowing asymmetries into the unfailing resonance of his
form. Brief moments of brutality, unfeelingness, inhuman coarseness
in the lives of his personae are set into powerful vibration against the
civility of Moss's formal craft. The instrument is shaken fiercely by a
few touches of tragedy, usually the pain of those who have grown
inured to the bitterness and life-muffling boredom of their lot.

In his early books, when Moss's style became too lean, too unobtru-
sive, it suffered from immobility. The price of so much suavity and
polish was, at times, a pallidness of manner, inertness. But, in many of
the best new poems, that surface pallor is an accurate gauge of the
bloodlessness, the spiritual anemia, of the modes of contemporary life
it mirrors—and quietly and tastefully deplores, as in the stunningly
unlurid spoof on the love-threesome motif, "Ménage à Trois":

> To say I was bored would overstate the case.
> I'm languid. They're worse. Desultory.

Howard Moss has emerged in his last two books as our master re-
porter of the modern plague of desuetudes, and this poem is his most
devastating exposure of that condition. For the three protagonists—
two men and a woman—even routine, perfunctory fornication has
grown obsolete through ennui. All human resources for self-
amusement, much less productivity, have fallen into a passionless

mire of monotonies:

> The dullness of the nights is hard to believe,
> Though, from outside, I gather we cause
> A sensation. Who's sleeping with whom?
> We keep them guessing: Nobody is.

In "The North Sea," the remarkable new poem that ends the collection, Moss undertakes a massive revaluation of the work of twenty-five years. He insinuates, though with a mild bitterness of self-mockery, that he has always found a healing power, a momentary stay against the heart's mistakes, in the perfecting of his verse:

> You dream the moment's sustenance
> Is working against all error, hands
> Hand you back your heart all healed.

He has now reached the point in his career where he can find no more solace in that assured "sustenance" of skill, the mastery of technique, and he renounces the safety of an aesthetic of glacially fixed forms. There are risks inherent in the very will to believe in the perfectibility of form, and it, too, is held suspect by this ruthless self-criticism.

And yet, at his best, there has been no more perfect and consistent technician than Moss. Above all, one sensed from the beginning of Moss's career that here was a responsible man—that rare, nearly extinct bird itself—translating a particularly high quotient of basic human reliability into poetic forms. There are at least a handful of virtuoso pieces at each stage in the growth of his art in which each note harmonizes ("O all the instruments agree") with the total orchestration. But in his last two books Moss has sought to cultivate and intensify disharmonies in his work, to keep his medium in step with the bizarre dissonances multiplying at an incalculable rate in city life, especially, as metropolis explodes into megalopolis. In the new poem "Radical Departures," Moss lards his brokenly stammered soliloquy with a surprising mixture of Big City colloquialisms, with no loss of the sophisticated irony and grace that marked the poems in *Second Nature*, as exhibited most impressively, say, in the poem "Arsenic," which explores a similar terrain of self-mutilations and suicides. But "Radical Departures" employs a strikingly new elliptical pizzicato style in which the lines seem to be plucked and twanged—Moss's bow has unlearned the accustomed smooth strokes, and bartered them for a rough strumming.

"The North Sea" routes the new direction in Moss's work, promising an artistic itinerary patrolled—indeed, policed—by a demanding inner censor squelching the charm-school voices of eloquence and poise, and calling for a balanced mixture of bitter and sweet, dread and desire, in the exquisite coda that ends the book:

> A mirrored dread comes closer slowly
> Dragging its wires across the snow.
> It narrows the distance gradually;
> It is watching you, yet it is you.
> It opens its mouth to speak. Silence.
>
> The mirror begins to melt and bleed.
> No music warms the baleful vision,
> No voices charm the unbearable.
> The desired and dreaded arrive at once,
> Their true proportions coming clear.

Retracing the steps of our brief tour through twenty-five years of Howard Moss's poetry, we discern that his best love went out to the word at first; now his best love goes out to the world, to be wounded over and over, returning to the word not to be soothed or salved—not for healing—so much as to let the open wounds have voice: to suffer in his own person the peculiar dread—that sickness unto death somehow beyond, or outside, pain—of our moment in history.

THE YALE REVIEW, 1971

Mark Strand

THE BOOK OF MOURNING

Reasons for Moving

Some readers of Mark Strand's *Reasons for Moving* will dismiss the book as being merely an assortment of clever stories set up to look like poems. For poetry to be as obviously interesting and readable as the pieces that open this book ("Eating Poetry," "The Accident," "The Mailman") is apt to arouse the intellectual reader's suspicion. Even the most difficult poems ("Man in the Tree," "The Ghost Ship") have a deceptive simplicity. They seem so perfectly transparent on first reading that it is puzzling to find, on repeated readings, that they wear as well as they do. Despite their initial sudden impact on our emotions, the poems deliver their full import to us slowly, after many readings. Trying to get under the skin of these poems to experience them more deeply is like trying to get inside a disturbing dream from which we have just awakened. We remember the dream, usually, as a sequence of events in time, and then put it out of mind, vaguely sensing that memory has cheated the inquiring self by reducing a powerful symbolic complex of being to a mere time sequence. But the searching intelligence is not content to be cheated by memory's tricks, not when a dream, or dream-poem, has struck like an ax into the deeper mind. As in the most powerful dreams, the events of the story in Strand's poems serve as a frame for a rich complex of symbolic images, gestures, human encounters.

The beautiful strangeness of "Man in the Mirror" and "The Last Bus" derives from the dual effect of an austere simplicity of events combined with an inexhaustibly rich overlay of images. The naturalness of Strand's verse movement allows for a maximum quantity of radical imagery to be carried without making the reader's ear feel overburdened:

> I was walking downtown
> when I noticed a man in black,
> black cape and black boots, coming toward me.
>
> His arms out in front of him,
> his fingers twinkling with little rings,

Reasons for Moving, by Mark Strand. (Atheneum, 1968.)

he looked like a summer night full of stars.

It was summer. The night was full of stars.

(from "The Man in Black")

The splendid transition between the last two lines of the passage demonstrates how Strand's imagination characteristically seizes upon a metaphor to suggest a just-hidden mystery behind the forceful appearances, the bright exteriors, of everyday things. The next moment, the scene is transformed by the metaphor into a new identity, one that retains the old clarity of outline but clothes it in the unsheddable garment of the poet's inner life. The poetry moves so swiftly and effortlessly from ordinary reality into dumbfounding spirituality that a reader is taken by surprise. And the surprise may not be lessened after several readings—the poem will catch the reader off guard every time. Somehow the lines sweep from day into night, waking to dreaming, humor to horror, serenity to hysteria, safety to ruin—to doom, with no appreciable shift in the plane of vision. Emotional and spiritual opposites of every sort exist side by side, and join hands, in the poems: "The end of my life begins," Strand reasons with absurd clarity, as if he were inhabited by two men—the living being and the dying being—and the birth of his extraordinary art is the progeny of the marriage between them.

The poems in this book are defined within a field that is governed by such clear-cut rules that any flaw in language or rhythm will show like an inkblot on white linen. No tricks will work. The poet has deliberately divested his style of every means to fool the reader. Everything he makes the poem do is inescapably in the open, in plain view. The cost of this method is an unfashionably thin book of finished work. The reward is a kind of elegantly flawless art—in a few poems—that bespeaks a perfect tuning of the instrument.

THE YALE REVIEW, 1968

The Book of Mourning

By all odds, Mark Strand's *The Story of Our Lives* has far less immediate sensuous appeal than his earlier volumes of poetry. The virtuoso performer of *Darker* has been supplanted by an elegist. *Story* is chiefly a book of mourning. Strand mourns the deaths of his father ("Elegy for My Father"), his mother and his childhood ("The Untelling"), his marriage ("The Room," "The Story of Our Lives," "Inside the Story"), and finally, the demise of the aesthetics that informed the spare,

The Story of Our Lives, by Mark Strand. (Atheneum, 1973.)

compact poems of his other books ("To Begin"). Evidently, for the moment, he has abandoned the assured popular instrument which appears to have acquired a school of followers—imitators and parodists, much as did the prototypal short, intense lyric of Merwin, Kinnell, Wright, and O'Hara of the generation before him spawn a coterie of idolators and apprentices. *Story* is a deeply haunting book, though not as disheartening as its prevailing timbre of somberness, on first acquaintance, suggests. The book culminates in a quiet joy, an intellectual ecstasy of a kind we would never have anticipated from the poetry's characteristic gravity. However, readers who were allured by Strand's elegant charm, as well as by the fabling gnomic terror and humor of his phantasmagoric dream-poems, may be disappointed by the expansive sprawl of the long new poems which, by a slow effervescence of incantatory rhythms, cast a gradual hypnotic spell over us. The new poems make far greater demands of our powers of concentration, but the rewards, after many readings, are equivalently greater.

In *Darker,* Strand had employed the mode of chanted litanies for the first time, a form which accounted for an important widening of imaginative range, releasing him from the strict contract of the stanza form, the exclusive mode of his first two volumes. In *The New Poetry Handbook,* he explored the associative logic of serial image-chains, an experiment related formally to the list-poem genre developed exhaustively in the brilliantly funny poems of Kenneth Koch, and in scores of cheerless imitations by poets of the New York school. It was an ostensibly non-programmatic structure, mystifying the reader with the illusion that the open-ended poems started or stopped at purely arbitrary points in an endlessly stretchable series of imagistic statements, as in Strand's two quasi-fragments deceptively entitled "From a Litany." And yet, Strand baffled the form, inveigling the reader's ear with a mastery of tonal resonance that left the aftertaste of an organic unity all but impossible to locate or account for by conventional inspection of the structure, while a few passages of lavish imagery contained a more elevated pitch of musical opulence than he had ever approached in his previous work.

In "Elegy for My Father," the stately, slow-paced, hypnotic dirge that begins the new volume, Strand amplifies the serial mode of litany. Exhibiting a remarkable range of technical virtuosity, he adapts the device of image-chains to six widely varying fantasias. In each, a simple statement—flat and blunt—is repeated at irregular intervals, and operates less like a conventional refrain than an aria or leitmotiv in an opera. The statement tends to fade, to become hidden, vanishing into a chanted monotony, but it subtly builds resonance in the reader's ear and accumulates a force of quiet, but irreversible, authority. "Nothing could stop you. You went on with your dying."

In "Your Dying," the midsection of the poem, the father's unswerving complicity in his progress toward death exalts the process of welcoming death into an austere discipline, an artistry which by its propulsive force of negation, by its revulsion from nature and human society, sends all things into orbit around itself. He achieves an absolute solipsism of dying, which is mirrored by the son's solipsism of mourning. The total psychic withdrawal from life, paradoxically, adds a dimension to being alive, a deepening and heightening of spirit, which threatens the comfortable world of the living, the friends and neighbors who "doze in the dark/ of pleasure and cannot remember." The living are shocked into a panic of opposition—they are wavery, unstable, flighty, aimless. The act of dying easily imposes its higher will and design on the chaos of life, its deathly order on the disorder that is prevalent everywhere.

The whole book is a profound act of mourning—hence, the aptly grotesque irony of the fifth section of the elegy, entitled "Mourning," a Kafkaesque caricature of conventional funerals in which the mourning process, so indispensable to healing the psychic wounds of bereavement, is debased and betrayed by self-pity. The common blind refusal to accept death is parodied as a procession of beggarly kin pleading with the corpse to come back to life, perverting the funeral rites into a litany of gamy ruses to pamper and coddle him into not dying, as if a complex gymnastics of undying could undo the death:

> They mourn for you.
> When you rise at midnight . . .
> They sit you down and teach you to breathe.
> And your breath burns,
> It burns the pine box and the ashes fall like sunlight.
> They give you a book and tell you to read.
> They listen and their eyes fill with tears.
> The women stroke your fingers.
> They comb the yellow back into your hair.
> They shave the frost from your beard.
> They knead your thighs.
> They dress you in fine clothes.
> They rub your hands to keep them warm.
> They feed you. They offer you money.
> They get on their knees and beg you not to die.
> When you rise at midnight they mourn for you.
> They close their eyes and whisper your name over and over.
> But they cannot drag the buried light from your veins.
> They cannot reach your dreams.

So far from resisting, or denying, the reality of his father's death, Strand's own mode of mourning is to follow his father into dying, taking as many steps down the path toward death as possible short of dying himself, and though this process culminates in a valiant entreaty invoking the invisible powers for release from the bondage to his father's corpse ("It came to my house./ It sat on my shoulders./ Your shadow is yours. I told it so. I said it was yours./ I have carried it with me too long. I give it back."), it is clear from the other poems of the present volume that the elegy is only the first milestone in an interior odyssey in which he follows a long, intricate course in developing a new poetics that recapitulates his vision of his father's dying. Strand is obsessed, in poem after poem, with absence, vanishings, disappearance of parts of his own psyche. The opening litany of the elegy, "The Empty Body," suggests that the author's obsession with disappearance grew initially out of the shock of witnessing his father's dead body. He could not fathom or accept the emptiedness—the spiritual evacuation—of the corpse:

> The hands were yours, the arms were yours,
> But you were not there.
> The eyes were yours, but they were closed and would not open....
> The body was yours, but you were not there.
> The air shivered against its skin.
> The dark leaned into its eyes.
> But you were not there.

The two dominant human situations in *Story*—the dying of a father, the dying of a marriage—are not simply fictive correlates, but clearly the occasions in the author's life which demanded for their successful embodying and execution in the poetry a commensurately barren, arid, desolate vocabulary. Strand subjects his style in this book to a severe cutback—approaching a strangulating *cutoff* in some passages— of his most dependable resources, and he adopts a starkly austere and reductive diction. In each of the central poems, the persona has come to a hopeless spiritual impasse—the necessity to change his life is as crucial to continued survival as the act of breathing. The author has reached the point in his career at which the full stretch of his technical powers, all the mastery of craft he can muster, is needed to accomplish an extra-literary goal, a task outside language. He must change his life. He must move beyond a life which threatens to suffocate his spirit into another life, and he will mobilize all human and artistic resources to achieve this—hence, this book's radical shift to a lean poetics of expediency. The process of writing is an act of heroic struggle to stay alive in the spirit against terrible odds, to maintain the life of a beleaguered sensibility. Thus, the stripping away of all but the most subtle artifice, and the divesting of all stylistic flourish, all super-fluities. Literary success is an accidental by-product of this enterprise.

The language in this book has grown so refined, so flattened and subdued, that it resembles ordinary poetry—or indeed, literature—less and less, and one may look for parallels to explain its technique more readily in other arts, such as painting, a discipline to which Strand submitted himself years before that of poetry. In "The Room," Strand creates the illusion that the high drama between the lovers at a time of crisis is dictated simply by the interior design of the room's furniture, by spatial and temporal arrangements of objects, by pacings—to and fro—of the two human bodies; but the poem's design is covertly propelled by movements of the characters' inner lives. Everything that happens between them appears to depend on moves toward and away from the few plain objects. I'm reminded of how much spiritual power of the kind that enables people to change their lives radically—to choose or leave their mates, to find their life's work, to risk and perhaps sacrifice their lives for love or some other faith—is contained in the subtle color shadings and spatial placements of pieces of fruit in a still life by Cézanne. Or rather, like the objects in a painting by Magritte, the objects in Strand's poem are so bare and plain and unembellished by ornament that a reader is dumbfounded by any effort to locate the source of the fierce supernatural energy that surrounds them:

> The room is long.
> There is a table in the middle.
> You will walk
> toward the table,
> toward the flowers,
> toward the presence of sorrow
> which has begun to move
> among objects,
> its wings beating
> to the sound of your heart....
> I know by the way
> you raise your hand
> you have noticed the flowers
> on the table.
> They will lie
> in the wake of our motions
> and the room's map
> will lie before us
> like a simple rug.
> You have just entered.

We are persuaded that the activity of writing such long poems and studying the enlarging drafts of each poem between writing spurts, by a slow unfolding of stages, was clearly the *only* way left—whatever others may have been undertaken—for a human being named Strand to survive in the spirit. Any careful reader must discover, unmistakably, that for their author the process of composing these mournful threnodies was not so much an act of writing them down as of slowly begetting and weaning them, coaxing and beguiling the lines out of a near-implacable muteness, a dark interior mausoleum of the soul in which the spirit's pulse has slowed down so much that its tiny flickerings are barely perceptible, and he must carry these slowest, quietest flickerings of the spirit's life through an almost unendurably long gestation from first mumblings into audible voice, and finally, the building into resonant utterance.

In "The Room," as in the two longer poems about the languishment of desolating love ("The Story . . ." and "Inside the Story"), the prevailing mental weather is anxiety. In "To Begin," the poem which I take to be the axis about which the artist slowly and agonizingly rotates from the poetics of his earlier books to his new metaphysics, the climate is a crippling dose of malaise:

> He lay in bed not knowing how to begin. . . .
> There was no reason to get up.
> Let the sun shine without him.
> He knew he was not needed,
> that his speech was a mirror, at best,
> that once he had imagined his words
> floating upwards, luminous and threatening,
> moving among the stars, becoming the stars,
> becoming in the end the equal of all the dead
> and the living. He had imagined this
> and did not care to again.

When so much radiance has faded ("The sun and moon had washed up/ on the same shore"), so much ambition and limitless aspiration played themselves out and been quenched, and youth's inflated dreams of infinite solipsistic power been punctured, a writer's disillusionment is total and spreads to every precinct of his being. His refusal of speech and the preference for silence go very deep, and the failure to summon up—or mobilize—enough energy to break the deadlock, the stranglehold on his speaking voice, reduces him to a state of vast spiritual torpor and lethargy:

> It took no courage, no special
> recklessness to discredit silence.
> He had tried to do it, but had failed.

He had gone to bed and slept.
The phrases had disappeared, sinking
into sleep, unwanted and uncalled for.

The last step in an unbroken chain of failures to endow faltering
speech with consequence before the plunging descent into muteness,
utter speechlessness, is the writer's attempt to "discredit silence," but
this is the one failure that will save him. It is by sinking far enough
into the silence, the sleep of language, that language may be restored.
Finally, the poet will honor the silence, not rival it, and celebrate
silence in speech that is torn from immense avoidance of speech, a
fierce intensity of passion contained in the unspoken, the untold. To
resist the impulse to tell falsehood, and to master the counter-impulse
of the *untelling,* is to revitalize the art of writing into a noble mental
discipline, a discipline by which he may become wedded to the silence,
transforming it from a rival into an ally. His lost dream of absolute
solipsistic power will return, but in a different form—he will be abso-
lute monarch and sovereign lord of the manor of his interior land-
scape, a possible topography for the rebirth of his deposed aesthetic
reign glimpsed for a few shaky moments in the midst of his struggle to
shake off the bonds of the dying love relation in "Story . . .":

> *A bleak crown rested uneasily on his head.*
> *He was the brief ruler of inner and outer discord,*
> *anxious in his own kingdom.*

But to rediscover exalted being, to come again into possession of the
deep, passional self, necessitates a slow, step-by-step chain of negotia-
tions with nothingness borne of a powerful, ruthless stripping away of
all versions of ourselves forced upon us by human society, by occa-
sions in a life—anniversaries, pacts, honors—all those data which the
world assumes are the loci for treaties and contracts between the
private life and the public theater that beget self-definition. The
popular confessional school in our poetry supports this despirituatiz-
ing of identity, but Strand's radically opposed strategy of self-
discovery challenges the narrowness of the public ego running naked
through the avenues of our verse, and aspires to restore to contempo-
rary poetry something of the lost multi-dimensionality of Yeats's "Dia-
logue of Self and Soul," by fashioning a self toughened in the crucible
of its warring with the timeless human spirit.

Perhaps the most remarkable single poem Strand has written to
date is "The Untelling," the very long poem that ends the new vol-
ume. The poem revisits a haunting scene from Strand's childhood, as
the persona tells the same story, again and again, in his struggle to
reconcile—or reconnect—his adult identity with a missing part of

himself locked in the past. The poem begins with maximum distance, remove, between the adult and the child, the twin moieties—or doubles—of the same psyche. The doubles move closer and closer, and by a cyclic progression—toward and away, toward and away—they finally coincide. The persona is training himself, by a sequence of scrupulously delicate entries and exits, to achieve a dialogue between the worlds of present and past, and thus to learn expertise as a traveler in the interior landscape of the self. He finds he must rehearse the recital many times, each time stumbling at different points in the script, the audition, the scenario, and beating a retreat to correct his blunders, then beginning again:

> Maybe something had happened
> one afternoon in August.
> Maybe he was there or waiting to be there,
> waiting to come running across a lawn
> to a lake where people were staring
> across the water.
> He would come running
> and be too late.
> The people there would be asleep.
> Their children would be watching them.
> He would bring what he had written
> and then would lie down with the others.
> He would be the man
> he had become, the man
> who would run across the lawn.
> He began again:

In writing a long poem, it is not unusual for the writer to make a good number of partial forays, or tentative excursions, into the field of his vision, withdrawing again and again to re-tune his instrument and alter his grip on his materials, picking up the weighty opus and laying it back down again in exasperation many times before striking exactly the right key or pitch for executing the vision. But I know of no other poem that dramatizes and explicates this very process, revealing the artist's many approaches and withdrawals, his to and fro rhythm of becoming attuned to the map, the layout, of his inner landscape, as exhaustively as this poem does—in fact, the slow discovery of the aesthetic outlined above is quite as much the poem's subject as the re-engagement with an experience of childhood which occupies the front of the stage.

The persona of "The Untelling" is an updated spiritual pioneer akin to the hero of Bunyan's *Pilgrim's Progress*, though in Bunyan's work, a chief ancestor of the modern novel, the external lineaments of plot are far more complex. But in both works it is the story within the story, the drama of the spirit's progress, that is always felt to be dominant, though subtly masked by the translucent overlay of the narrative line. The events of consequence are always internal, and must be inferred obliquely from the play of figures and scenes that populate the surface. In "The Untelling," the constituents of nature are a few ordinary, bland stage props of setting—the lake, the woods, the lawn; the human events recounted are pedestrian, colorless, pale. Strand divests all surface glamors and sustains an utmost faith in the power of the barest scene, robbed of all picturesque trappings, to assert a hidden emotional turbulence, avoiding at every step the expected opportunities to exploit strong overt feelings. He explores, instead, the cataclysmic events in the self which occur only when the life of intense personality appears to have slowed and slowed, nearly dying out, like the pulse of a hibernating bear. The active life of ego and consciousness is etherized into a slow lento, the music a stately, dispassionate minuet which, toward the end of the poem, approaches a rhythm of somnolence, a meter that mimics indolent breathing:

> It was late.
> It did not matter.
> He would never catch up
> with his past. His life
> was slowing down.
> It was going.
> He could feel it,
> could hear it in his speech.
> It sounded like nothing,
> yet he would pass it on.
> And his children would live in it
> and they would pass it on,
> and it would always sound
> like hope dying, like space opening. . . .

Hesitant, slow, halting. Slower and slower, from andante to larghetto to largo. The short, end-stopped one-line sentences, especially, bring the poem's rhythm near to a dead halt, the meter all but standing still. The music is holding its breath, and in listening, a reader finds that if the tone of poetry is superbly well modulated, a poem can stop breathing, but its life continues, as it probes for a hidden inner rhythm of the heartbeat. Another music—subliminal—imperceptibly emerges and overtakes the fading tempo:

> . . . he was alone in the dark,
> unable to speak.
> He stood still.

He felt the world recede
into the clouds,
into the shelves of air.
He closed his eyes. . . .
He felt himself at that moment to be
more than his need to survive,
more than his losses,
because he was less than anything.
He swayed back and forth.
The silence was in him
and it rose like joy,
like the beginning.
When he opened his eyes,
the silence had spread, the sheets
of darkness seemed endless,
the sheets he held in his hand.

As a child, Strand had felt alienated—as if the scene did not belong
to him, nor he to the scene—because he witnessed the events from a
clairvoyant and enchanted darkness. He had seen beyond the natural
world, through the bodies, past the faces, heard beyond the voices,
and penetrated into the mysterious heart of things, but tragically he
could not recognize the sacred beauty he saw and heard, much less
share his revelations with the adults. Later, in the process of writing
the poem, these visions are recalled, revivified, and given a public
form in the writings—hence, this poet's power to share his most pri-
vate and intimate recollections with readers. But to do so, he had to
find a way to be in the scene and outside it looking in, at once, to be
himself as a child and adult, simultaneously, to see through the eyes of
both, and thereby to repossess—by the genius of his art—the leap of
spiritual transcendence that had occurred in childhood:

> . . . *I shut the window*
> *and saw them in the quiet glass, passing*
> *each time farther away. The trees began*
> *to darken . . . The shapes among the trees kept changing.*
> *It may have been one child I saw, its face.*
> *It may have been my own face looking back.*
> *I felt myself descend into the future.*
> *I saw beyond the lawn, beyond the lake,*
> *beyond the waiting dark, the end of summer,*
> *the end of autumn, the icy air, the silence,*
> *and then, again, the windowpane. I was*
> *where I was, where I would be, and where I am.*

The Untelling is a Wordsworthian vision of self reborn, as in *The Pre-
lude*, from dwelling on the few enigmatic and haunted moments of

childhood in which the natural world flooded our being with an annihilating quiet—half ecstasy, half terror—lifting us out of the net of human society, both its protection and its constraint, and shaping our hidden core of identity. These events occurred at mystical, unforeseen moments, but each at a definite locus in time, in place. The child in the poem, though dazed, poignantly contained, and carried away within him, the scene, the locale in which the mysterious psychic events occurred. To walk away physically was in no sense to leave that geography ("Though I walked away, I had no sense of going"), since the scene had been miraculously ingested and transformed into an inner landscape of himself. For the grown man to recall those moments, and that scene, within the vision, by a disciplined and controlled tautology of self-hypnosis, is not simply to relive or re-experience them, but to re-enter the vivid flux of total spiritual elasticity of childhood, that utmost availability for change. Those deep situations, stories begun but left unfinished in our inner lives, may be resumed, continued as if the two or three decades of young manhood have never intervened or interrupted the process of their unfolding. Thus the powerful rewards made accessible by this aesthetic of reentries into an earlier life of being, born accidentally of itself in childhood.

POETRY, 1974

David Wagoner

THE COLD SPEECH OF THE EARTH

I

Stretched out on the ground, I hear the news of the night
Pass over and under:
The faraway honks of geese flying blind as stars
(And hoof—or heartbeats),
The squeaks of bats, impaling moths in the air,
Who leave light wings
To flutter by themselves down to the grass
(And under that grass
The thud and thump of meeting, the weasel's whisper),
Through the crackling thorns
Over creekbeds up the ridge and against the moon,
The coyotes howling
All national anthems, cresting, picking up
Where men leave off
(And, beneath, the rumble of faulted and flawed earth
Shaking its answer).

In "One Ear to the Ground," the chorale of sound images orchestrates cries of creatures that fly, scurry, flutter, crawl, or burrow, tunneling under the earth's crust, with the rustlings of foliage and brush. The deep, low-pitched voice of the earth itself, maestro and impresario combined, presides over the chorus and provides the solo bass (music of the lowest audible register), the poem's dynamic blend of aural effects beginning and ending at ground zero. David Wagoner's ear is perfectly attuned to all keys of the chromatic scale of ground music. Owing to this supersonic acumen, which distinguishes Wagoner's most current poetic language, his masterful new sequence of backpacker poems—his song of the earth—comprises the most profound and accomplished work of his career to date. In this cycle of nine meditations (which launch the "New Poems" section of Wagoner's *Collected Poems,* the book's release date synchronized with the author's fiftieth birthday)—naturalistic and metaphysical, at once—Wagoner maps out a topography which earns him the creditable claim of exclusive squatter's rights. It is his own unique stakeout in contemporary writing. Wagoner's lone surveillance of this territory

Collected Poems, 1956–1976, by David Wagoner. (Indiana University Press, 1976.)

in the American Northwest of the psyche keeps unearthing fresh
resources in the land. It proves to be a forestscape fully equal to his
lavish talents, a locale proportionately challenging to his substantial
lyric and contemplative gifts.

In his last three volumes (*Riverbed, Sleeping in the Woods*, and "New
Poems" in the *Collected*), Wagoner has, characteristically, taken a
poised stance at the bewitched thresholds between interiors and ex-
teriors:

DOORS

All over town at the first rattle of night
The doors go shut,
Flat hasp over iron staple, bolt into strike,
Or latch into groove;
And locked and double-locked and burglar-chained,
All of them wait
For the worst, or for morning, steady in their frames:
From hinge to lock stile,
From hard head-casing down to the plinth block
The doors hang still,
One side for knocking and one for hiding away,
One side for love
And one for crying out loud in the long night
To the pounding heart.

Wagoner deciphering life-signals at the charmed doorsill, the window
frame (indoors vs. outdoors), the city limits, the magical earth itself
(aboveground vs. below). Wagoner listening, with "one ear to the
ground," to subterranean chase for survival, the scuttle of hunter and
hunted, *the cold speech of the earth.* Wagoner discovering that the mole's
death-shriek is one heartbeat away from his own early-warning-
system previsions and forebodings of death: the rapid-fire heart pal-
pitations that fling him down panting and gasping for breath on the
fairway of the golf course ("Tachycardia at the Foot of the Fifth
Green"); Wagoner himself a human equivalent to the salmon washed
ashore in "The Survivor," its precarious life or death subject to a
chance flick of Wagoner's boot, freeing the puzzled creature—fallen
quirkily out of its element—from ripples of the hopeless shallows ("we
saw its humpback writhe ashore, then tilt/ upright in an inch of
water"), sending it back into the saving flow of the downstream cur-
rents. A strong kinship between humans and fellow creatures is
evoked, recurrently, by scenes in which mortal and bestial frailties are
juxtaposed, as in the remarkable poem "In the Open Season": the
human lovers find themselves unexpectedly sharing victimization
with wild animals as targets for the hordes of hunters swarming near

their carelessly selected campsite. Their only recourse against the cacophony of the guns is to bed down on the earth's matted "duff," their love cries of copulation fending off, or counter-balancing, the symphony of discords—an odd mixture of gun blasts, animal squeals, thrashings and flailings in the brush, the terror sounds sizzling and ripping through the air all about them:

> ... blue and ruffed grouse
> Went booming and rocketing slapdash deep under the branches
> Beside us, beating our hearts, and the guns began slamming
> Their blunt, uninterrupted echoes from valley to valley.
> We zigzagged up through the stunted hemlocks, over stumps and snow
> Into shale, into light, to a ridgecrest frozen hard as a backbone
> And lying down as if breathing our last, caught the air
> One burst at a time. When the world came back, we looked
> At dozens of miles of it crumbling away from us
> Where bears and deer were spilling out of hiding.
> The overlapping thumps of shotgun and rifle
> Froze us around each other out of the wind ...

II

The new sequence of poems, though it draws on many of the same virtues of style and imagination as in the earlier works, offers a remarkably expanded breadth of vision. As in Theodore Roethke's great *North American Sequence,* Wagoner's cycle of backpacker poems achieves a poised surveillance of three worlds at once: the citizen-naturalist of America's Northwest, the creative artist, and the passionate lover of fauna, flora—and woman. The poems are obsessed, chiefly, with questions of survival—in the woods, in love, and in the art of the poem. Three worlds—no fewer—resonate in all the best images. And yet, Wagoner's advanced style is so level-spoken, so gentle and even-toned, it is baffling for a reader to try to account for its power to bear up under so much wealth of human reference and density of overtones. Somehow the phrasing is well ventilated with no loss of tautness in the line. A remarkable complexity and versatility of syntax dynamically accentuates shifts in rhythm. The resultant effect, unlike anything I have encountered in American poetry, is that of an apparently low-keyed, spare lyricism, of moderate emotional intensity which gathers force and verve from a steady build-up of pitch accruing from the perfect control of nuances and overtones over a wide stretch of purely hypnotic, clean writing. In some passages, the stylistic blend is so transparent in its radiance, its discharge of energetic intelligence, that Wagoner's unwavering assurance of voice may be misperceived by readers as mere fluency or glib facility.

In "Breaking Camp," the short introductory poem of the cycle, we are implicitly forewarned not to read the sequence narrowly as a metaphor for the creative process, but to see symbolized in the backpacker's adventures and travels a graph of Wagoner's entire life-odyssey, his aging process a cyclic *traveling*, punctuated by vivid, life-giving returns to his first self:

> Having spent a hard-earned sleep, you must break camp in the
>   mountains
> At the break of day, pulling up stakes and packing,
> Scattering your ashes,
> And burying everything human you can't carry. Lifting
> Your world now on your shoulders, you should turn
> To look back once
> At a place as welcoming to a later dead-tired stranger
> As it was to your eyes only the other evening,
> As the place you've never seen
> But must hope for now at the end of a day's rough journey:
> You must head for another campsite, maybe no nearer
> Wherever you're going
> Than where you've already been, but deeply, starkly appealing
> Like a lost home, with water, the wind lying down
> On a stretch of level earth,
> And the makings of a fire to flicker against the night
> Which you, travelling light, can't bring along
> But must always search for.

Wagoner finds, as he edges past mid-career, that very nearly all the human riches and poetic resources he had ever prized have survived the wear of years with minimal slippage. While he has cultivated a clear-sighted rigor in owning up to losses ("burying everything human you can't carry"), he is finding that there is precious little of value that has not been frugally salvaged. There are few ashes to scatter, no squandered human means, gifts, to be written off and buried behind him. Facing into the cold winds of middle life and beyond, Wagoner has armed himself with the backpacker's code of "travelling light," "lifting/ your world now on your shoulders." And this creed will suffice. It is a lean style he now writes, carrying little, if any, excess freightage. This poetry is pervaded with the tenor of buoyancy, a floating grace of movement. The verse measure oscillates periodically: in form, it approximates a sine wave pattern, but the apparent regularity of movement is merely typographic, not rhythmic. Wagoner adroitly modulates the musical cadences of his verse paragraph, his rhythms never falling into a deadening consistency, though his craftsmanship might be mistaken for run-of-the-mill conventionality by careless or hasty readers. In recent work,

Wagoner's language has grown less ornate, shorn of the word-play and surface flashiness that many admirers of his earlier work may have come to regard as a welcome trademark of his personal style. But if they take pains to get in step with his new pacing, a momentum which often may sacrifice verbal pungency to luminous thought, a continuity of rhythmic sweep, and a purity of tonal pitch held taut from first line to last, they will find ample new rewards. In the most stirring passages, the powerful spell over a reader's ear is such that the lines seem to glide, or drift, weightlessly on Wagoner's breath like flotsam on a wave crest.

III

The weakest poem in the sequence, "Meeting a Bear," fails largely because it lacks the true sense of drama:

> If you haven't made noise enough to warn him, singing, shouting,
> Or thumping sticks against trees as you walk in the woods,
> Giving him time to vanish
> (As he wants to) quietly sideways through the nearest thicket,
> You may wind up standing face to face with a bear.
> Your near future,
> Even your distant future, may depend on how he feels
> Looking at you, on what he makes of you
> And your upright posture
> Which, in his world, like a down-swayed head and humped shoulders,
> Is a standing offer to fight for territory
> And a mate to go with it.

A reader is perhaps too demanding in his expectations, given the wealth of bear portraits in our literature, ranging from Faulkner's totemic projection of the demon of primeval America (half flesh-and-blood mammoth, half phantasm) to Galway Kinnell's hunter magically transfigured into the bear he hunts. Since Wagoner clearly establishes a metaphysical rhetoric as the prevailing discursive under-tone, a reader does not anticipate either a strong narrative line or lurid naturalistic detail of raw encounter between man and beast, but he could well wish for a few select items of brute physiognomy to at least suggest the palpable actuality of bear—a few deft strokes, say, like those skillfully abbreviating the anatomies of the killer whale in Wagoner's earlier poem, "The Keepers" ("heaved and lapped by its own backwash./ I couldn't have closed my arms around its head ... Its mouth a foot below/ as wide as a window"), or the rattlesnakes in "Snake Hunt" ("pale bellies looping out of darker diamonds/ in the shredded sunlight, dropping into his sack ... Like the disembodied muscles of a torso . . ."). The poem begins on its strongest nuance, a graphic snapshot of the bear's unique style of locomotion, his near-invisible "sideways" departure that almost perfectly blends with the surrounding foliage, recalling Faulkner's spectre-bear. The poem returns to the crisp, vigorous language of this passage only once again, as the trapped persona is admonished to escape the bear by simulating his body-moves:

> But if you must make a stir, do everything sidelong,
> Gently and naturally,
> Vaguely oblique. Withdraw without turning . . .

For the most part, however, the poem is written in feeble, essayistic language, its meter slackened, the over-civilized voice of the author-as-seer intruding as it explains the bear's psychology:

> He won't enjoy your smell
> Or anything else about you, including your ancestors
> Or the shape of your snout. If the feeling's mutual,
> It's still out of balance:
> He doesn't *care* what you think or calculate; your disapproval
> Leaves him as cold as the opinions of salmon.

There is a false note here—Wagoner posturing as social commentator; his fixed, unyielding attitude toward events manipulates the poem's action and forcibly leads its language. In the remaining poems of this otherwise superb sequence, the natural events lead the reticent will of the speaker, his tacit reverie and contemplative flux of ideas unfolding, haltingly, from the succession of moves across a landscape—terrestrial and cosmological, at once—with a sparkling inevitability.

IV

"Walking in a Swamp" is the pacesetter for the remaining seven poems of the sequence. Tracing the stages of inextricable entrapment in a swamp, the poem explores new modes of staying afloat and "means of moving"—while reclining—for survival:

> When you first feel the ground under your feet
> Going soft and uncertain,
> It's best to start running as fast as you can slog
> Even though falling
> Forward on your knees and lunging like a cripple.

The protagonist finds he has been crippled—to struggle to walk, or even to remain "upright," is to sink and drown. In short, to cling, regressively, to the most fundamental definition of a man—*the upright biped*—is to die. His very species, as it has been envisaged since the caveman's wall murals, is challenged, gainsaid, negated. The most rudimentary questions of how to be a man, how to function as a man-organism, must be reassessed, relearned:

> But if you're caught standing
> In deep mud, unable to walk or stagger,
> It's time to reconsider
> Your favorite postures, textures, and means of moving,
> Coming to even terms
> With the kind of dirt that won't take no for an answer.

Dirt. Man's fraternal earthmate, the submissive partner in his life travels, ungrudging ally, always heretofore the one "that takes without question whatever comes its way," has suddenly grown waspish, unconciliatory. There is no way to modify, or become divorced from, the inhospitable morass that has *chosen him* ("the ground under your feet/ going soft and uncertain"). To survive, he must set about to radically alter his own *inborn* physiology. Wagoner's empirical reconstructionism tackles, equivalently, lifestyle and art mode. The pilgrim woodsman will have to endure many trial efforts of clumsiness, ungainly moves and awkward missteps, like any half-crippled victim training his body to compensate for the malfunction. Slowly he develops an entire new set of routines, improvising novel habits of mobility to fit the countless new small emergencies forced upon him by the uncivil environment. "Coming to even terms" with this misanthropic dirt requires an austere self-training, the re-styling of sensory impulse and response to stimuli, a program of exercises and minigymnastic feats that could eventuate in a reconstituting of the human creature's central nervous system.

In subsequent poems of the sequence, a variety of distinct human crises lead to this common solution—the rigorous fostering in the persona's sensibility and physiology of new modes of expression, the adventure of self-renewal carried to such exhaustive limits as to feel like a rebirth. But the new vision of himself, following the violent shake-up and dissolution of his patterned response, has a surprising familiarity about it. It seems as if, in forging ahead, he has accidentally found his way back to a much older state of his own being. Perhaps the original moment of pure awakening to full consciousness has been restored—a primal condition salvaged from childhood in all its "first wildness," but now coupled with a mature guiding intelligence:

> . . . searching
> Among this second growth of your own nature
> For its first wildness . . .

In other poems, the triggering misadventure, or catalyst to the "second growth," ranges from a bullet wound ("Being Shot"), to being lost in the woods ("Missing the Trail"), being perplexed by mirages in search of hills ("From Here to There"), falling helplessly under the spell of an enchanted garden ("Waiting in a Rain Forest"), and voyaging deeply into trackless, snow-buried hinterland ("Travelling Light").

"Walking in the Swamp" is the first poem in the sequence to decisively break new ground in its experimental language. In this compact lyric, though Wagoner shies away from the more glamorous pyrotechnics of his popular early style ("The March of Coxey's Army," "The Apotheosis of the Garbagemen"), he explores an exuberant vocabulary of sensory excitation which superbly enhances the new body language of the protagonist:

> You must lie down now,
> Like it or not: if you're in it up to your thighs,
> Be seated gently.
> Lie back, open your arms, and dream of floating
> In a sweet backwater.
> Slowly your sunken feet will rise together,
> And you may slither
> Spread-ottered casually backwards out of trouble.

"Slither/ spread-ottered" hits exactly the right note, the moment of finding the language—musculo-skeletal, as well as literary—of survival, the lexicon of rescue. The cumulative sound-effects of this poem have accrued over an exquisite build-up of verbals with approximate similarity of music, but widely differing meanings, the action-words searching out the new "means of moving," the new "postures, textures" of body expressiveness that survival of the crisis demands:

> [slog/lunging/scampering/bogged down/stagger/slither/swivel/wallow]

Though all verbals in the chain except "slither" represent failed tries to engineer a locomotion of escape, the versatility in the poet's aural range mirrors—and resonates with—the persona's trials and tests, the risks and possibilities of stretching his musculature. The poet has found a sinewy body-language of daring athleticism, the many near-to-right words falling a shade to one side or the other of the precise nuance, circling the moment of truth, and shoring up—at last—the exactly apt phrasing to give it voice, a process of narrowing and keen selection expertly controlled by successive approximations, modulated and evoked by half-tones, like a guitarist tuning the strings of his instrument.

Survival, in this primitive barrens, requires that a man dredge up

lost or forgotten animal skills, supersensory acumen that he can re-
cover by traveling backward across the evolutionary chain in his
psyche to disinter his animal forbears, re-living his kinship with the
snake and the otter ("slither/spread-ottered"), borrowing their spe-
cialized expertise. And Wagoner does not stop there, but escorts us
further back in time to the earliest links in the life cycle, when the
first unicellular animalcules and plantlets were conceived out of the
muck. He suggests that we can retrieve our "first wildness" by resum-
ing our shared familial linkage with the muck. To keep from sinking
and drowning in muck, one must dig up the hidden muck in the
human. To recognize the swamp's survival in us is the key to our
survival in the swamp:

> If you stay vertical
> And, worse, imagine you're in a fearful struggle,
> Trying to swivel
> One stuck leg at a time, keeping your body
> Above it all,
> Immaculate, you'll sink in even deeper,
> Becoming an object lesson
> For those who wallow after you through the mire,
> In which case you should know
> For near-future reference: muck is one part water,
> One part what-have-you,
> Including yourself, now in it over your head,
> As upright as ever.

We note the correspondence between syllabic overtones and the
poet's implicit metaphysics, as registered in the reader's ear by the
successful warring of potent, monosyllabic whole-earth-thuds [swamp/
mud/dirt/mire/muck] against frail, intangible, brain-bred polysyllabic
man-blips [stay vertical/above it all/immaculate/upright], and the con-
sequent orchestral vanquishing of the synthetic head verbiage by the
indigenous ground music. *The cold speech of the earth.*

V

In "Tracking," Wagoner departs from the customary passivity of his
persona, who now becomes the aggressor, a hunter tracking an un-
known human quarry. As in Henry James's magnificent story, "The
Jolly Corner," the psychology of the hunt is an unspoken collabora-
tion, or partnership, between hunter and hunted. The one role com-
plements and elucidates the other. The strategy of pursuer is the
obverse of the pursued. Briefing, or self-training, in either role is apt
discipline for its counter-role, which perhaps explains Wagoner's

adopting the unlikely stance of huntsman in "Tracking." For hunter or hunted, pursuer or fugitive, the moment of recognized onset of the hunt miraculously sharpens attention—the powers of concentration are heightened, focused on minutest detail of the natural environment. In "Tracking," the drama of survival—the single man's life-death struggle, matching his civilized wits against the uncivilized forest—is complicated by a power struggle between two human antagonists.

In "Walking in a Swamp," the persona was forced to evolve a new system of instant reflexes, to discover secrets of his joints, bone levers and nerve endings ordinarily unlocked only by great athletes after years of training, to enable him to cope with a forbidding natural habitat. In "Tracking," too, the chief preoccupation is the extemporizing of a new language to cope with unanticipated rigors of physical survival, but this time the perils that menace life are human in origin, not issuing directly from the natural environs. Once again, however, the necessity to find a new language of sensory response is absolute, and requires a similar jolting of the persona's sensibility, a series of shocks to his nervous system that initiate a process of re-learning in his nerve endings and sense organs. In the battle of wills between hunter and hunted, the land itself becomes a neutral intermediary, neither enemy nor ally to either party in the hunt. But this poem's special crisis and distinctive habitat ("this empty country") demands a more sensitive and delicate new body-intelligence in the persona, coupled with an intricate and exquisitely wrought diction to mirror the new body-language. The tracker must cultivate a new consciousness in his senses to detect minimal shifts and alterations in a low-keyed, even-toned monochromatic landscape. The man whose body can learn to become intimately attuned to fine shades of nuance in the bleak terrain will be equipped to outwit his opponent.

He enters into a close communion with the territory, as if mated to the landscape. He comes to know every patch of this special geography as well as he might know the delicate slopes, valleys, contours, hollows of his lover's naked flesh. The knack he develops for detecting any traces of human or animal movements, maneuvers that have disrupted the "natural disorder" of the landscape, is a power akin to that of learning to read a profoundly difficult foreign language, a language not remotely akin to his native tongue. He develops the paramount art of the woodsman, the hunter, the tracker—the discipline and art of readership:

> ... in this empty country
> You must learn to read
> What you've never read before: the minute language

> Of moss and lichen,
> The signals of bent grass, the speech of sand,
> The gestures of dust.

"Tracking" evolves through several distinct clusters of language, differing vocabularies of interrelation between the protagonists—huntsman and victim—and their shared landscape. The central vocabulary, or phrase-cluster, is the lingo of tracker expertise. The passage quoted above is a good compendium of the language of expert tracking. Self-schooling in the logistics of the hunt entails mastering the alphabets of the lay of the land, the vocabulary of earth dialects. "In this empty country," a treeless and bushless terrain, all key signs of ground lingo occur at ankle level and below. The tracker must investigate and decode clues in ground-cover foliage (moss, lichen, grass), closely inspecting, as well, the surface of the barren topsoil itself (sand, dust).

A second vocabulary, with which the poem begins, is a bunching of the language of laxity, heedlessness, expressed by the undisciplined moves of the traveler who, at first, does not guess that he is being tracked by another:

> The man ahead wasn't expecting you
> To follow: he was careless,
> At first, dislodging stones, not burying ashes,
> Forgetting his heelmarks,
> Lighting his fires by night to be seen for miles,
> Breaking dead silence.
> But he's grown wary now...

[dislodging/not burying/forgetting/lighting fires/breaking dead silence]

A third vocabulary groups the language of trickery and concealment, a language of failed attempts to fool an expert tracker:

> No man can move two feet from where he is,
> Lightfooted or lame,
> Without disturbing the natural disorder
> Under him always,
> And no sly sweeping with branches, no bootless dodging,
> No shifting to hardpan,
> Not even long excursions across bedrock
> Should trick your attention.

[lightfooted/sly sweeping/bootless dodging/shifting to hardpan/ excursions across bedrock/trick your attention]

A fourth, and final, vocabulary is the phrase-grouping of masterful detective sleuthing, which extends and completes the language of tracking expertise illustrated earlier:

> And so, at dogged last,
> If you've shuffled off the deliberate evasions
> And not been sidetracked,
> Have followed even blind trails, cutting for sign
> Through slides and washouts . . .
> . . . your dead-set face . . .

[dogged last/shuffled off evasions/not sidetracked/followed blind trails/
slides/washouts/dead-set face]

The dramatic contest between the two men provides the narrative logic and pretext for the poem's successive development of an existential diction of survival tactics. But these clusters of language evoke the solitary nuance of sequential phases in only one man's private struggle to wrest *a living* from an extremely primitive environment. The poem's true drama curiously appears to devolve around collisions between the successive blocks of language clusters, rather than centering in any actual human encounter between the two characters, who gradually merge, it would seem, into two antithetical sides of the same man, deepening the parallel I drew earlier to James's story, "The Jolly Corner." As in the later poem in the sequence, "Being Shot," the two men are doubles, the man hunted a disguised fantasy-projection out of the psyche of the hunter in "Tracking," and vice versa in "Being Shot," a second doubles-fantasy poem complementary to the first.

The doubles genre serves multiple functions in both poems. The implicit relationship between antagonists, two men who have never met, intensifies the reader's absorption in the story—the human-interest level, however superficial at first reading, is arresting in itself, a narrative dimension which fails absolutely in "Meeting a Bear." The conflict between the men, though they be disguised warring factions of the same personality, provides the occasion and impetus for exploring supplementary dimensions of language, widening the range of stylistic resources, since any kind of relation between humans invites verbal resonances not afforded by a diction strictly confined to the lone backpacker's struggle in the wilds. Finally, it is entirely feasible for a man several days lost in the woods to fantasize, and even hallucinate, about a human enemy—a trick the subconscious mind plays on the cognitive intelligence as a kind of shock therapy to scare up surplus, or residual, psychic energies, and thereby to extend the lost travelers's powers of endurance, whereas he might otherwise have sunken into a malaise of premature exhaustion and defeat.

Both doubles poems conclude with an encounter between hunter and victim that is tinged with a wry humor which intriguingly contradicts, or belies, the tone of tragic entrapment:

(1) You should be prepared for that unwelcome meeting:
     The other, staring
     Back to see who's made this much of his footprints,
     To study your dead-set face
     And find out whether you mean to kill him, join him,
     Or simply to blunder past.

                          (conclusion of "Tracking")

The strange play of irony about these lines, evoking quixotic am-
biguities, underscores the element of unreality in the victim, who, like
a mirage-like figure in a dream, dissolves in smoke mists when ap-
proached too closely. The poem's drama halts with a significant thud
of vague finality—"or simply to blunder past." What else is there to do?
One cannot seize a phantom by the throat. How can the hunter go on
believing in the reality of a victim who vanishes at close range? How,
indeed, continue to give credence to his own identity as hunter?

(2)   . . . seeing things
     In a new light
     Which doesn't come from the sky but from all loose ends
     Of all your hopes, your dissolving endeavors
     To keep close track
     Of who you are, and where you had started from, and why
     You were walking in the woods before this stranger
     (Who is leaning over you
     Now with a disarming smile) interfered so harshly.
     Not wishing to make yourself conspicuous
     By your endless absence
     And having meant no harm by moving quietly, searching
     Among this second growth of your own nature
     For its first wildness,
     You may offer him your empty hands, now red as his hat,
     And he may grant mercy or, on the other hand,
     Give you as gracefully
     As time permits, as lack of witnesses will allow
     Or your punctured integrity will stand for,
     A graceful *coup de grace.*

                          (conclusion of "Being Shot")

"Being Shot" is a poem of Kafkaesque disorientation, a nightmare
vision in which the victim's debonair acceptance and absurd civility to
the murderer intensify the dream's credibility and terror. To be
wounded by a bullet—perhaps fatally—is to enter a foreign territory,
another unfamiliar and uncharted landscape. And once again, the
expert traveler starts right in to discover the lay of the new land, so to

speak, first noticing—with a degree of concentration and sensitivity much more intense than was possible before: his powers of observation have multiplied breathtakingly—the actual forest floor beneath his fallen body. Then gradually he discerns and colonizes the newly discovered topography of his body, slowly succumbing to each of the inevitable symptoms of shock:

> And if you haven't fallen involuntarily, you may
> Volunteer now and find what ease waits here
> On the forest floor,
> The duff of sword fern and sorrel, of spike moss and beadruby
> That takes without question whatever comes its way,
> While you begin to study
> At first hand now the symptoms of shock: the erratic heartbeat,
> The unexpected displeasure of half-breathing,
> The coming of the cold,
> The tendency to forget exactly why you're sprawling somewhere
> That has slipped your mind for a moment, seeing things
> In a new light . . .

As in "Missing the Trail," the new light comes from an inescapable void in the psyche that forces the traveler to get newly in touch with the self, the seat of his being, if he is to survive in consciousness at all. Everything within, everything without—both worlds are seen in the "new light." The old light has vanished, put out by a killing shot.

VI

In "Missing the Trail," the persona discovers that all trails followed, all roads taken, are uncertain and arbitrary, whereas the violent shake-up of finding oneself trailless, lost in "the middle of nowhere," is the beginning of true self-awareness:

> Only a moment ago you were thinking of something
> Different, the sky or yesterday or the wind,
> But suddenly it's yourself
> Alone, strictly alone, having taken a wrong turn
> Somewhere behind you, having missed the trail,
> Bewildered, now uncertain
> Whether to turn back, bear left or right, or flounder ahead
> Stubbornly, breaking new ground out of pride or panic,
> Or to raise your voice
> Out of fear that screaming is the only universal language.
> If you come to your senses, all six, taking your time,
> The spot where you're standing
> Is your best hope. . . .

The full coming "to your senses, all six," is the recovery from half-being, half-awakeness. The woodsman has been lost, perhaps unknowingly, for much of his life. Thus, when he awakens to this unmistakable palpability of finding himself lost in the woods, it accidentally triggers in him an awareness of the pervasive disjunction of his whole sensibility. His being is out of step, out of touch with his body, and consequently out of touch with the earth, with Nature. This full recognition of dividedness is a locale on the self's map, the site where everything is beginning again ("the spot where you're standing/ is your best hope . . .").

The persona of "From Here to There," in his rage to connect with "the reality," subjects even his senses to scrutiny and ridicule. His flawed sense-organs threaten to trip him at every step. Moreover, as he travels "from here to there," every medium or element that fills the space between himself and the place viewed "in the distance" is held suspect:

> Though you can see in the distance, outlined precisely
> With speechless clarity, the place you must go,
> The problem remains
> Judging how far away you are and getting there safely.
> Distant objects often seem close at hand
> When looked at grimly,
> But between you and those broken hills (so sharply in focus
> You have to believe in them with all your senses)
> Lies a host of mirages.

The pilgrim backpacker's training, his program of stern self-discipline, is extended to the befuddling and complex schematics—an exact science, it would seem—of mirages. He grapples with the vast, elusive continuum, ranging from optical illusion to hallucination, and pursues these phantoms with a scientist's unfailing objectivity and skepticism. He trains his keen eye, augmented by a clairvoyant mind's-eye, upon all the disguises reality wears.

What can we trust, if anything, to lead us safely from one indispensable place in our lives to another, "from here to there"? The poem, in addressing itself to this central question, tangentially explores a number of searching questions of epistemology. What is the nature of air, light, and earth, as they can be known and experienced directly by human senses? What are the validity and limits of such information about the world of nature as reaches us via our senses, the messages and data having been relayed to our sense receptors by such more or less reliable intermediaries as water, air, etc.? Provisionally, the speaker elects to trust his senses, though he finds that they grow less reliable to the degree that they are separated from the object by mediators which intercept the raw data transmitted by the object, and thereby filter, refine, dilute, or otherwise distort the information en route to our senses. Since habitually he has surmised in good faith that air, water, and light are neutral and non-interfering mediators (allowing for the usual margin of error compatible with routine or median daily experience), it comes as a great shock to his nervous system to acquire, passively, the following wisdom:

> Passing through too much air,
> Light shifts, fidgets, and veers in ways clearly beyond you,
> Confusing its weights and measures with your own
> Which are far simpler . . .

One by one, the common elements he'd complacently depended upon to tell him the truth about his world are exposed as a gallery of necromancers, frauds: subverted from their role as his faithful counselors, all participate in a confederacy of treason, turning his own senses into defecting agents in the service of his enemy—the mirage:

> . . . between you and those broken hills (so sharply in focus
> You have to believe in them with all your senses)
> Lies a host of mirages:
> Water put out like fire, the shimmer of flying islands,
> The unbalancing act of mountains upside down.

Water, fire, air, light, and the land itself—whether it masquerades as "flying islands" or "mountains upside down"—are in league to deceive his senses. How, then, in such a topsy-turvy landscape, can he continue to believe *in,* or *with,* his senses to guide him? One by one, each in its turn, he reassesses his sense organs, eliminating from his trust those which cannot provide him with unmediated passage to the reality he seeks, "the Land Behind the Wind": sight, smell, hearing are suspect, since each of these senses invites deceptive mediation—all are hopelessly vulnerable to the mirages. Only immediate contact will suffice as a safeguard against nature's legions of disembodied spectres. The sense of touch is the one unimpeachable and incorruptible counselor:

> A man on foot can suffer only one guiding principle
> Next to his shadow: One Damn Thing After Another,
> Meaning his substance
> In the shape of his footsoles against the unyielding ground.

At last the scrupulous woodsman, following many amputations and reductions, is ready to "come to even terms" with bedrock reality. Likewise, the writer lurking within the backpacker persona, having stripped away all expendable ornaments and excesses of his style, and

having disciplined and honed down the tools of his craft, is now ready
to wield the sharp cutting edge of his blade of vision to finding imper-
ishably solid poetic terms, and to shore up the architecture of his
vision with this irreducible language of substance. He can trust only
naked quantities, materiality, flat, hard surfaces—body surface
planted squarely on earth surface, flesh and bone pressing the land:

> ... his substance
> In the shape of his footsoles against the unyielding ground.

Not even all touch receptors are to be trusted implicitly, nor is all
ground above suspicion. Naked footsoles are the one flat patch of
bare anatomy which receives incontrovertibly valid data from the
earth beneath. Seemingly, too, firm ground must be tested until it is
proven solid through and through, lest it collapse under his life-
risking, life-bearing step:

> When you take a step, whatever you ask to bear you
> Is bearing your life:
> Sound earth may rest on hollow earth, and stones too solid
> To budge in one direction may be ready
> To gather no moss
> With you, end over end, in another. You've been foolhardy
> Enough already to make this slewfooted journey...

"Slewfooted" is the pivotal word, remarkably fusing the potential fal-
libilities of the human foot and the earth. This word operates as a
hinge in the poem between two shelves of language, and once again
the center of gravity—the main thrust—of a poem's drama shifts from
the narrative overlay (the semblance of a dynamic story-line) to the
lyric conflict between vocabularies tugging and straining toward op-
posite poles.

The language of substance, of materiality, is pitted against the lan-
guage of the mirage, of incorporeality. The first cluster is prompted
by the persona's full recognition of his self's anchorage, and his be-
ing's center, in his senses. But all of his senses gravitate downward,
earthward, converging finally in his body's mass, the give-and-take
exchanges between his full bulk and the earth under each step he
takes:

> [weights and measures/substance/shape of his footsoles/unyielding
> ground/sound earth/stones too solid to budge/rap knuckles against
> the reality]

This language bunching is rivaled by a second cluster which emerges
toward the end of the poem, triggered by the cue phrases "watching
your step, having shrugged off most illusions": the persona then re-

counts, or rehearses, the language of illusiveness, partly to reassure himself that he has in fact mastered the pitfalls of the mirage, but mainly for catharsis, to purge out of his sensorium any last residues of susceptibility to the demons and spectres that might trip him up, impede his vision, and throw him off the straight and narrow course to reality:

> [light shifts, fidgets, and veers/through thick and thin air/dumb shows
> of light/cloud-stuff/flimsy mock-up/world spun out of vapor]

This is a heavy cargo of mirage verbiage, and a reader is almost physically dizzied by it, learning that it is indeed a long and exacting vigil to maintain—as this writer does—a clear-sighted, unshakable pursuit of bedrock reality in a universe wholly permeated and shrouded with cobwebbiness. But we feel that the strength of the poet's restraint and skepticism triumphs at the finish. His humble plea to continue to be a learner and struggler in the blind wilds is wholly authentic and persuasive. Unconditional belief in the reliability of his senses, which launched this poem, has been tempered indeed ("an infirm believer"), but his singleness of purpose is as steadfast as ever:

> ... your hope should be,
> As a hardened traveller,
> Not to see your trembling hands passing through cloud-stuff,
> Some flimsy mock-up of a world spun out of vapor,
> But to find yourself
> In the Land Behind the Wind where nothing is the matter
> But you, brought to your knees, an infirm believer
> Asking one more lesson.

His faith shaken, the "man on foot" has sunk to his knees, but he finds perhaps more honor and strength in the acknowledged infirmity than a proud self-assurance could ever afford. It is the burden and complexity of his whole past life assimilated and swept up into the voice of the dynamic present moment that he shoulders, all gracefully folded and tucked into his one lightweight backpack, whether he stands erect, upright biped on his two flat footsoles, or sinks to his knees in prayer:

> When you take a step, whatever you ask to bear you
> Is bearing your life...

Wagoner's calm authority in these lines is a serenity of earned arrival, a power to face the future and the reality of death with undiminished bravery, conserving and bearing up under his full human and artistic allotment in every step.

VII

The natural marvels of the rain forest, a unique locale, project an instant metaphor. The special idiosyncrasy of the region awakens the visitor/guest to a dream-life native to the habitat. The rain forest is a country in its own right, shielded by its own low ceiling of treetops ("a green sky"). It imposes a tariff, *a duty,* on the traveler, the immigrant-sojourner who punctures its territorial borders and would seek refuge in its salubrious retreat. To be eligible for passport to this land, he must achieve in himself—the tariff on his corpus—utmost metabolism of passivity, but not vague drift of mind, diminution of wits, or dilution of consciousness—not *absence!* Rather, he must cultivate a heightened *presence* of mind in leisureliness, a peace of body which accompanies—indeed, fosters—total alertness, a state of intensified consciousness. His body must be actively vulnerable in stillness: the *being* of prolonged incubation, a temperament of limitless receptivity, will then fertilize in him new dawnings of consciousness. Then he will see and know, as with his mind's eye, the very rare light which is a by-product of the rain forest's unique interplay of shade and refracted sun-rays filtering through the dense, high overhead foliage. The forest and the earth, acting in concert, will offer the voyager a healing umbrage of a quality he has never before encountered.

For him to lie down, trustingly, in this fructifying darkness compounded of magical half-light, a light so refined by many-layered leaf overlappings and branch intertwinings that its eerie glow seems supernatural, shall be for him to assume the splendid, mystifying identity of a "fallen nurse-log," which both remains itself and slowly transforms into a fantastic nursery harboring and nurturing a countless variety of *other* lives, moving into his flesh, finding and sharing his one life in parasitic or symbiotic weddings not unlike the lichen's symbiotic coupling of fungus and alga. His body shall move from a keener grasp of its own singleness, its aloneness, than it has ever achieved before into a recognition of the blessed state whereby a human corpus becomes "a wild garden" in which a variety of other lives may take root. His body, "a fallen nurse-log," shall convert into a botanical municipality providing free and equal interchange of tissue fluids between all plant species and itself; his body, with the help of the healing moss-catalyst ("moss mending your ways"), idly burgeoning into a remarkable new phase of its biological health, reaching backward across the evolutionary chain to claim its kinship with the family of plants.

Not altogether surprising in a poet who, in other recent poems, registers an anguish over the deaths of trees as excruciating as the pain of loss a reader might expect to be prompted only by slaughter of other humans dear to the writer. (I refer, principally, to the splendid trio of poems which impugn the maniacal squandering and decimation of "three square miles" of a forest of fir trees by so-called selective loggers in the employ of the ubiquitous Weyerhauser Company.) I can think of no other contemporary poet who so readily experiences an intense and authentic *fellow feeling* for trees: who finds, while reclining on the matted duff of the forest floor for refreshment, travelwearied, that he can "taste the deepest longing of young hemlocks":

> And know whatever lies down, like you or a fallen nurse-log,
> Will taste the deepest longing of young hemlocks
> And learn without fear or favor
> This gentlest of undertakings: moss mending your ways
> While many spring from one to a wild garden
> Flourishing in silence.

To have arrived at a condition of spirituality in body which bespeaks an ardor of compassionateness flowing with fraternal kinship and allegiance even to trees, as well as to other flora of the forest community—is it not to have made of one's own body, in Mark Strand's phrase, a "final embassy of flesh"?

"Waiting in a Rain Forest" is an exercise in the calisthenics of artful lingering, dallying, delaying. The rain, in this beatific haven, is endowed with special powers that could not have been predicted from its normal properties in ordinary landscapes. It is unlike rain anywhere else, and hence, in its capacity to awaken and evolve hidden efficacies in its usual static constitution, it can serve as an evolutionary guide to the human being who, though he has stumbled into this precinct of forest quite by accident, is searching for a formula, or prescription, for achieving the "second growth" he feels is latent and dynamically waiting to be realized in his own nature. Inadvertently, he finds himself taken into the tutelage and guardianship of this enchanted rain:

> The rain does not fall here: it stands in the air around you
> Always, drifting from time to time like breath
> And gathering on the leaf-like
> Pale shield lichen as clearly as the intricate channels
> Along the bloodwort gleaming like moths' eyes,
> Out of the maidenhair
> And the running pine and the soft small towers of club moss
> Where you must rest now under a green sky
> In a land without flowers
> Where the wind has fixed its roots and the motionless weather
> Leaves you with nothing to do but watch the unbroken
> Promises of the earth . . .

The pale, otherworldly light of this charmed atmosphere is luminous, despite the indirect source—many layers removed—of the lighting: delicate and minute details of the flora glow with unearthly clarity, "the intricate channels/ along the bloodwort gleaming like moth's eyes." Things are more starkly visible in this muted light—not *less,* as one might expect—than in ordinary daylight, and this eerie highlighting, or italicizing, of the borders and outlines of things hypnotizes the woodsman-poet, creates the illusion that he views objects as if they are lit by mind's light, by a shine emitted directly from the inner spirit. The garden landscape comes to seem a projection of the poet's interior landscape of consciousness, and he feels as if he is peering into a scene cast forth by his own skull's lantern, alit by brain light. Hence, this foreign place beguiles him with flashes of odd familiarity.

Later in the poem, the mental process of confusing interior and exterior landscapes is fascinatingly reversed. Whereas, in the poem's opening lines, the protagonist seems to experience the illusion that he is witnessing a scene that has been mysteriously externalized out of his own human psyche, or exhaled by his human lungs, "the rain . . . drifting from time to time like breath"; in the closing lines, the beholder seems to have imbibed and internalized the natural landscape that surrounds him—which is the container, which the scene contained?—his own body playing host to the many phyla of the plant kingdom, his physiology itself gradually undergoing metamorphosis into a "wild garden/ flourishing in silence."

In this haze of perplexing transpositions between the world's body and the body's world, it may seem natural and inevitable for the traveler to take the cues for a new mode of his sensibility from the superior intelligence of the rain's being, letting the rain's spirit set the pace and rhythm of his moves as he, too, finds himself content to simply glide and sway and drift from side to side (as does the poem's versification), modeling his motions after the endlessly hovering, floating mists of "the motionless weather" in which "the wind has fixed its roots." The small shifts and modifications, the gentlest maneuvers, are all suggested to him, and indeed, hypnotically induced in him by the rain's ghostly identity, an apparitional presence so palpable as to seem a personation haunting the air, such that he might put out his hand and touch the rain's limbs. All life, here, hangs in suspension. It seems as if time stands still, as does the unfalling rain. "The motionless weather" is slowness incarnate, a slow country of timelessness and weightlessness. All bodies seem lighter than air; they, too, seeming to float aimlessly between the "green sky" and the earth. The rain tutors, counsels, the guest to follow its lazy halfway meanderings: observe, with the arrested traveler, the rain's vocabulary of min-

imal comings and goings, of least risings and lowerings. No thing
abruptly sails away or falls. All things droop, or loll, or slide. The rain
"stands": it moves, imperceptibly, by gradual shades or shifts:

[drifting/gathering/gleaming/running]

The sharpest movement of the rain is water running down the sleek
sides of the pines, but even that steady flowing is so clean, unrippled,
and level-slipping (which is *running,* the water or the pines?) that the
unwavering flow of water down slick tree-bark may appear to be no
water at all. It may pass for a dry flickering.

Thus follows, in the poem's concluding passage, a matching vocabu-
lary of least human moves, of slowest, most delicate leanings and
sprawlings of the human body, as it incubates and opens itself to
invasion and transformations by the minimal plantlet-lives of the
forest:

[rest now/nothing to do but watch/lies down/taste the deepest longing/
gentlest of undertakings/mending your ways/flourishing in silence]

The reader can envision a battalion of healers and menders, com-
mandeered by the wizardry of the moss, in what comes to feel, at the
very last, like a wonderful fantasy-prevision of Wagoner's own bodily
death and slow, tender reincarnation on the forest floor through the
roots, stems, and foliage of the plants. (*The cold speech of the earth.*)
How, indeed, can the reader separate a consummate vision of rebirth
from the vision of a death which both preceded the new self coming
into being and foretells, with sapience, the full individual human
death to come in the indefinite future? The apparent still point at
which the poem ends is a "flourishing" silence, since the fully em-
braced moment of the present is a fulcrum about which the great
forces of past death and future death struggle, matched in perfect
balance.

The rain forest is "a land without flowers," since no flower species
are needed in this fertile oasis to assert the spirit of freshness and
wildness—the role, say, of a wild rose in the desert, or on a sandy plain
otherwise barren of vegetation. Everything is flowering here, where,
in the "motionless weather," all active physical life comes to a
standstill. Overt energies are all held in check, rechanneled into a total
garden universe, a wildflower charge of blossoming that spreads
equally in all directions, inflating with bloom every patch of earth and
every cubic foot of rain-saturated air. Here, in this fertility, the earth
will never break its most extravagant promises to the pilgrim who
faithfully keeps his contract to quietly suspend his will to ambition,
and sits to keep his watch:

... The motionless weather
Leaves you with nothing to do but watch the unbroken
Promises of the earth ...

VIII

Sleeping in the Woods, Wagoner's last full collection of poems before
the *Collected,* concludes with a prayer to the earth, granter of good
sleep, good death—"For the sake of my joys, sleepmaker, let me in."
The poem is entitled "Death Song," and the final line—"I sing for a
cold beginning"—is a prevision that has been borne out lavishly in
"Travelling Light," the superb poem which ends the backpacker se-
quence. In "Travelling Light," all of the most distressing human in-
terrogations that had obsessed the woodsman persona—ranging from
the earthy to the metaphysical—are brilliantly resolved by the poetry's
exhaustive vision of transfiguration by cold. Robert Frost had au-
gured in his small classic, "Fire and Ice," that the vision of bitter cold,
the spiritual radiance of ice sight, has as much power to radically
change the inner man as the vision of fire, the blaze of sensual
passions. "Travelling Light" has fulfilled Frost's prophecy, but in a
form and style befitting David Wagoner's own idiom and craft.

What I find to be most remarkable in the whole sequence of poems
is Wagoner's consistent pattern of working through harrowing physi-
cal crises to questions of survival as a human identity. Devising skills to
survive in spirit, breaking new ground in the territory of second
growth in the psyche, is intimately bound up, after all, with the body's
struggle to perpetuate its wholeness. The two missions, both poten-
tially grueling enterprises which may demand all the human energies
each of us can mobilize, are indissolubly yoked together at some more
or less distant phase in our racial past. No backpacker who has gotten
lost in the woods for weeks, or even days, and has had to train himself
to imitate small animals in improvising ways to make a living off the
land can ever forget that minimum sustenance to support his
body's—or his mind's!—vital functions may be snatched away from
him at any time; so, as Frost foretold, *we had better be prepared for cold.*
The adventure into the metaphysics of cold has been carried to its
limits in "Travelling Light," and Wagoner's voyaging to the North
Pole, the arctic ice-cap, of his dream gives all readers of poetry a
welcome impetus to begin our own travels into the Ice Age of the
spirit, and to find such healing manna of ice breath as may await us
there.

Beyond all other virtues of the poem, I am most struck by the
unwavering and astonishing elevation of its language. The very crux
of major poetry is the successful improvising of an experimental lan-

guage, the finding of a vital new idiom with roots in common speech. In "Travelling Light," Wagoner plays the most dangerous game with language, like a man juggling chunks of dry ice without asbestos gloves to protect his fingers from burns or frostbite. The lovers in the poem know how great a risk they take journeying into the center of the ice storm of vision, the "dazzling white-out." But the promise of a wisdom and revelation that can transfigure their identities—the very seat of their sensibilities—awaits them, and the anticipated rewards clearly surpass the austere trials and deprivations they are braced to welcome. The transfiguration by cold is illimitable. It touches everything, from the air they breathe to the act of breathing itself, and everything touched by this cold is changed utterly, changed permanently. A terrible chilled beauty is born.

If the dozen vultures in Wagoner's short poem "In the Badlands" could read English, and if this poem were to be inscribed on the "level claybed" below, they might well honor its extraordinary language by mistaking its accents—just as they mistook the lovemaking movements of the amorous couple—"for the thresh and crux and sprawled languor of death": such a writing style, in common with exalted acts of love, both resembles the process of dying, and embodies secrets, enigmas, unmistakably wrenched from death itself.

In "Travelling Light," the only poem in this sequence with two *central* protagonists, Wagoner completes a cycle of nature-hike love-poems that have spanned about a dozen years in his career, initiated by the poem which I take to have been his first work of major stature, "Guide to Dungeness Spit." "Travelling Light" is a strange voyage into snow country. The traveler-beloveds do not guess what they shall find here, but their first impression is that they glidingly traverse—as in a dream of floating—a once-familiar terrain turned foreign, but inviting ("deeply, starkly appealing/ like a lost home," as he'd foreseen the next night's campsite would be, in the first poem of this sequence, "Breaking Camp"). It is their homeland, the country they have known all their lives, but it is completely transfigured, despite the many recognizable outlines of known "landmarks" buried under the deep snow:

> Through this most difficult country, this world we had known
> As a cross-grained hummocky bog-strewn jumble of brambles
> Stretching through summer,
> We find after blizzard and sunlight, travelling in the winter,
> A rolling parkland under our snowshoes
> Where every color
> Has drifted out of our shadows into a brittle whiteness.

The poem's second line wonderfully condenses and epitomizes the various landscapes comprised by the word *country,* deftly investing this word with a broader range of metaphorical overtones than would seem possible so early in the poem's discourse. It is America, to be sure. It is, too, the homestead of lavish sensual pleasures, a bounty shared by the lovers in their youth's long summer. Finally, it is the homesite—or birthplace—of Wagoner's art in the language of sensory excess. All of these landscapes survive, persisting under the deep blanket of snow, but they are transfigured—their difficult complexities simplified to a stark oneness, a singleness: or rather, it is a landscape characterized by total absence of color, "a brittle whiteness," a colorlessness borne of the whole rainbow continuum of hues absorbed, and transcended. The color void is strikingly imaged as the non-color of human shadows cast upon the snow.

> A man on foot can suffer only one guiding principle
> Next to his shadow,

surmised the persona in "From Here to There," but if our shadows, even, have been drained of all color, such that they fade and blend in with the landscape, they, too, must lose their power to guide our travels. *White shadows!* What better image for a transfiguration by cold so total that it proceeds, by one stroke, from our visible faces to the hidden visage of our identities mirrored by our shadows. Color is magical. For the hiking lovers to perceive, slowly, that "every color has drifted out of our shadows" is equivalent to their observing the process of transfiguration of self at firsthand, lost color by color by color:

> And so we begin shuffling our way forward
> Above the invisible
> Deadfalls and pitfallen brush, above the deeply buried
> Landmarks and blazes we had found misleading,
> Above the distraction
> Of flowers and sweet berries and bird-songs that held us
> Back, breathing and tasting, sitting, listening.

Without even shadows for guides, the travelers advance slowly and cautiously into their new cold heaven/ cold earth. They proceed at a "shuffling" gait, partly to keep from falling, partly to allow time for the new reality to sink in. They would slowly savor, together, the visible remnants of their old buried landscapes, surveying whatever survives from their past as they advance into the uncharted territory of the future. The catalog of milestones in the sunken terrain is anything but arbitrary, "deadfalls" and "pitfallen brush" signifying two categories of traps, those set by hunters to catch their prey and those that may trip up the hunter himself. These images enable the author to re-experience, in memory, the valuable lessons of existence related in detail in the two hunting poems, "Tracking" and "Being Shot." "Landmarks" and "blazes" were found to be "misleading," since, as in "From Here to There," our sensory perceptions of these earth signals and fire signals are so often confounded and distorted by the mirage. These phenomena, imperfectly witnessed in detail, are now viewed as having pointed us in the wrong overall direction as well: the province of sensory awareness. The next two lines recount separate but interdependent lists of data which, taken together, constitute our "distraction":

(1) The list of nature's luxuriant beauties—"flowers and sweet berries and bird-songs."
(2) The list of human agencies—the breath, the senses—for inhaling and imbibing these beauties—"breathing and tasting, sitting, listening."

Both catalogs enumerate data which are now perceived to have "held us/ back," but nature's beauties and our senses are not so much revoked as transcended—hence, the three repetitions of "above," expanding the word's overtones from a term of physical positioning to a term denoting scales of mentality. The lovers are voyaging into a snow Elysium, a more elevated spiritual condition which passes beyond the life of sensual beauties, but contains and assimilates them rather than repudiating the youthful heyday of their earthly passions. Their passage upward into the cold heaven of purification proceeds through a series of graduated steps up a ladder, though they maintain to the poem's finish the illusion that they travel on a horizontal itinerary across a conventional flat snowscape, bordered by a visible horizon.

Having severed themselves from the tug of sensual excesses, still lurking seductively under the snow crust, they take fortification from having shrugged off those burdens, much as if they had emptied some material contents from their backpacks to lighten the load of freightage, and, traveling lighter, they find themselves able to augment their pace from "shuffling" to "hurrying":

> Now we are hurrying
> With the smoothswift scuttling of webs, our feet not touching
> The earth, our breath congealing, our ears hearing
> More than we can believe in
> In the denser air, disembodied by the cold, the shouting,
> Shouting from miles away, the slamming of gunfire,
> The ghosts of axes.

This passage achieves an amazing concentration of craft as it enumerates, in rapid succession, each of the baffling hypnotic symptoms of the ascent from a condition of mortality into the dream-life of the cold heaven: the sensation, in body, is experienced as lightening of physical mass (as a man might experience, say, walking on the moon—indeed, much in the poem's second half suggests the magical luminosity of a lunar landscape, divested of color, a landscape which never darkens, but is always aglow with a muted light like neon), approaching weightlessness, their footfalls growing lighter and springier, their bodies seeming to levitate as in a dream of floating. What I take to be most impressive in this passage—an aspect of the whole poem's prevailing style, but more intensified in these lines—is Wagoner's power to evoke otherworldly resonances with undistorted naturalistic detail, the haunted dimension of experience seeming to well up naturally and irresistibly from normal daily events. The delineation of mundane happenings with precision and lucidity never deters the supernatural aura which envelops the narration, and it is difficult for a reader to begin to guess how it is that the ghostly radiance deepens, rather than beclouds, the credibility of the life-resembling details:

(1) "The smoothswift scuttling of webs, our feet not touching/ the earth": This unarguably accurate rendering of the literal experience of walking on snowshoes projects, simultaneously and mysteriously, a vision of the shoes transfigured into weblike wings, sky-sails, lifting the walkers, their feet levitating. (Likewise, the other varied metamorphoses that dazzle across these lines. In all instances, the mystical echoings and re-echoings are generated purely and without strain by events reported with photographic realism.)

(2) "Our breath congealing": Exhaled breath not only fogs in bitter cold air, but also appears to crystallize into particles, and it may seem to an observer as though his own breath is strangely acquiring supernatural mass and density.

(3) "Our ears hearing/ more than we can believe in/ in the denser air, disembodied by the cold, the shouting,/ shouting from miles away": Sounds in the distance are greatly altered, in transit, while traveling across a wide expanse of snowscape, and may indeed hypnotize walkers into feeling as if they hear disembodied voices of the dead, voices out of the past, both the air and the ears seeming bewitched. The literal sounds do seem enigmatic and strange, an eerie combination of distortions produced by the snow and cold. The reverberations muffle the clarity of sound, while the starkness and crisp reception in such air makes the fidelity of sound seem enhanced, suggesting clear voices traveling an abnormally long distance. The distances traversed seem to convert from spatial to temporal quantities, land expanse transforming into time expanse. The voices heard

in this air, "disembodied by the cold," are experienced as voices lifted from graves, voices escaping the bodies which housed them in life.

(4) "The slamming of gunfire,/ the ghosts of axes": As with the disembodied human voices, so it is with the reports of guns and axes, drifting into the present across a timeless expanse of hundreds of years of America's past.

This air is enchanted, charged with the yelps and howls of warring ancestors, the white men and the red men trading threats, exchanging deaths. Their shouting spirits tear through the air yet, to be beheld, overheard, by those few who pass beyond the limits of ordinary sensory experience into a timeless geography in which America's past, present, and future merge, in flux. The ears of these most fortunate travelers still operate in this sphere, but their senses have grown otherworldly, clairvoyant, traveling backward and forward in time, freely spanning generations in seconds. The author, like his protagonists, finds himself moving across great distances in his personal life and career. He gravitates, predictably, back to recurrent themes that have brought him long-standing grief and pain, his countrymen's unscrupulous decimations of wildlife ("the slamming of gunfire"), the heedless devastation of forests ("the ghosts of axes"). No one man can ever correct or offset moral wrongdoing on such a vast scale, but in his own person David Wagoner has undergone strenuous rites of purification in this poem's healing vision of cold, the events in his private memory converging with the events of his country's history, and both are transfigured, his soul cleansed by the ice vision embodied in the deep-earth-frost of his language.

What began as a journey, spatial and horizontal, across a snowy plain, ends as a flight, temporal and vertical, backward in time and descending into the mind's interior snowscape, "the simply amazing world of our first selves." The traveling lovers, innocently taking a walk together in snowshoes across a great expanse of snow, find themselves unexpectedly swept back into their youth, back into their country's stretch of past history, and back into earlier phases of the evolution of their race; at last they find themselves swept forward, voyaging ahead into a prevision of their deaths, surviving the exposure to death's secrets in full consciousness, and returning unharmed, but enriched with a haunted, unearthly intelligence, a gift of the grave:

> And then the cold-spelled morning will make us stare
> Into each other's eyes
> For the first signs of whiteness, stare at the ends of fingers,
> Then into the distance where the whitening

> Marks the beginning
> Of the place we were always looking for: so full of light.
> So full of flying light, it is all feathers
> Which we must wear
> As we had dreamed we would . . .

They are approaching a condition of spirit in which all things of this
world appear to be giving up their mass, shedding their substance,
their bodies, and growing weightless like feathers, the feathers an
American Indian wears when he dances a prayer to light, dances to
blaze with "flying light" in the spirit. They have moved from light-
weight to featherweight to "flying light." The travelers, who had sup-
posed their destination was to be a geographical place, a region that
can be pinpointed on the map of a horizontal landscape, have found,
instead, that they have been traveling *into* light, light itself the place, a
condition and site combined, and they themselves are becoming the
light they enter, a new inner light by which all things beheld are
observed to glisten with a ghostly luster, filling the void of snowblind-
ness with a new structure of vision, supplanting the old sensory vision
of the retina:

> But snowblindly reaching
> Into this dazzling white-out, finding where we began,
> Not naming the wonder yet but remembering
> The simply amazing
> World of our first selves, where believing is once more seeing
> The cold speech of the earth in the colder air
> And knowing it by heart.

"Dazzling white-out" is indicative of the crowning moment of trans-
figuration by cold, the voyaging lovers reaching the end-point of
their odyssey, fulfilling the implicit message of the title. They move in
their diversified passageways, as in the countless tunnels, corridors, of
a labyrinth, and, as the radius of their travels expands, their orbits
resembling a series of widening rings of light, nimbuses around a
planet, the word *traveling* opens outward, embracing a steadily
broader spectrum of human and trans-human experience. The word
itself is sprung into a metaphor which radiates tributaries of meaning
in all directions, and most pertinently, the author finds he is traveling
back to earlier stages of his own career, lower rungs of his ladder of
authorship. Perched on each of these steps, in turn, he finds he is
ideally placed to take inventory of his present stockpile of resources,
his workmanlike supplies, and he can make ready to launch a fresh
start, a new itinerary of travels in the world of poetic language: "The

cold speech of the earth," a new rich lode, or vein, of ore to be lifted straight from that indigenous mine of so much surpassing American poetry—Whitman, Frost, Masters, William Stafford—the ground of common speech. David Wagoner had broken new ground in that mine-shaft before, but now he has excavated a much deeper trench.

James Wright

WORDS OF GRASS

Shall We Gather at the River

There is a stubborn, manly honesty in James Wright's new book of poems. He is beautifully resolute in his refusal to make any bargains with life or art. The man in these poems (and we can never forget he is inside their skins) has an unquenchable craving to find "my secret, my life" and to say it in poems. This last, pure demand of his spirit speaks from the very roots of his being—the words have the finality and unshakable authority of self paying its dues, and claiming its total due:

> But my life was never so precious
> To me as now.
> I will have to beg coins
> After dark.

Nearly every poem in the book contains lines which bespeak a man who has been so lost, so hurt, so dumb, so wrong . . . and he knows it to his bones. Now, in his fourth and best book of poems, he is at last able to say it out and nothing can stop him, not even the words. Indeed, he is at war with the very words of his poetry. They will never be enough. If he could, he would change them to grass:

> The earth is hard now,
> The soles of my shoes need repairs.
> I have nothing to ask a blessing for,
> Except these words.
> I wish they were
> Grass.

But I mustn't mistakenly suggest that Wright is exclusively taxed with introspection—a squaring with his personal demon—in this book; rather, he reaches out to others, and achieves a passion of common humanity, a commonality of fellow feeling for the least of mankind, to a degree not witnessed in his earlier work. In this book, Wright is obsessed with the lives and dyings of people from whom life has taken everything except the inner life of spirit: the arthritic man

Shall We Gather at the River, by James Wright. (Wesleyan University Press, 1968.)

who "takes coins at the parking lot/ He smiles with the sinister grief/ Of old age"; the old woman in the gambling casino who "has been beating a strange machine/ In its face all day"; Uncle Willy Lyons, who "was buried with nothing except a jacket/ Stitched on his shoulder bones"; Wright's father, who, though his life was "caught among gird-ers that smash the kneecaps/ Of dumb honyaks . . . He came home as quiet as the evening"; Jenny, who "has broken her spare beauty/ In a whorehouse old. She left her new baby/ In a bus-station can"; as well as the whores of Wheeling, West Virginia, who "could drown every evening [in the river]," yet each dawn "they climb up the other shore,/ Drying their wings." Is it possible to doubt the scoured authenticity of such lines, lines that have won their ductility and steely durableness from being eaten into by the acids of living pain; lines which, despite their pared-down, wiry tautness, are stained with the irremovable residue of lived terrors as surely as particles of soil cling to tree roots?

Irresistibly drawn to the souls of beings who have wasted their lives—or who have been devastated *by* life—Wright's soul becomes, at last, hopelessly and lovingly entangled with theirs. He has the large-ness of heart of the great empathizers, and worse, a mind suicidally honest, a mind hellishly bent on stripping away all self-protective devices. His best poems enact the drama of a mind struggling, usually with punishing success, to resist the temptation to take solace from its own compassionating ardor. The pain he feels for another never becomes a disguised way of cheering himself up. It is a tougher thing. The poems in this book are nearly identical in form to those of Wright's last book, but they have advanced to an altogether new spiritual magnitude. Perhaps the most serious obstacle to the new life of spirit is brevity of form. I feel that this tendency has become a handicap which impedes a full blossoming into the massive, raw-boned jaggedness of form which, as in the superb *Minneapolis Poem,* can provide the structural leverage needed to render the fuller sense of life newly available, but somehow left unbodied, in many of the short poems. The best work in this volume demonstrates clearly that Wright has the skill and fortitude needed to rid his art of the leaning to premature closure that often stifles his ablest, most incandescent vision.

POETRY, 1969

Two Citizens

One afternoon,
At Aetnaville, Ohio,

Two Citizens, by James Wright. (Farrar, Straus and Giroux, 1973.)

A broken goat escaped
From a carnival,
One of the hooch dances
They used to hold
Down by the river.
Scrawny the goat panicked
Down Agnes's alley,
Which is my country,
If you haven't noticed,
America,
Which I loved when I was young.

That goat ran down the alley,
And many boys giggled
While they tried to stone our fellow
Goat to death.
And my Aunt Agnes,
Who stank and lied,
Threw stones back at the boys
And gathered the goat,
Nuts as she was,
Into her sloppy arms.

In "Ars Poetica: Some Recent Criticism," the long poem which opens James Wright's new volume, this shrewdly recalled anecdote serves as an intermediary between fragments of family history and Wright's searching diagnosis of America's soul-sickness. Employing his memory of childhood, then, as a go-between, Wright traces the origins of family tragedy and links its genesis, enigmatically, to the roots of various catastrophes in the current national life. We witness the two tragedies in tandem, a river of recollection and deep human sympathy flowing back and forth between them; Wright aching for the waste, brooding over the desolation of squandered beauty and human resources—so much promise, so much endowment of natural gifts depleted in a single generation; Wright agonizing—not without bitterness, not without a few flare-ups of raw hatred and plotted vengeance—over the downfall and the ruins of his two beloveds: his family ancestry, his country.

Out of this duet of heartaches Wright fashions his new *ars poetica,* which takes shape as he tours through France and Italy in the bewitchment of a second duet, the *Two Citizens,* he and his wife Annie, unfashionably and unabashedly falling deeper in love with America—as with each other—the more they find she has betrayed her citizenry, the more they discover her to be despicable in the quality of her national character as they wander and sample the glories of classical antiquity that beset their wayfarings down public roads, coun-

In Wright's main line of defense of his father's credentials to join
the elect friends to Horace in Elysium, the logic for arguing a basis for
affiliation is, of course, serio-comic:

> Now, if I ask anything, I would ask you
> How to gather my father to your bosom.
> He knew, after all, how to love Italians.
> Others said dagoes....
>
> Every time I go back home to Ohio,
> He sits down and tells me he loves Italians.
> How can I tell you why he loves you,
> Quintus Horatius?

The rich overtones of this passage point to a dramatic frame of refer-
ence beyond the context of this poem to the larger scheme of the
whole volume. If Wright is taxed by his efforts to put his father over as
a great unacknowledged friend and kindred to Italians, how much
severer are his anxieties lest the Italy of his European travels turn a
deaf ear to his prayers for his own spiritual passport, in retaliation for
the vulgarity and outrageous incivilities of many of his fellow coun-
trymen who visited or emigrated to Italy before him, as in "Names
Scarred at the Entrance to Chartres":

> P. Dolan and A. Doyle
> Have scrawled their names here....
> I have no way to go in
> Except only
> In the company of two vulgars...

Wright's forerunners—maybe rich aristocrats in America—think
they can earn a place in Olympus by hacking their names at the
entrance gate to the cathedrals. But the poet knows himself to be, at
best, a second-class citizen here, a full cut below the peons. Arriving
with virtually no baggage—of class, of ancestry, of nobility, or of
peasantry's natural grace of person—he pleads his humble case for
admission. The poet waits and waits, his country's ugliness and dis-
honor weighing down his head, his spirit's shoulders hunched,
America's disgraceful bad manners underscored by the scars of
"scrawled" signatures, "P. Dolan and A. Doyle," whom he cannot
repudiate without forfeiting his American heritage. So he must carry
the burden of his countrymen's disreputable acts, as well as the weight
of his own crippled prosody ("the crude/ Rhythm of my time"), with
no help but his pride in his love, Annie, to solace and support him:

> The cracked song
> Of my own body limps into the body

Of this living place. I have nobody
To go in with
But my love who is a woman,
And my crude dead, my sea,
My sea, my sepulcher, the crude
Rhythm of my time.
This cracking blossom is my second America.

His true passport among the Olympians is the authentic, vast awe he feels before the indecipherable magnitude of beauty in the cathedral. How can his mere stripped-down humble song do homage to this masterwork of scores of anonymous—X's, nameless and forgotten— geniuses? By finding its modest life in the form of no more than a "cracked song," a broken-voiced mortal prayer to the immortals.

In a number of poems revering great works of sculpture and architecture, Wright guides the reader through an exquisite chain of paradoxes. How can we tell the monuments from the native people they were modeled after?

The Last Pietà, in Florence

The whole city
Is stone, even
Where stone
Doesn't belong.
What is that old
Man's public face
Doing sorrowing,
Secretly a little,
A little above and
A little back from
A limp arm?
What is that stone
Doing sorrowing
Where stone
Doesn't belong?

Wright's ardors to the statues and the people are indistinguishable. Works of sculpture and cathedrals burgeon into supernatural life. The stone trembles and breathes. The stone erupts. It is flesh, and the poet feels embarrassment, shame—at moments, horror—before so much naked exposure of beautiful, soulful bodies in public.

How appropriate, then, for the archetypal woman to greet him unbidden from the eyes of the saints. In Bologna, Mary Magdalene is the muse whom Wright entreats to "give me this time . . . a poem about gold." Arrival in Italy, finding his true place and center at last, is a matter of raw encounter with the presiding supreme holy woman of the place. She rewards him with one of his best poems, "Bologna: A Poem about Gold." In a wonderful passage celebrating Mary's secret earthiness ("her love/ For the golden body of the earth"), Wright swiftly composes a synthesis of sublime women—the Wife of Bath, Cleopatra, and his own privately mythic Jenny, all perceived as off-spring of Mary, the prototypic complete woman who subsumes her descendants much as Yeats's Maude Gonne is canonized as a spiritual heir of Helen of Troy:

> White wine of Bologna,
> And the knowing golden shadows
> At the left corners of Mary Magdalene's eyes,
> While St. Cecilia stands
> Smirking in the center of a blank wall,
> The saint letting her silly pipes wilt down,
> Adoring
> Herself, while the lowly and richest of all women eyes
> Me the beholder, with a knowing sympathy, her love
> For the golden body of the earth, she knows me,
> Her halo faintly askew,
> And no despair in her gold
> That drags thrones down
> And then makes them pay for it.

Mary is sublimely guiltless and undespairing. Self and soul are bal-anced in her, the human and goddess comfortably wedded in the poet's vision of her icon.

THE YALE REVIEW, 1974

PART II

W. H. Auden

> Each year brings new problems of Form and Content
> new foes to tug with: at Twenty I tried to
> vex my elders, past Sixty it's the young whom
>   I hope to bother.

So reads the inscription on the dedicatory page of W. H. Auden's new volume, *Epistle to a Godson,* and this reader, close enough to the midway age—give or take a few annual furlongs—between Auden and his "new foes," may gropingly undertake to act as referee. In the title poem, Auden envisages a time of world crisis in the imminent future in which the survival of the race would depend on a survivor corps who

> may be called to opt for a discipline
> that out-peers the monks, a Way of obedience,
> poverty and—good grief!—perhaps chastity . . .

and Auden quite soberly sets himself the task to write works that will nourish such a hardy crop of rugged caretakers of our future. He would set an example to the young less in what he writes than in the exacting discipline of the style and form:

> Nor shoddily made: to give a stunning
> display of concinnity and elegance
> is the least we can do.

The lines hearken back to Yeats's

> Irish poets, learn your trade,
> Sing whatever is well made,
> Scorn the sort now growing up
> All out of shape from toe to top,

but Auden, adopting the posture of a much-weathered Anglo-American oldster, evidently isn't addressing young poets so much as haranguing a featureless, universal new youthster. How seriously does he take his role as mentor? Indeed, fancy his striking the pose of ambassador of global politics, while adopting a tone and manner not far from light verse, despite the uniformly elegant prosody and stately—if not perhaps often statesmanlike, magisterial—syntax.

In most of Auden's recent work, his chief predilection is a flair for

Epistle to a Godson and Other Poems, by W. H. Auden. (Random House, 1972.)

artlessly speaking his mind. His serio-comic tone is scrupulously well-pitched to accommodate a mode of discourse that fluctuates whimsically from clowning gossip to impassioned thought. Speaking with utmost candor in the epistle to his godson Philip Spender (*"turn your toes out as you walk, dear,/ and remember who you are, a Spender"*), he negotiates gracefully from a cantankerous survey of the spoils of our illiterate political bosses ("Global Archons") to a more telling outline than is to be found elsewhere of the improbable poetics that has been gaining ascendancy in his last three volumes of poetry, starting with *About the House:*

> its dominant
> mood should be that of a Carnival.
> Let us hymn the small but journal wonders
> of Nature and of households.

In radical departure from the classical emphasis on subjects of high consequence that characterized the poems of his early and middle periods, Auden now gravitates more and more to "small but journal wonders," domestic and local occasions assuming the forefront in his gallery of common wares. But usually, the scales of the balance are tipped pronouncedly away from the avowed subjects to the unmasked dialectics of Auden's speaking voice, happily and luminously at war with itself, but inviting the reader to clandestinely eavesdrop on the self-bemused conversation; and it is no accident, surely, that the book concludes with the charming "Talking to Myself," an intellectual vaudeville act in which Auden soliloquizes jokes to his mate, his mute beloved, his own body:

> My mortal manor, the carnal territory
> allotted to my manage. . . .
> Our marriage is a drama, but no stage-play where
> what is not spoken is not thought: in our theatre . . .

Auden, confessedly, is importing into his new gabby art of the lyric "a sense of theater" borrowed from his verse plays, as well as distilled from his decades as an erudite and shrewd entertainer on stage in the lecture circuit. His own distinctive personality, droll and caustic by turns, a favorite character from one of his plays, steps into the spotlight of the poems. He carries it off with the insouciance of a casual man shooting the breeze, but secretly ruminating in strictist prosody. Yes, for all his liberal outspokenness, the audacious and garrulous speaking out of a sagely opinionated mind, he remains a staunch formalist in his craft, and a strict rationalist in his cognitions. Hence, he dismisses the current avant-garde with gruff obstinacy:

No, Surrealists, no! No, even the wildest of poems
  must, like prose, have a firm basis in staid common-sense.

His unrelenting, if obsessive, adherence to overt sanities of craft and
vision exceeds all limits in a marvelous passage addressed to his body,
again, in the last poem. I fancy I hear the snorts and grunts of a
medieval knight bracing himself to behead a fire-breathing dragon!
Auden threatens to uproot his own dream-life as, with comic arro-
gance, he would bully his "nocturnal manias," too, into learning the
correct rules of versification:

For dreams, I, quite irrationally, reproach You.
All I know is that I don't choose them: if I could,
they would conform to some prosodic discipline,
mean just what they say. Whatever point nocturnal
manias make, as a poet I disapprove.

THE YALE REVIEW, 1973

Michael Benedikt

Michael Benedikt's surrealistic poems are a highly serious form of
play in which easily recognizable chunks of human and non-human
reality are reordered in enchanting and luminous fantasies. In Ben-
edikt's world, people and objects are interchangeable: people are
deadened from within; things are vivified from without—invested,
layer by layer—with personality. Benedikt skillfully controls the queer
humor generated by the disparity between his subjects and his grace
of treatment.

Many of Benedikt's poems, however, are mere intellectual curios,
clever exercises in which a vivacious display of technique conceals an
emptiness of subject. His best poems are parodies of intellectual self-
consciousness and moral decadence. They are compact allegories, or
narrations, which project with the stunning clarity of animated car-
toons the de-spiritualization of all beings into gadgets, self-imitating
inventions. An outstanding example is "Some Feelings," in which
people's feelings are visualized, as in an op-art poster, first, as so many
electromagnetic lines of force issuing upward from their appendages,
and finally, as threads from which the people are suspended like
marionettes:

The Body, by Michael Benedikt. (Wesleyan University Press, 1968.)

> Only somebody
> At the level of the ground may see
> That each feeling is connected by a thread
>   to a forehead, an arm or a leg
> And that individuals
> At the heights of their tragic moments
> Resemble porcupines or pincushions

At its best, Benedikt's method quantifies fanciful ideas into memorable concoctions that have the zany resourcefulness of a highly talented child's inventions with Tinkertoys and Erector sets, though the ingredients of his structuring are likely to be portions of human anatomy and of the human psyche. Face parts are displaced, as in a Picasso painting; body organs and itemized quantities of the inner life are juggled and dissected, all reduced to a common scale of thingness: "I had this picture in my mind of carrying around my lungs/ As if they were valises I was trying to smuggle through/ Customs, perhaps as if to slip my heart through/ My mind."

The one intrinsic weakness in his writing is a failure of passion, perhaps owing to the studiedly ironic offhandedness of his manner. But in the lines concluding one of his best poems, "The Debris of the Body," he does achieve high passion by converting provisionally vulgar materials—body wastes, body sloughings—into a strangely beautiful synthesis:

> There, the sea is inundated with the flower of fallen hair, worn skin, fingernail parings, nose pickings, oozed blood, used sperm (love's leavings!), annoyed old scabs, tears accidentally escaped in wind, tears meant to be wept, the nether wastes, the shit and piss of the skin, superannuated wart parts, etc.

POETRY, 1969

Robert Duncan

Robert Duncan's struggle in his new volume to overhaul his technical apparatus to make it able to accommodate political denunciation may be likened to Yeats's metamorphosis in *Responsibilities,* the volume in which he explicitly set out to bury his allegiances to "old mythologies" and to intensify reality in his work. In the effort to de-mythologize his medium, Duncan is undertaking a similarly exhaustive labor of self-

Bending the Bow, by Robert Duncan. (New Directions, 1968.)

effacement and self-renewal. Duncan has desperately needed for many years to retrieve his poetry from the incantatory monologue of private reverie and myth, and to initiate a return to subjects of public consequence. In the years since the publication of his best volume, *The Opening of the Field,* Duncan appears to have succumbed more and more to debilitating preciosities of mannerism, mostly derived from the poetry of Ezra Pound: abbreviated spelling, philological queries, overt pedantic scholarship. This defect of artificiality sinks to a new low of self-consciousness in the poem "Spelling," which humorlessly explicates stylized misspelling in the manner of a gloss to an Old English text.

The Opening of the Field had announced the birth of a surpassingly individual talent: a poet of mysticism, visionary terror, and high romance. Duncan's work is outstanding among his contemporaries' in having rehabilitated from three hundred years of relative disuse and stagnation the emblem—not the image, or the symbol—as the central vehicle of the poem's drama. Duncan's emblems are populated by flaring presences who, like crucified angels, blazingly dance out of the "black pit" of blindness, and into "the beginnings of love." But in his recent books he has produced numerous exercises—lacking all vividness—while he waits for the return of his demon. These many autotelic performances are like prayers to the absent spirits urging their return: they may serve, for us, as a record of soul-priming, the readying of fallow poetic ground for the next major theme, whenever it may strike.

Such a theme is the Vietnam war. In the best new poems, "Up Rising," "Transgressing the Real," "The Soldiers," Duncan's new aesthetics of political engagement embodies his outrage in the most viable, grotesque emblems he has produced in any poetry: "The Grand Poker Table," where "the hydra" (heads of state), "shuffling cards, beyond number," gambles away the lives of thousands: Lyndon Johnson's "Texas barbecue," a gargantuan super-feast "swelled with the votes of millions" of pampered, overfed, innocently criminal Americans, "good people in the suburbs turning the/ savory meat over the charcoal burners and heaping their barbecue/ plates with more than they can eat." It may well be that these agonizingly Dantesque, emblematic hymns point ahead to a full resurgence of Duncan's demonic genius.

David Galler

Leopards in the Temple, David Galler's second volume of poetry, brings together an impressively large number and variety of substantial poems. He writes poetry of solidity, quantity, substance; his poems never suffer from thinness of style, or lack of consequence.

Galler is strongest in poems which are detectably anchored in his experience. There is so much prolixity and indirection in his manner to start with that he can't afford to distance the reader still further by interposing a vast historical remove between him and the subject. Though I've spoken elsewhere against the trend to self-conscious personal journalism in contemporary poetry, Galler is most interesting when his subjects are, or seem to be, most obviously tied—sometimes with direct intimacy—to experience. I'm speaking here of the inevitable built-in hazards of a given method. Galler's style grows heavy, morose—his lines tend to shuffle under the burden of historical names and references—in some of the poems dealing with mythical or classical figures. But in the poems dealing with contemporary life, as well as in the controlled absurdities of his original, Kafkaesque parables ("Colloquy in a Motel," "The Passion," "The Witness"), his manner operates as a full-bodied language of fine density and precision:

> Informed my father had for years maintained
> My seat beside him in the *shule* . . .
> I saw myself the stranded child again . . .
> Again the child rose by his side,
> And back and forth began to sway—stiff little
> Brows in frantic imitation—
> Watching its elder's eyes to find the place.
> Each time their eyes would meet, the child
> Convulsed its lips toward every shape, faking
> The foreign sounds at quickened pace.
> *Hold on!* I cried, fixing the youngster with
> A spurious eye, *Your legs in pain*
> *Mouth parched, your mind by language raped, my strength*
> *Be yours to see it out in a*
> *Cool rage at old men kissing silk . . .*

In these lines from "The Dybbuk," a poem that demonstrates the power of art to exorcize demons—the dybbuks—of the mind, the

Leopards in the Temple, by David Galler. (Macmillan, 1968.)

persona projects himself back into a childhood catastrophe, and traps himself into re-experiencing the unbearable guilt he felt when he committed spiritual treason against his lovingly authoritarian father and God, simultaneously, by deserting his seat in the *shule*. The psychological device successfully employed by the poem is a self-induced, but controlled, schizophrenia. The dutiful son and the rebel, two halves of Galler's childhood self-image, are separated and forced to mystically confront each other in the poem's drama. Father and son are pitted in a holy war, each seemingly against, but truly (if secretly) *for* the other; and the sustained love—in opposition—between them provides the spiritual fortitude necessary for the conquest of self over anti-self, rebel over slave. In Galler's vision, a man's true identity heroically emerges out of successful desertions, apostasies, from the many anti-selves thrust upon him by the world. How well Galler has been able to crystallize for the reader in beautifully exact particularity of detail those moments when the child's (and through it the man's) identity can somehow be miraculously preserved—and indeed, toughened—in its warring against the combined forces of family and society that conspire to confound it.

Galler is a virtuoso technician. He usually creates fresh stanzaic patterns for each subject, and he manages to exploit to advantage all the special resources of rhythm and line movement made available by the shape of the stanza. If he tends to be, at times, an over-ambitious craftsman, often thickening his lines and stanzas where a thinning out of verbal saliencies seems to be demanded by the flow of his thought, perhaps it is because he must constantly exercise and maintain his technical means at full stretch in the weaker poems to enable him to be fully equipped to write poetry of the highest order when a subject of the massive proportions of "The Archipelago," or one of the profound human consequences of "The Dybbuk," falls into his hands.

THE YALE REVIEW, 1968

Paul Goodman

A full human personality streams through Paul Goodman's *Hawkweed:*

> Indeed, these days my contempt
> for the misrulers of my country

Hawkweed, by Paul Goodman. (Random House, 1967.)

>is icy and my indignation raucous.
>Once American faces
>were beautiful to me,
>I was their loyal lover,
>but now they look cruel
>and as if they had narrow thoughts.
>Their photographs in *Life*
>devastate my soul
>as their gasoline denudes
>the woods of Indochina.
>Let me go into exile
>—a poet needs to praise.
>It is wicked to live
>where I do not care for the people.

The quality I find most refreshing in Goodman's poetry is his constant bearing down on the diamond-bright bedrock of experience, and his ability to transmit those rare, invigorating moments of beauty of personal revelation from the wide stretch of his years of intense productivity. Much of *Hawkweed* reads like a diary or journal. The many poems entitled "Long Lines" recall to mind, but only as a device, Norman Mailer's "Short Hairs." While Mailer's marginal poetry is merely a slick medium for incidentals, Goodman's marginal poems are telling, often painful to read, footnotes to his public life. I'm constantly reminded of this, even as I chide at the evident scrappiness of so many of the poems. They are a vital testament of one of the most interesting minds of our time.

Goodman's uncompromising judgments of American society and politics are delivered with thunderous honesty and clarity in his prose. In the poems, he vacillates between raw self-exposure and bewilderment at his failure to set things right for himself, his family, or his country, despite his incredible creative energy and output, as well as his genius for getting across to the younger generation:

>Three years I made a thousand pages
>And a hundred flights across America
>And kept an ill-starred love affair alive.

It is his lover's quarrel with the country that I'm grateful to find he's keeping alive in the poems, and that is what gives his poetry a kind of superabundant life that is rare today. Goodman is constantly spilling over in his art, as in his love life: "Oh the beauty and the madness and the strangeness/ of my six lovers astonishes me," but we can allow his excesses if we view them as a necessary surfeit of his Elizabethan dynamism.

Arthur Gregor

Arthur Gregor is surely one of the most deeply spiritual poets of our time. The development of his art can be viewed as the cultivation of a purely transparent medium in which language becomes a vehicle for transmitting moments of luminous being. To many readers, his poems may appear to be moving toward a total absence of style, the condition of stylelessness. Yet he is an experimental stylist in the truest sense. In Gregor's work, we find the nearest approach in American poetry to what Susan Sontag has identified as "spiritual style" in the films of Robert Bresson. To a generation of readers accustomed to a garish obtrusiveness of style, Gregor's style is apt to seem invisible. Simply to compare Gregor's style with the bland, featureless style of most poetry in translation, poetry without any face, is to be struck with the distinctive serene beauty and simplicity—the austereness—of his lines:

> Yet we were driving to get to her
> who we feared might soon be gone.
> And how were we to reconcile
> exuberance with what we were about?
>
> That a car was taking us
> to the condition we call death,
> that extinction could occur
> when the day showed itself
> in a display so bright
> it seemed a game of light,
> that disappearance should
> make sense when all about us
> objects we could not name
> flared up in a cold winter sun
> and shone until we had to turn
> from them as from a flame,
> nothing in us could reconcile,
> nothing in us could explain.
>
> (from "Irreconcilables")

A special quality of Arthur Gregor's writing is his power to hold a long sentence in breathless suspension over many lines, lines which instill the feeling of softness, gentleness, lightness. In Gregor's medium, tone must be perfectly pitched and mood everywhere sustained, since

Figure in the Door, by Arthur Gregor. (Doubleday, 1968.)

any slip in rhythm or phrasing will be accentuated by the stark crystallinity of his line movement, and may be picked up instantly by the careful reader.

Gregor's fervent preoccupation with images of subtle and delicate movements in nature is indicative of a search for living correlatives to the stillness-in-motion he aspires to in the refinement of his poetic line:

> Silence shivers as if touched by sounds
> subtle as the air that holds
> the heron's spread blue wing . . .

Gregor has evolved a poetic manner that serves as a frictionless conveyor for his thought. Ideas in the poems are as inseparable from the style of their expression as wave from water, wind from air. Because Gregor's work is more a poetry of ideas than we are accustomed to reading today, it is easy enough to make the mistake of dismissing him as merely a philosopher in verse. But these poems are not doctrinaire; rather, they employ ideas as one of many elements in the service of projecting an inner luminosity of being. Philosophy is subordinate to the stream of intensely devotional feeling running through most of the poems.

In a few pieces, ideas do dominate the poetry. Similar motifs may be employed repeatedly, and the weaker poems fail to give any new life to the theme. Philosophy must be lifted above a minimal threshold of linguistic and imagistic adventurousness to become poetry, and some poems lag much below that minimum. Another of the difficulties in Gregor's art is the tendency to sameness in line length and line movement. He evidently has a nearly irresistible affinity for shorter lines, perhaps because they nearly always so aptly facilitate the free flow of his mind.

But in his longest and best poem—the one that concludes the present volume ("The Unworldliness That He Creates")—he achieves an altogether new line movement: supple, pulsing, taut or slack by turns, long or short, adaptable to multiple rhythms. The new mode intersperses prose passages in a matrix of expanding sentences of poetry, sentences that employ a Whitmanesque paralleling of clauses in sequence to encircle a larger and wider landscape of vision. The one constant in the poem—which marks a perfect arrival and fulfillment of many of the central motifs in the book's philosophy—is the movement from beauties of art, nature, urban scene, into the space in the persona's being in which all "things he looks upon achieve themselves."

Gregor's power to envision for the reader the quality of spiritual beauty in strangers, "foreigners," is an ideological mainstay of many of his poems. He seems to be proposing a theory of personality which gives a new validity to the romantic axiom of love at first sight by annexing it to its antithesis of classical restraint:

> On your way home you stopped to shop,
> looked around as you were going in,
> and recognized yourself in me
> some steps away. Then you went in
> and I went on. Of course the outcome
> could have been otherwise, but not
> what had already taken place.
> That we had seen each other in
> each other's face without disguise,
> had beheld what is not yours nor mine:
> a nameless recognition we might not
> have reached, had our shyness and
> each other's namelessness been breached.

Again and again Gregor dwells on the kinds of recognition—the radiances—that are possible only between strangers, the momentous flash in the eyes of "the figure in the door." The sensibility in the poems is one that has learned to guard against the damages—the subtle losses—that result from frail intimacies. The fashionable glamor that attends all forms of personal involvement today leads to serious, though nearly imperceptible, injuries to the self. Gregor revives the power in us to respond to beauties in people that transcend their worldly personalities. This impersonal—or trans-personal— beauty is, for Gregor, the supreme reality.

THE YALE REVIEW, 1968

John Holmes

For twenty-five years John Holmes had been a good poet, and a steadily productive one, when his untimely death jolted the poetry world in 1962. As I thumb the pages of the *Selected Poems,* I can see why the poem "The Fortune Teller" took me (and swept me away) by surprise when I first read it in 1957. I had been reading this poet for years with lukewarm interest, and I remember feeling that while his subject matter was usually tame and his language lacked piquancy,

Selected Poems, by John Holmes. (Beacon Press, 1965.)

there was often a pang of urgency in the voice of the poems that compelled me to read on. I sensed that Holmes had something remarkable to say to me—something personal about experience we mysteriously had in common—but he couldn't plug his voice into the right outlet. He sang off-key. There are surprisingly few traces in the earlier work of the "tender and terrible" vision that blossomed suddenly and seized this poet out of himself in "The Fortune Teller" and in so many of the later poems. The early domestic poetry suffers from a smug sense of safety. What can go wrong, or right, in the world of the poem seems too conveniently settled in advance. The poems cannot accommodate much discomfort, much chaos.

In the selections from his third book, *The Double Root*, there *are* moments when he verges on the perilous abyss of the inner self, forecasting vaguely the central motif of his best work. The four stanzas beginning a long poem entitled "The Core" come as close as any lines in the early volumes to the poet's truest voice. (I think the fourth stanza would have ended the poem beautifully, but it goes on and on *and on*—his ear is simply not attuned to his voice yet.)

All children sound the same.
Walking today, I came
Near small boys counting loud
The words of a game.

A voice there seemed my son,
Again and again the one
I would know in any crowd.
But I knew none.

I thought, if he were dead
How always in my head
Would sound in any street
Something he said,

Until I could not bear
To walk out anywhere,
For fear that I might meet
His voice in air.

The terror of the unknown and the strange is more chilling when it emerges, unexpectedly, in oneself and one's loved ones. This insight is a direct link with the apocalypse of "The Fortune Teller": the discovery that the most lethal disasters may lurk behind the most commonplace experience, and deadly poison may spring at any moment from familiar and apparently calculated relationships. The closer to home, the greater the threat.

In "The Thrifty Elephant," "Death in the Back Yard," and "On a Magazine Picture of a Mass Burial," the peculiar blend of humor and terror marks the arrival of Holmes's most distinctive personal voice. The concluding image in "The Thrifty Elephant" projects an unforgettable picture of spirit maintaining itself intact under the burden of a grotesquely lame and dying carcass:

> Who's seen an old bull elephant lately, old
> Red-eyed, foot-dragging, single-minded blunt-
> Tusk, lugging his bones to the bones piled?

"On a Magazine Picture of a Mass Burial" is the one poem that makes no attempt whatever to soften the ghastliness of death. The surface lightness of tone and rhythms renders the nightmare landscape more terrible. The poem moves from the scene of a mass burial following an accident to a contemplation of mass death in nuclear war:

> What is there that people do in eighteens?
> Sing, eat, sit in a bus, march in threes.
> I could die, but eighteen is too many.
> Forty thousand is incomprehensible,
> Or thirty or sixty-five thousand deaths,
> Or one death . . .
>
> But this—we might as well all jump in,
> Be the dead the dirt and the desolate . . .

Here is the sort of underplay of humor you find in *King Lear*. The grotesque ironies of statement heighten the tragic sense. The short, snappy phrases and sentences, some of which read like advertising copy, suggest modern man's helplessness and impoverishment before the instruments of death he has constructed. By juggling the small numbers with the large ones, Holmes demonstrates the futility of the IBM or the computer grappling with the fact of death. This is the one death in Holmes's poetry from which there can be no escape, no salvation. (I might add that the images of death in John Holmes's work are unalterably fused in my mind's eye with the searing image of Holmes dying of cancer, portrayed in Anne Sexton's poem about him, "Somewhere in Africa." It's such a painful image to recall, I'm not at all sure that I'm grateful for it. But the poem is a touching benediction to Holmes's memory by one who clearly drew much of her poetic powers—her forthrightness, certainly—from his influence.)

THE HUDSON REVIEW, 1965

Edwin Honig

Rigorously trained in the classics, Edwin Honig's high-spirited, droll intelligence is wearing its scholarly decorations and credentials lightly in his new poems. He is a formal, disciplined talent backing away from thoroughbred sophistication into an easy-going, open-ended artistry. There is enough assured firmness—an earned austerity of control—in the very accents of his cavalier, lazy-speaking lines to free him from the need for pre-given formal structures. His relaxed meters draw their surprising zest from indolence of being, a falling away into "the power of idleness." In the shorter poems, Honig is cultivating an art which is stylistically hospitable to pressing recent experience of bereavement and fatherhood—deaths and births—and he knows he can best acquire suppleness by leaning toward the raw impulse-telling of folk art, as in his poem to a jazz musician: "You'll never make great music . . . Great? Who knows, who cares./ Why talk art these days?/ Now with so much dying/ Music's got to shake you,/ feel like you're spilling guts." Like "life, this lowgrade infection," which eludes the stethoscope of the kibbitzing "highgrade" family doctor ["(say ahhh) forever"], Honig's new poetry is low-keyed; his lines, moving with a soft and easy quietness, catch unexpected fire from the lowbrow, unschooled rhythms of routine living. The seriousness of vision in the long title poem, "Spring Journal," avoids introspective stuffiness because it is never far from spilling over into adjacent planes of easygoing, disenchantingly affable, happy being. Honig returns us from the transcendental abyss to the plain actuality that life requires us to deal with in most of our moment-to-moment frustrations. It is a poetry keeping its cool despite the worst of things, of selves, a poetry finding its nourishment and fortification in managably confronting those worsts.

One difficulty in the long poem is that the rambling, gabby, discursive manner of the persona grows too slack, windy, in some sections of the sequence. At such times, the writing loses its texture and grows to resemble a shapeless, chopped-up prose. More usually, though, the jet stream of Honig's loquaciousness is tempered by the fine cutting edge of his wit, and the interplay of these two constitutional leanings of his personality furnishes his long, spiraling verse sentences with astonishing permeability to experience. This enlivened medium is

Spring Journal: Poems, by Edwin Honig. (Wesleyan University Press, 1968.)

porous enough to absorb all shades of the vivid flux of lived, thought, and felt act—the ongoing and inrushing drift—of the poet's energetic daily life.

POETRY, 1969

Katherine Hoskins

Excursions gives us a fine cross-section of Katherine Hoskins' career, with a definitive selection from her three earlier books and an ample section of new work. Until now, Miss Hoskins' poems have been mistakenly ignored by most readers, and it is apparent why she did not win an early popularity. Clearly, it is difficult to acquire a taste for her poems, but I find that they grow steadily more appealing on long acquaintance. Her work offers some of the same obstacles to an impatient reader as do the poems of Thomas Hardy: lumbering, choppy meters; eccentric, hand-picked oddities of diction; unnatural syntax. And these qualities are not so much overcome as improbably *made to work* in many of her good poems. In others, her cumbersome style and the invented intricacies of her stanzas grow unwieldy, as in the long final piece, "A Journey," which maintains a slow, clippety-clop jog-trot on its belaboring metrical hoofs for many pages:

> But lulla-blue dissolves with sun's declension.
> And quick and quivering she flairs fox-season.
>   Skies are delicate,
>   Grasses fritillate ...

But if, by cultivating a capricious style, Miss Hoskins risks unreadableness in the good many poems on subjects that don't perfectly jell with her manner, she more than makes up for this drawback by preparing herself to write, occasionally, a superb poem like "An Education." In this long, story-telling poem, recalling Randall Jarrell's verse fairy tales, she entrances the reader with a bewitching dreamspell in which life's outer extremities—old age and childhood—flow into each other as companion streams from an ever-renewing fountain, each re-living, and thereby doubling, the life of the other. It is that beautifully rare specimen of poetry, in any age, that seems to spring from a bedrock of daily experience that is but scantily explored in literature—the purely uncritical love that exists between the very

Excursions, by Katherine Hoskins. (Atheneum, 1967.)

old and the very young. And this is one subject Miss Hoskins has made perfectly her own.

In her new poems—many of the best of her career—she has learned to reveal her very rich poetic gifts and show them to advantage as never before, by developing a new line movement, and a new variant of form that is much closer to free verse than her previous work. The loosening of form surely must be a major factor behind the success of "A Guided Tour," "Da Ming," "An Education." It would seem that formally patterned stanzas usually have a constricting effect on Miss Hoskins' line, a line which is typically overloaded with word-thickness, and the demands of rhyme and traditional meter compound the rhythmical heaviness. But a relatively open form frees her line, and gives her busy verbal antics a wider, more elastic field to move in. The result is that we find a new authority—even a kind of necessity—inhering in her very special vocabulary, which, in these new poems, seems to be perfectly rooted in the experience she transmits to the reader. One senses that not only is this an apt language to express her unique sensibility—it may well be the only possible language for its expression. Almost any poetic manner that seems peculiar at first acquaintance will grow attractive if a reader's ear can be persuaded by the adherence of words to the quality of each mental act they render into art. And a few of these poems incontrovertibly persuade me.

THE YALE REVIEW, 1968

Langston Hughes

Langston Hughes's new poems, written shortly before his death last summer, catch fire from the Negro American's changing face. To a degree I would never have expected from his earlier work, his sensibility has kept pace with the times, and the intensity of his new concerns—helping him to shake loose old, crippling mannerisms, the trade marks of his art—comes to fruition in many of the best poems of his career: "Northern Liberal," "Dinner Guest: Me," "Crowns and Garlands," to name a few.

Regrettably, in different poems, he is fatally prone to sympathize with starkly antithetical politics of race. A reader can appreciate his catholicity, his tolerance of all the rival—and mutually hostile—views

The Panther and the Lash, by Langston Hughes. (Knopf, 1967.)

of his outspoken compatriots, from Martin Luther King to Stokely Carmichael, but we are tempted to ask, what are Hughes's politics? And if he has none, why not? The age demands intellectual commitments from its spokesmen. A poetry whose chief claim on our attention is moral, rather than aesthetic, must take sides politically. His impartiality is supportable in "Black Panther," a central thematic poem of *The Panther and the Lash*. The panther, a symbol of the new Negro militancy, dramatizes the shift in politics from non-violence to Black Power, from a defensive to an offensive stance: Hughes stresses the essential underlying will to survival—against brutal odds—of either position. He is less concerned with approving or disapproving of Black Power than with demonstrating the necessity and inevitability of the shift, in today's racial crisis.

"Justice," an early poem that teaches the aesthetic value of rage, exhibits Hughes's knack for investing metaphor with a fierce potency that is as satisfying poetically as it is politically tumultuous:

> That justice is a blind goddess
> Is a thing to which we black are wise:
> Her bandage hides two festering sores
> That once perhaps were eyes.

But this skill is all but asphyxiated in many of the new poems by an ungovernable weakness for essayistic polemicizing that distracts the poet from the more serious demands of his art, and frequently undermines his poetics. Another technique that Hughes often employs successfully in the new poems is the chanting of names of key figures in the Negro Revolution. This primitive device has often been employed as a staple ingredient in good political poetry, as in Yeats's "Easter 1916." But when the poem relies too exclusively on this heroic cataloging—whether of persons or events—for its structural mainstay, as in "Final Call," it sinks under the freight of self-conscious historicity.

POETRY, 1968

Richard Hugo

Richard Hugo merely needs to arrive at an enchanted place in nature to recognize the primitive spirits lurking in water, trees, rocks, and immediately he starts to cross over the mystical barriers to make con-

The Lady in Kicking Horse Reservoir, by Richard Hugo. (W. W. Norton, 1973.)

tact with all the hidden gods of the place. They all begin to sing in his
hand at once as he writes, rows his oars, or casts his fishing line:

> Spinning hymns downstream is fun. The worm spins
> warm to German Brown, and warm to bad sight
> Rock Creek splits the day in hunks a hawk can't count.
> A fragment of a trout, half tree, half elk,
> dissolves in light and could have been a cliff.
> Current and a cross can blind a saint. . . .
> All sermons warp with one slight knock.
> Eyes are hands. Nylon sings and reassembles day
> and day is cracked in silver jokes: whip and tug
> and whipping rod, red ladder and white play,
> a mottled monster ages down the net,
> brighter than answer, big enough to see.

The Northwest landscape that Hugo knows best is haunted by the
spirits of many generations of dead Indians, and in poem after poem
he touches the deep roots of memory in the ghost town, the ghost
ranch, the fallen mine or mission, the neglected graveyard. He knows
he can trust the spirit of each place, setting, locale—if accurately
rendered—to breathe its own hidden life into the image cluster that
whirls and spirals down the plunging columns of his verse. No other
recent American poet of my acquaintance shares Hugo's power to
evoke the magic of place names: the Indian names assert a quiet
intelligence in his poems—they carry a musical authority as well as a
hidden Indian mystique into the very texture and integument of the
poem's action. A name may be repeated several times for its sheer
musical and rhythmic beauty, while the core of meaning latent in the
name may be revealed late in the poem, suddenly emerging in a
surprising new context which releases a hidden river of associations:

> They named it Sweathouse Creek because
> somewhere way upstream from here
> the Indians built houses over hot springs
> where the sick could sweat bad spirits out.

Indian names are demonstrated to be irreplaceable avatars of the
spirit of a place or region. The gods asleep in the names are wakened
in the "Indian wind" of the poem's physical climate, as weather, too, is
revealed to be supernaturally alive; the primeval wind, or rain, or
snow becoming a dominant symbolic motif that orchestrates the var-
ied elements of a poem's voluptuous music.

   The rhythmic intention behind Hugo's poetry, the impetus and
thrust behind his meters, is to achieve a lean, spare prosody, stream-
lined to accommodate itself to a stylized illusion of conversational

rapids, words tumbling like water and heavy currents traveling at very
high velocity, shattering over rocks. Or, as in "Driving Montana," his
identity is projected as a constellation of live receptors. His total re-
ceptiveness is a fervor to take in whatever the landscape and weather
may be pleased to bombard him with:

> The day is a woman who loves you. Open.
> Deer drink close to the road and magpies
> spray from your car. Miles from any town
> your radio comes in strong, unlikely
> Mozart from Belgrade, rock and roll
> from Butte. Whatever the next number,
> you want to hear it.

To throw the car throttle wide open, flooring the gas pedal ("Never
has your Buick/found this forward a gear"), is to accelerate the rate of
bombardment. He hurtles down the speedway of those plummeting
stanzas of variable decasyllabics as if he would strip away all traces of
artifice and ornament, all harnesses of literary convention, to achieve
a pure, unshackled flow of loquacity:

> I got three bulls and a native cutthroat, lover.
> I'm phoning from the bar in Victor.
> One drunk's fading fast. The other's fast
> with information—worms don't work in August.
> I found a virgin forest with a moss floor.
> You and I can love there. Pack the food.

Many poems erupt with ardent impulsiveness, blurted messages
phoned in haste and breathless passion from a noisy bar. The visita-
tion has struck. Here. Now. You better listen, reader. Lover. This may
be our only chance. Listen with all your heart in your ears—over the
bad connection, the jukebox, the snores of the drunk Indian brave
laid out on the table. Listen to the priceless, sage lore veteran drunks
and wizened Indians (those "aging eagles") squander on the unde-
serving likes of me. This is the moment, this the place. The world is all
rich, trembling voices; they all speak to me at once, a wonderful,
aching music of human misery and ardor. This moment and this
place are ever-changing, perishable, fleeting in time. Come share it
with me while it lasts ("You and I can love there"). He has won the
sweepstakes of the human spirit, the daily double, struck oil, hit a gold
lode, and is burning to report and share the lucky claim.

The other world Hugo explores is the cosmos of inured boredom:
the small-town mountain communities, has-been boom towns
wrecked by the "Silver Bill repeal"; or rest-cure havens ("Hot
Springs") which cater to the imagination of convalescence, a psychic

condition of chronic half-aliveness supported by a total hospital-ward world:

> You arrived arthritic for the cure,
> therapeutic qualities of water
> and the therapeutic air. . . .
> You have ached taking your aches up the hill.
> Another battery of tests. Terrible probe
> of word and needle. Always the fatal word,
> when we get old we crumble.

It is a world of all faint grays, the "Degrees of Gray in Phillipsburg." There are no decisive whites or blacks ("with so few Negroes and Jews we've been reduced/ to hating each other, dumping our crud/ in our rivers, mistreating the Indians"), no exploding lights or darks, only pale and fading neutrals—neutral colors for sexless humans. All the senses have atrophied, not just sight; but the psychic malaise is expertly portrayed as a chromatic wasteland, a world robbed of its color, reduced to bland, diluted fakes of color. Hugo suggests that the greatest poverty, in Stevens' phrase, might be to live in a colorless world; the surest antidote to our impoverishment would be to restore radiance of color to the world by retraining the faculty of color perception, and discovering—with Hugo—the remarkable spiritual aliveness that lurks just below the brilliant, iridescent surfaces of wildlife, woods, rivers:

> . . . he comes lightning
> out of nothing at your egg. Best of all,
> the color. It could be the water, but the bulls
> are damn near gold and their white dots
> stark as tile. The orange spots flare
> like far off fires. The body's tubular and hard.
> Cuts are rose and peach, all markings definite
> as evil, with a purple gill.

Galway Kinnell

Even when he operates on just two cylinders (in disproportionately many of his new poems, unhappily), Galway Kinnell is the poet the young writer will now watch—for tips of voice and stance—as he

Body Rags, by Galway Kinnell. (Houghton Mifflin, 1967.)

might have watched W. D. Snodgrass five years ago. There are individual lines, images, and whole passages in nearly every poem in *Body Rags* that are unforgettably poignant. Kinnell's generosity of spirit—a keenly piercing reverence for society's derelicts—and his self-scalding empathy for the mutilated souls of the crushed, the beaten, the solitary proud victims of back alleys and backwoods, give all his work the rare quality of that which has been profoundly seen, witnessed, lived to the bones, before being translated—however fumblingly or gracefully—into words.

But most of the poems in *Body Rags* are conspicuously marred in structure. There is altogether too much random collecting in these poems. They simply do not cohere. The author seems to assume his sensibility will automatically invest his random samplings with implicit linkage. Regrettably, whatever connects these fragments in Kinnell's inner life is not available to the reader. Can this sort of defect in structure be an indulgence catered to by readers and editors over-eager to give assent to Kinnell's second-rate work because they feel so much natural affinity to his personality—human and poetic? If so, I hope he will learn to resist this sort of popularity.

If I seem to be ungratefully severe in my judgments of the scrappiness of form in nearly every poem in this book, perhaps I've been spoiled by the last two poems, both major performances, immeasurably superior to the rest of the collection. "The Porcupine" and "The Bear" are fiercely self-transcending invasions into the incredible otherness of mysterious animal being—as in D. H. Lawrence's best animal poems—and when the reader crawls back out of the bear hide and drains away the last drops of bear blood that Kinnell has injected into his veins, he knows the poem has punctured him where he lives:

> I hack
> a ravine in his thigh, and eat and drink,
> and tear him down his whole length
> and open him and climb in
> and close him up after me, against the wind,
> and sleep.
>
> And dream
> of lumbering flatfooted
> over the tundra,
> stabbed twice from within,
> splattering a trail behind me,
> splattering it out no matter which way I lurch,
> no matter which parabola of bear-transcendence,
> which dance of solitude I attempt,

which gravity-clutched leap,
which trudge, which groan.

Kinnell's poetry achieves a focus and intensity of vision when, as in "The Bear," he becomes thoroughly drenched in his subject. Only then does his poetic structure—saturated with a bizarrely extra-human creatureliness—become solidified, from start to finish.

THE YALE REVIEW, 1968

Stanley Kunitz

Again! Again!
Love knocked again at my door:
I tossed her a bucket of bones.
From each bone springs a soldier
who shoots me as a stranger.

Stanley Kunitz has had to go away farther to exile, and to stay away longer, than perhaps any other major poet of his generation. *The Testing-Tree*, Kunitz's first book in the thirteen years since the publication of his Pulitzer Prize-winning *Selected Poems*, resounds with the upheaval of a spiritual recluse coming back to the world, to voice, after a long self-banishment: the voice surprised at its own return from muteness with intense shocks of awakening like those of a body amazed to have exhumed itself from a premature burial. It is the body of a sixty-four-year-old ghostly stranger he sees mirrored in his collegiate daughter's eyes:

Outside your room
stands the white-headed prowler
in his multiple disguises
who reminds you of your likeness.
Wherever you turn . . .
he waits for you,
haggard with his thousand years.

Kunitz's repatriations in his new book are wrenchings of the "creature self" ("he is not broken but endures") out of its stony sleep of slow recovery from the ravishment—which drove his friend Mark Rothko to suicide—by the worlds of country, family, "adversaries." His recov-

The Testing-Tree, by Stanley Kunitz. (Atlantic–Little, Brown, 1971.)

ery occurs with the violence and rage of a self-disinterment, no less than a full return at the age of sixty-four to the "fugues of appetite" of his lost youth.

In "King of the River," a small masterpiece in a Roethkean vein and worthy to stand beside much of Roethke's best work, he sighs from the body of the spawning salmon (now his body!) nearing its hastened death, following its remarkable two-week escalation of the aging process ["the same geriatric process in humans takes some twenty to forty years"—S. K.'s note]: "Nothing compels you/ any more, nothing/ at all abides,/ but nostalgia and desire,/ the two-way ladder/ between heaven and hell." In "Journal for My Daughter," he blurts out a message to the beloved daughter estranged during the years when "the resentment weed" grew "in the crack of a divided house," hoping to rebuild lost affections: " 'What do I want of my life?/ More! More!' " By turns, in the same short poem ("The Mulch"), he communes with the "indefatigable gull/ dropping a piss-clam on the rocks/ to break it open./ Repeat. Repeat," and he feels enticings of empathy for the old man who loves to roam the seashore "gathering salt hay/ in bushel baskets crammed to his chin" to take home and spread out on the earth in his garden—even though his garden "prepares to die," " 'Try! Try!' clicks the beetle in his wrist." And he unhesitatingly throws himself into the ravages of love, "Again! Again!"

Nostalgia and desire, heaven and hell, More! More!, Repeat. Repeat, Try! Try!, Again! Again!—these paired outcries, crackling like pistol shots in poem after poem, are the systole-diastole heartbeats of a man who, though he admits "I spoiled . . . my own left ventricle," is far from ready to throw in the towel in the tournament of his "unshattered, unshatterable" life passions:

> In a murderous time
>   the heart breaks and breaks
>   and lives by breaking.
> It is necessary to go
>   through dark and deeper dark
>   and not to turn.

Kunitz is so powerfully drawn to the imagination of estrangement into that "deeper dark"—"What's best in me lives underground,/ rooting and digging, itching for wings"—it is a marvel that he *ever* returns from exile. Note his tone of emulation in speaking of Dante's unshakable exile, as well as his sympathetic participation in both Mark Rothko's escapist suicide and Pastor Bonhoeffer's political suicide, in the failed plot to assassinate Hitler.

Despite a recurrent impulse to regain his lost affiliation with the community of mavericks by joining his daughter in the youth movement—"Oh to be radical, young, desirable, cool!"—he is an incorrigible loner, and part of him must always hang back: "Demonstrations in the streets./ I am there not there,/ ever uneasy in a crowd." He knows his repatriations must always be partial, incomplete. He is fatally condemned, and perhaps secretly blessed, to a life stance poised halfway between exile and return, between banishment and inheritance. In "King of the River," he hovers at the threshold between these antipodes. Midway in each of the poem's four symphonic stanza-movements, the *impossible* steps over into the *actual,* man alchemizing into animal and angel, by turns ("you are changing now/ into the shape you dread/ beyond the merely human"), generating the remarkable incandescence—half-demonic, half-ecstatic—of this poem's vision:

> On the threshold
> of the last mystery,
> at the brute absolute hour,
> you have looked into the eyes
> of your creature self,
> which are glazed with madness,
> and you say
> he is not broken but endures,
> limber and firm
> in the state of his shining,
> forever inheriting his salt kingdom,
> from which he is banished
> forever.

For all the pain, the loneliness, the helplessness of having chosen "a damnable trade/ where winning is like losing!," his happiest moments of exalted vision come to him as he balances, survives, on the edge, belonging neither to this world or to the other world, but vacillating between them:

> The sands whispered, *Be separate.*
> The stones taught me, *Be hard.*
> I dance for the joy of surviving,
> On the edge of the road.

There are a handful of masterful poems in this book, but the collection taken as a whole lacks body. Too many pages, I feel, are given over to translations from the Russian poets which are scattered, rather arbitrarily, over three of the book's four sections. "Hand-rolled Cigarettes," after Yevtushenko, is a splendid political spoof on the Russian custom of rolling cigarettes by hand in old newspapers; the charming mixture of humor and political allusion is rendered with gusto in Kunitz's crisp, rhythmical quatrains. But the other translations are written in a bland, colorless style, lacking the vivacity, say, of Lowell's *Imitations.* The source seems to dominate overmuch both the voice and vision of the English versions. Kunitz's own unique human personality is too well hidden. One gathers from the quiet austerity of tone that the poems are diligently faithful to the originals, and a whole volume of these vignettes, which we are told is soon to be published, will clearly be an engrossing and readable book. The abiding clarity and restraint of his style, spread out over an ample range of selections, will enhance the majesty and dignity of the Russians.

THE YALE REVIEW, 1971

Archibald MacLeish

On an oak in autumn
there'll always be
one leaf left at the top of the tree
that won't let go with the rest and rot—
won't cast loose and skitter and sail
and end in a puddle of rain in a swale
and fatten the earth and be fruitful...
                                        No,
it won't and it won't and it won't let go.

"It already rained today and there was only a 20 percent chance," my daughter says tearfully, shaking me awake, and I am at the point of correcting her: "No, honey, the weatherman isn't God. It's his job to guess wrong. He only predicts, like me." But before I can get the morning leaf of my tongue untied from sleep, I see a whole brown autumn leaf tangled and matted intact in the ends of her long, straight hair.

In his lordly moments, the poet is a more gifted weatherman, a prophet. That strangely familiar survivor-leaf haunted me last night, *reappearing* at the top of the oak in the very memorable recent poem

The Human Season: Selected Poems, 1926–1972, by Archibald MacLeish. (Houghton Mifflin, 1972.)

"Survivor," significantly placed at the end of the first section—
"Autobiography and Omens"—of Archibald MacLeish's new volume
of selected poems. I knew it instantly for a recurring leaf, but where
had I seen it before? Hastily leafing through another sector of the
book—"Love and Not"—hunting for old favorites, I halted at the
familiar early anthology piece "'Not Marble nor the Gilded
Monuments'" and lit upon the immemorial shadow-leaf in the lady's
hair of the closing lines:

> I will not speak of the famous beauty of dead women:
> I will say the shape of a leaf lay once on your hair.
> Till the world ends and the eyes are out and the mouths broken
> Look!
> It is there.

I was stunned afresh by the poem's exquisite reversals, its power to
wrest new life from a dying tradition by successfully warring against
the clichés that encrusted the motif, and then rescuing what was still
authentic and contemporary in the romantic impulse behind it. The
leaf would last and last as an emblem of the lady's beauty—now,
enigmatically, the leaf has been reborn in the oak. Its original sur-
vivor power, and saviorship, was not held lightly, but written in dead
earnest.

The leaf is just one offspring of a family of durable recurring im-
ages in MacLeish's imperishable canon of well-made poems, all beto-
kening an obstinate survivor spirit that "won't let go." If the doomed
poet foresees, or accidentally foretells, his own suicide—the gist of
MacLeish's pained words for Hemingway ("The laughing man . . .
waits for the gunshot where the play began. . . . The gun between the
teeth explains")—may not the poet blessed with long life augur his
own immoderate survival? Moreover, the survivor-poet may take a
guiding hand in the afterlife of his work's future. He forestalls the
deaths of many of his poems at the hands of leaf-color-blind poetry
anthologists by daring to send his aged words hurtling like so many
live leaves spinning end over end through leaf smoke over the heads
of old men who, raking leaves and setting small leaf fires, "smell of
burning leaves":

THE OLD MEN IN THE LEAF SMOKE

> The old men rake the yards for winter
> Burning the autumn-fallen leaves.
> They have no lives, the one or the other.
> The leaves are dead, the old men live
> Only a little, light as a leaf,

Left to themselves of all their loves:
Light in the head most often too.

Raking the leaves, raking the lives,
Raking life and leaf together,
The old men smell of burning leaves,
But which is which they wonder—whether
Anyone tells the leaves and loves—
Anyone left, that is, who lives.

Turning his back on those mourners, MacLeish propels his fire-resistant words beyond even his own breath into "Immortal Autumn," the human season of deathlessness:

It is the human season. On this sterile air
Do words outcarry breath: the sound goes on and on.
I hear a dead man's cry from autumn long since gone.

I cry to you beyond upon this bitter air.

MacLeish's sole new poem in this volume—call it a prose-poem—is his eightieth birthday "Forward":

At eighty you have to begin to look ahead.

The critic in the poet has designed the present volume as another bold gesture of survival, a way of avoiding inclement weather in the poetry's climate of continued readership. He would provide the student reader ("and there are more student readers of poetry in our society than we suspect . . . a generation raised on samples") with a detour around the dead end of anthology set-pieces by arranging his own choice of works that can best claim to be a "representation *of*," not a "choice *from*," his marathon career, gathered in thematic clusters, each nucleus of poems offering a sampling or cross-section spanning some fifty years in his art, and suggesting avenues to the ardent or ambitious reader for further exploration of his oeuvre. Acting in both his own best interests and ours, MacLeish has achieved in the inspired editing of this volume one of the many unacknowledged tasks of indispensable high criticism, a service usually rendered by a close friend or associate of the artist's years after his death.

THE YALE REVIEW, 1973

Josephine Miles

Josephine Miles's new poems contain great moral beauty. Their abiding generosity of spirit would seem to prescribe a socio-religious faith that is rare in our times—the belief in a community of the heart. The credo I find in these poems advances a more comprehensive theory of oneness than the credo of the mystic, who is so often merely a social escapist. Hers is a religion of ordinary human commitments: the kind of affection she puts most store by is the kind that admits—requires, even—"measureless distances" between people. Like Arthur Gregor's empathy, it is a tenderness and caring that may easily occur between people who are perhaps no more than strangers. In fact, a degree of acknowledged strangeness is necessary to support this kind of affection, so that any possible meshing of personalities—in conflict or in harmony—will be kept to a minimum, freeing the individual's attention from the emotionally charged demands of personal involvement, as in "love at a distance." The more the love is refined in "filaments of thought, in lines as thin/ As the lines latitudes rest upon," the more available it will be for worthy and productive tasks:

> In a morning of clarity and distinction
> Students and I exchange questions and answers about a book
> As if we had all been reading it.
>
> Then stepping over a rough place
> I hold out my hand for balance, and someone gives it.
> And someone writes a letter for help I can give.

Above all, these poems celebrate each "day's simple fact," the small kindnesses that effortlessly occur—in mutual supportiveness—between people who busy themselves with a common task, each giving of himself to the utmost in concentration of being to the common labor, to workmanship "so austere, thank or praise/ Only by use."

Frugality is her mode for experiencing emotion; at times, she can't help admitting that she is sacrificing something of value by denying herself extreme passion, but she will not—perhaps cannot—let herself be drawn into the oblivion of mindlessness, the risk taken by the emotional addict:

> Addicts progress from saturation
> To saturation, ache, thirst, slake,
> To a plenitude, an oblivion, then they wake

Kinds of Affection, by Josephine Miles. (Wesleyan University Press, 1967.)

> And ache, until gradually as the sun climbs the heavens
> They thirst again toward that oblivion.

Miss Miles's frugality of being extends gracefully from her inner to her outer resources: conservation of spirit is complemented by conservation of language and syntax. Unlike the political conservative who protects and preserves accumulated interests, her conservative spirit is a daily, moment-to-moment dutifulness toward human exchange, a conservation of the frail beauties and liberties that arise spontaneously in talk with friends and associates, beauties that are usually missed because we are in such a rush to get to what is important that we pass over what is ourselves, the *real* of us:

> When I can be
> A moment glad, repletion
> Lasts me the day through, or so I say.
>
> Nibbling greed . . .

Miss Miles's mind moves delicately between two poles—the will to surety, the will to doubt all positive surety. Many poems attain a rare seesawing buoyancy from the difficulty of balancing these two extremities of thought. Her handling of lines and meters, too, achieves a teetering effect, a rhythmical vertigo set in motion in the reader's ear by her technique of framing "lyrics of speech or talk" in sentences with inverted syntax and grammatical ellipsis. The easy-to-hear speech idioms give the poems a very readable surface, despite a highly compressed and compacted style:

> Grievances . . .
> I keep one or two and press them in a book,
> And when I show them to you they have crumbled
> To powder on the page. So I rehearse.
>
> But I do not believe. I believe rather,
> The stems of grievance put down their heavy roots
> And by the end of summer crack the pavement.

The movement from surety to doubt—the cost of honesty—is dramatized here. Miss Miles is an expert in the art of puncturing false comforts. She loves to catch her mind, as one might pounce upon a thief, in the act of evasion, duplicity. Her intellect is the shrewdest of culprits, and the contest in her between the artist-censor and the mental gymnast—a conflict which parallels her twin careers of scholar and poet—is one of her favorite subjects. The aspiring self's struggle to break out of all mental enclosures, to tear down the mind's defenses, limits, to remove obsolete habits of self-protection that carry over from the past—these themes are appropriately complemented by a new fluidity of line movement, a free play in the management of lines and stanzas unlike anything in her earlier work, with no loss of Miss Miles's customary precision and conciseness, or the depth of her absorption. Whereas most of her earlier poems were as symmetrical and as tightly wound and coiled as a watchspring, in the new poems, though she continues to lean toward lines of middle length—three to five accentual feet—now she can adroitly maneuver into the very short or very long line. She frequently employs the new metrical agility to suggest the careless to-and-fro pacing of spontaneous talk, or relaxed conversation between friends:

> Dear Frank, Here is a poem
>   I dreamed of you last night;
>   It makes me happy
>   Because it makes sense to me.
>
>   We went to the Greek Theater to see a play
>   And as we entered were given elaborate menus
>   Of the players' names.
>   Dinner was three dollars.
>   It was served on the little round tables from cocktail lounges.
>
>   I kept leaning back against your knees,
>   Because of those backless benches, and you kept moving
>   Further and further away in the amphitheater,
>   I following, until finally you said,
>   Jo: I am having the six dollar dinner.

Often, in reading these poems, I am pleased and surprised to find it is the sounds and tremors of my own breathing that are mysteriously being returned to me. The poems do not simply speak *to* me, but they somehow manage to talk (or whisper) directly into my ear; and when I stop reading for a few moments, it seems as though the poem's discourse continues, survives, in my mind's ear, since many of the poems don't begin or end in a conventional way, but are more likely to be framed at either end by chance remarks. They are informal, though intensified, cross sections of talk—lifted from street corner, kitchen, or classroom—and sagaciously trapped on the page.

THE YALE REVIEW, 1968

Vassar Miller

Vassar Miller, who continues to be one of our best religious poets, is a perennial spiritual convalescent. Her poems are recoveries of the

Onions and Roses, by Vassar Miller. (Wesleyan University Press, 1968.)

spirit's lost footing, lines exquisitely rebalancing from dizziness. Her technique in these short, tight poems is a rage of alertness, as she shapes her few lines to fit her spirit's cagiest, most slippery, sidesteps. The poems in conventional rhymed stanzas, like much of her earlier work, suffer from rhythmical sameness. But the poems in freer forms employ a halting, backward-leaning syntax, describing events of her inner life by slanting away from them, purging them of their disquietude by slow degrees. Miss Miller defends her religious faith in this book with a tenderness of outrage, a comely defiance. Her lines inveigh against an always encroaching spiritual void. In the fiercely gentle poem "Embarrassed," she pits herself, tooth and nail, against the enemy—automatic response in prayer. Her private spontaneous impulse is precious to her, no matter how quirky or misguided it may seem at the moment, and she will forego all safeties of self or soul to guard it:

> No propriety of an Amen ends my prayer.
> I stumble from
> this wrong room while my apologies
> freeze my tongue tight.

Flatly refusing all half-truths, partial faiths, she will settle for nothing short of a fully conscious participation in every religious ritual.

In the poems which center her religious inquiry in ruminations about her dog, she is apt to expend whole stanzas in the service of insipid notions of pathetic fallacy ("your mystery/ deeper than any thinking," "wagging dumbness turned eloquent"). But her power to reach out feelingly to another being is entirely believable in the warm elegy to Rosa Sells, her Negro maid who has died: "I grieve, not for your death but for your life,/ worked, like the flowers in your skimpy yard,/ from lumpy clay. My race guilt I shrug off/ as too abstract a tribute for a friend./ I view your untouched ironing with a sigh."

POETRY, 1969

W. R. Moses

Identities, by W. R. Moses, is a first collection of poems by a man who has been writing and publishing poetry for over thirty years. In view of the many programs for publishing books of poems that have emerged in the last ten years, it's difficult to imagine why such a substantial poet as this did not find a publisher long before. A surpris-

Identities, by W. R. Moses. (Wesleyan University Press, 1965.)

ing number of poems in this book strike me as being fully realized
works of art, and I rather feel as though I'm reading the collected
poems of a long-established seasoned technician, rather than the work
of a *new* poet in any sense. Yet I'm sure I must have read many of
these poems when they appeared originally in periodicals, and practi-
cally none left a lasting impression in my memory.

Most of the poems achieve a slow, even pace, and emotional content
is subdued. The poems do not have much immediate impact; they
usually have to rely on repeated readings (and at least one slow read-
ing) to get their full import across to the reader. Perhaps that is why
book publication of this poet's work has lagged.

It occurs to me, after reading many pages of Moses' work at a single
sitting, that most of his poems gain power and authority from appear-
ing in a collection; that is, the honesty and patience with which he
examines experience, in poem after poem, instructs the reader in the
special style of perception that is ideal for reading any one of them.
And toward the end of the book the rewards are so great, and so
different from what one has been led to expect from poetry, that a
reader begins to question and reassess some of the other kinds of
goodness in poetry he has taken it for granted he admires.

In "Of Cabbages and Kings," the ruined pea-vines are a metaphor;
they represent art or other experience that is brought to a premature
climax, instead of being nurtured to a slow, quiet, but intense ripen-
ing, such as this poet, and many of his poems, have undergone:

> The peas that I planted too late in Kansas
> Leaped to the light, into it, through it.
> They were all extension; they never thickened
> In stem enough, or darkened enough in leaf.

Many of the best poems in the book are "contemplations" of young
boys engaged in sports: hunting, boating, baseball. "Boy at Target
Practise: A Contemplation" celebrates the uniqueness of each event
"in the world's swarm of things." The bullet holes in the tin cans are
"new bits of subtraction," suggesting that vacancies, where formerly
there was matter (like negative areas in a painting or silences in a
poem), have unique identities, too. This poem provides the book with
its striking cover: a punctured tin can sitting near the bull's-eye (black)
of a target (in red and white) bent at right angles. This example of
pop art curiously enhances the book's emphasis on the fascination of
random objects: wrecked autos, old clothes, mummies.

In "One Time on One River," Moses reminisces about a boyhood
experience of getting stuck on a river:

> Why try to look out for a stump
> Under the surface, when one is hurrying home?

> The oar stroke that grated us home on the covered top
> No other stroke could undo. The boat hung still
> As the sky above it.

Most of the savored experience in this long poem happens to the boy incidentally as he waits on the water and contemplates an escape. Finally, the wish to escape is dissolved in the small beauties that engulf him:

> The struggle in darkness, shoving, shifting;
> The empty heaving at a useless fulcrum—
> I remember these. Growing silent
> And listening, so, to the smallest sounds of darkness,
> The plops and gurgles near, and the tiny
> Rustling and calling yonder in the dark shoreward—
> I remember that. What I do not remember
> Is ever feeling pine wood moving on pine wood
> Until we were off.

The poem, like so many in this volume, reaches beyond the given setting to imply an attitude to poetry and life. One needn't rush here and there to encounter experience; it is better to sit patiently and quietly in one place and wait for the experience to come to you, upon you, into you, through you, over you.

Moses' careful and graceful renderings of natural phenomena (always taking the identity of the objects described as primary before anything they may be taken to stand for) lends itself particularly well to fable and parable. The "message" arises subtly, but inevitably, from the pictured vision, usually late in the poem. The poem has examined the objects with such quiet precision, one little expects a piercing discovery that stretches to the limits of perception. The power of understatement in "nature poetry" is largely a consequence of the surprising clash with the traditions of Wordsworth and Whitman, and it is a mode bequeathed to us by Robert Frost. Most recent poetry of nature has thrown away the opportunity to exploit this legacy of our language.

THE HUDSON REVIEW, 1965

Howard Nemerov

Howard Nemerov has perfected the poem as an instrument for exercising brilliance of wit. Searching, discursive, clear-sighted, he has

The Blue Swallows, by Howard Nemerov. (University of Chicago Press, 1967.)

learned to make the poem serve his relaxed manner and humane insights so expertly that I can only admire the clean purposefulness of his statements, his thoughtful care, the measure and grace of his lines. Most of the satirical poems in *The Blue Swallows* have indoor settings—podium, committee room, supermarket, library stacks, the museum, the motel—and these inner sanctuaries inflict their sterile personalities on their occupants. Nemerov perceives as acutely as any poet now writing the life-devouring bleakness of our domestic and workaday surroundings:

> In this motel where I was told to wait,
> The television screen is stood before
> The picture window. Nothing could be more
> Use to a man than knowing where he's at,
> And I don't know, but pace the day in doubt
> Between my looking in and looking out.
>
> Through snow, along the snowy road, cars pass
> Going both ways, and pass behind the screen
> Where heads of heroes sometimes can be seen
> And sometimes cars, that speed across the glass.
> (from "The Human Condition")

In his meditations, a rational, even-tempered consciousness is always securely at the controls. If in most of these poems Nemerov seems to lack inwardness, what a relief it is to find him dropping the grim philosophical abstractions before they can shut his mind off from the physical world, as the same ideas predictably would do in the discourse of most professional philosophers. Not that Nemerov takes the big questions—the weighty unanswerables—any less seriously than they do; rather, he stretches his mind to its limits, acknowledges thought boundaries (as few philosophers are willing to do), and gracefully eases into adjacent planes of experience, moving from idea to image, images that embrace and interpret ideas more acutely than thought processes ordinarily can. Nemerov is, I feel, a very serious thinker in his poetry. His wit facilitates the deepening and freshening of his thought precisely because he anticipates the contemporary reader's suspiciousness of philosophical poetry (or any usefulness of poetry outside a pure aesthetics), and constantly disarms the reader with gentle ironies.

At times, Nemerov frets about what must seem to himself to be an obsessive sanity of vision, obsessive balance of forms, in his art. Perhaps something of the spirit of adventure has gone out of his work, since he has come to know his limits so well. Or perhaps he feels somehow victimized by a talent for plain statement that was clearly his most dependable gift from the start of his career, a talent which, in my view, he has consistently refined with honest fidelity.

THE YALE REVIEW, 1968

John Peck

Since the surface luster of unabashedly well-made poems by a new-comer occasions immediate distrust in some quarters today, many readers may dismiss John Peck's first volume of poems, *Shagbark,* as weak-spined, after a first glimpse of the obvious control, the unobtrusively handsome glamors of technical firmness. No poet novice is likely to imitate Peck's style; perhaps not many will even notice him; he may loom a little outside their sights. This book first strikes a reader's ear with the overtones of antique familiarity—but reading further, any initial coziness, or easy chumminess, quickly fades:

> What is it throws the light back
> In steady points from the valley?
> He said, that is the sheer face
> Of granite sliced and smoothed by this,
> The tributary ice.
> A horse strange to this country
> Will smell the polished stone
> And test it with his hoof,
> Thinking it water.

Peck is a poet who knows how to ask the right questions of old men with more horse sense than a novitiate horse. He knows how to listen to old *foreigners*—"His language is alien/ But I can see that he is/ Confident, precise"—who have quietly, in solitude, grown wise in mother wit and the fund of that most magical wisdom of all: plain know-how, information, strictly technical data about how things work the way they do. So often, in describing actions or the use of tools—from athletics, carpentry, woodsmanship, mountaineering—the words chosen bespeak an authority of firsthand experience.

> We made camp, my hand stung
> Back into feeling over fire,
> Remembering sundered heft
> Of things they made once.

Shagbark, by John Peck. (Bobbs-Merrill, 1972.)

The hand's memory of made things is indeed a most palpable nuance in Peck's style: rock flakings, wood parings, filings of iron, sifted, but still clinging to the close-meshed sieves of phrase and line; lines which have the handmade, hand-turned quality.

In Peck's writing, at its best, the simple mechanics of nature, both animate and inanimate, disclose inexhaustible mysteries. His careful fidelity to the properties of objects in nature carries over into the close-knit mechanics of the poems, both shaggy and polished, intricate and rough-edged as bark. Grayish, curled, tart-smelling. Shagbark.

The longest and most ambitious poem in the book, "Cider and Vesalius," exquisitely mediates between worlds of modern man's psyche, and like the "first articulated skeleton" created by Vesalius—compiled from bone by stolen bone of an executed criminal—Peck's poem is assembled of skeleton parts gathered from night gibbets of art history, medical scholarship, the annals of crime and modern war. Recovering those moments of terror and awakening in which Vesalius' pioneering consciousness rode over a border, a subliminal, as yet unbroken threshold, in the racial mind of us all, the poem re-enacts the aura of discovery, a kind of mental seizure so intense and terrible that Vesalius must have felt a criminal-saintly queerness arising as much from the fear of entering forbidden frontiers of man's brain as from fear of capture by the police during his secret night thefts of the dead man's dangling skeleton "dressed in half its muscles":

> The young
> Student went from Louvain
> Out to the roadside gibbet
> Late at night, and he pulled
> The femur off the hip—
> The bones were bare, still joined
> By ligaments—and then
> Each night thereafter, piece
> By piece, till finally
> Only the thorax hung
> From its chain. His desire
> Was great: he clambered up
> And yanked it off, and made
> His first articulated
> Skeleton. Then he said
> Discreetly that he'd bought
> The thing in Paris.

Scaling the mental abyss between Vesalius' "woodcut blocks" and the drawings of Hieronymus Bosch—both highly accurate human anatomies—the poem marries two converging streams of human expanded awareness in unbroken confluence, the mind of science and the mind of art, Vesalius and Bosch twinned in genius, disclosing through their opposite disciplines facets of the same mysteries, the unplumbed secrecies of bodies in various phases of nakedness and dismemberment. Both oracles, prophets. Both illuminating by a kind of graphic fluorescence the hidden miracles of the body: the one the body's architecture, the craftsmanlike beauties of the temple's masonry; the other the body's demonic, infernal essence, the spiritual kinetics no less a tangible property of the body than the architectonics.

In many shorter poems of the book's final section, which I surmise were among the earliest writings collected here, the rhythm of Peck's verse is stiff and mechanical, as if choked by inflexible repetitions of the set form—usually rhymed triplets in pentameter. The language of the weaker pieces is gnarled, knotty; much of the writing smells of the poetry laboratory, the self-conscious technician and his toolkit. Only an occasional line or phrase in the dense meshwork of these lyrics flashes with the clarities born of density and tension that characterize Peck's best work. But how well he manages to tell a story in near-rhymed couplets, as in "The Factor Remembers His Lady." The language is so richly textured that the rhymes are usually half-hidden ear-rhymes, rarely eye-rhymes:

> And the house itself wrinkling like an old coat
> Over shoulders that are smaller now, that fit
>
> Nothing they once wore—no, I feel otherwise,
> Who managed her fields, affairs, and policies.
>
> I can still see, beneath nets hung through her trees,
> Squat bombers nestled in storage, tail to nose,
>
> Waiting to jolt along strips near the orchard,
> Often without lights rising from the dark yard.

The easy, meandering flow of a long sentence across many couplets is sharply punctuated by saliences and exactitudes of word and phrase, giving each line a memorable cast and character of its own despite the riverine sweep and contour of rhythm. And what a pleasurable freedom Peck finds as he escapes, at last, from intractable boxed-in stanzas into open forms, as in "Leaving the Coal Cellar," "Smoke Around the Bell," and "Spring Festival on the River," in which the line movement pivots, swivels, sideslips and modulates in dance step with the rhythms of a remembered experience.

THE YALE REVIEW, 1973

Theodore Roethke

Theodore Roethke had just begun to write his major poems in the late fifties, and wrote his very best poems near the end of his life—one waits in vain for the final flowering of his genius. I shudder every time I think of the poems he might have written had he lived just another year or two. I am reminded of the premature deaths of John Keats and Kit Marlowe. These poets were in their twenties, whereas Roethke was fifty-five when he died; and yet, like them, he was just beginning to reach his creative prime.

Apparently Roethke had some foreboding that death was near. In his last collection, *The Far Field* (published posthumously), there is a very touching poem to his wife, "Wish for a Young Wife," that sounds like a last will and testament:

> My lizard, my lively writher,
> May your limbs never wither,
> May the eyes in your face
> Survive the green ice
> Of envy's mean gaze;
> May you live out your life
> Without hate, without grief,
> And your hair ever blaze
> In the sun, in the sun,
> When I am undone,
> When I am no one.

In another piece, "Infirmity," he has the air of a man who has been ill for a long time, a man who struggles to find a meaning and even a kind of fulfillment in disease of the body:

> Sweet Christ, rejoice in my infirmity;
> There's little left I care to call my own.
> Today they drained the fluid from a knee
> And pumped a shoulder full of cortisone;
> Thus I conform to my divinity
> By dying inward, like an aging tree...

For me, Roethke is strongest in moments of tenderness. Curiously, his many poems depicting sexual experiences do not reveal the profound humanness and tenderness in the man nearly as well as those describing subtler love experience, such as the gentle endearment he

The Far Field, by Theodore Roethke. (Doubleday, 1964.)

feels toward his wife and even toward his own body in the poems discussed above, and the strange, quiet compassion he speaks over the grave of his student thrown by a horse (a student to whom he had never spoken a single word) in the well-known anthology piece "Elegy for Jane."

Perhaps the most moving expression of tenderness in all his writings appears in one of the last poems, "The Meadow Mouse." The poem begins with directness and naturalness of expression:

> In a shoe box stuffed in an old nylon stocking
> Sleeps the baby mouse I found in the meadow,
> Where he trembled and shook beneath a stick
> Till I caught him up by the tail and brought him in,
> Cradled in my hand . . .

The images Roethke uses to describe the mouse suggest an amused tenderness and a keen sensitivity to frailness:

> A little quaker, the whole body of him trembling,
> His absurd whiskers sticking out like a cartoon-mouse,
> His feet like small leaves,
> Little lizard-feet,
> Whitish and spread wide when he tried to struggle away . . .

The end of this poem extends the poet's tender concern to include all vulnerable and fragile forms of life:

> But this morning the shoe-box on the back porch is empty.
> Where has he gone, my meadow mouse,
> My thumb of a child that nuzzled in my palm?—
> To run under the hawk's wing,
> Under the eye of the great owl watching from the elm-tree,
> To live by courtesy of the shrike, the snake, the tom-cat.
>
> I think of the nestling fallen into the deep grass,
> The turtle gasping in the dusty rubble of the highway,
> The paralytic stunned in the tub, and the water rising—
> All things innocent, hapless, forsaken.

In another mode, the long series of meditations on North America, Roethke tries to identify with the American Indian ("Old men should be explorers./ I'll be an Indian./ Iroquois."). These poems combine life-enhancing descriptions of weather and landscape with the poet's psychic responses ranging from despair to joy. The moments of praise and affirmation outweigh the gloomy passages, and even death becomes a way back to life ("The Far Field"):

> I am renewed by death, thought of my death,
> The dry scent of a dying garden in September,
> The wind fanning the ash of a low fire.

What I love is near at hand,
Always, in earth and air.

The meditations are his most powerful works. In them he pursues a
spiritual reverie that, at times, borders on a too personal abstractness
but usually erupts into distinct images out of the poet's urgent past,
such as the picture of his father lifting him over the "four-foot rose-
stems in the six-hundred-foot greenhouses," and his memory of reck-
less speeding over gravel and rock roads of America. The search for
self and beyond self in these poems is the prevailing motif in Roeth-
ke's later work.

THE ANTIOCH REVIEW, 1964

Muriel Rukeyser

Muriel Rukeyser is a poet of dark music, weighty and high-minded.
The Speed of Darkness, the title of her new book, is indicative of the
oracular soothsaying quality of much of her writing—for me, a defeat-
ing tendency of her style which often nullifies any attentiveness to
detail. Her mystical vision is so dominant in the mentality of some
poems that the writing becomes inscrutable, as she packs her lines
with excessive symbolism or metaphorical density.

Her firmest art is in the linear and straightforward delivery of her
story-telling anecdotal poems, the longer biographical poems, and
letter-poems to friends expressing an open declaration of personal
faith. In all of these genres, her symbolism is balanced by clean, open
statement. In "Endless" and "Poem" ("I lived in the first century of
World Wars . . ."), personal lyrics irradiating pathos from the recollec-
tion of harrowing life-moments, Miss Rukeyser achieves a naïve
forthrightness—an artlessness—which, as in the most lastingly valu-
able personal letters (those of Keats, for example), derives a universal
moral faith from plain-spoken events authentically observed and re-
corded. In these poems, Miss Rukeyser is most nearly able to make
her experience—her recollected terror and madness—our own. Her
absorptively sympathetic portrait of the German artist, Käthe
Kollwitz, one portion of a continuing sequence of biographical works
("Lives"), is the most arresting long poem in the new collection. Miss
Rukeyser displays wisdom as self-critic in choosing to adapt so many
recent poems from biographical and historical studies, since the task

The Speed of Darkness, by Muriel Rukeyser. (Random House, 1967.)

of accurately restoring a human lifetime in verse compels a precision in the enumeration of items of dailiness that offsets her frequent tendency to drift into cloudy abstraction.

POETRY, 1969

Karl Shapiro

"I am of the race wrecked by success. The audience brings me news of my death"—in these lines from *The Bourgeois Poet*, Karl Shapiro is speaking for a generation of poets who—with the single exception of Roethke, towering higher and higher like Faulkner's bear as night overtook him—wrote a disproportionate number of superbly good poems in early career, became decorated overnight with honors (Pulitzers, or the like), and spent the next twenty-odd years trying to outpace a growing critical notice of decline. Of this group, Shapiro and Robert Lowell are the poets who recognized early on the futility of endless repetition of the well-made, handcrafted poem. Both writers took the lead from younger talents—Lowell looking to Snodgrass, Shapiro to Ginsberg—and both produced books in mid-career that recast the poetic instrument to embody formerly intractable large sectors of their personal lives. In *Life Studies* and *The Bourgeois Poet*, they won a precious freedom to extend the limits of their art, but the fuller expression and amplification of personality in poetry was soon to impose new limits which, in turn, would have to be overcome if the new emotional scale was to survive in the poems. In their more recent work, they appear to have retreated to forms—indeed, to an aesthetic—very similar to their early practice, and hence may risk losing the impetus and revived momentum they so laboriously earned.

Karl Shapiro's ongoing career in poetry, viewed in its extensive entirety, is an incarnation of the crisis of the critic/poet—the artist/ intellectual—of our time. In most of his best poems—"Auto Wreck," "The Leg," "Elegy to a Dead Soldier," "F. O. Mathiesson: An Anniversary," "The First Time," to name a few of my favorites—the difficulties of investing a crucial human drama with verisimilitude arrests all of Shapiro's intensely energetic intelligence, and the extraneities of his opinionated mind are refined out of the medium. But

Selected Poems, by Karl Shapiro. (Random House, 1968.)

much of his most precise writing—imagery of mathematical accuracy—is wasted on artificially worked-up subjects, as in the poem "Ego." A subject must arouse a penetrating sympathy in Shapiro if it is to elicit his best poetic energies, passions, and thereby to overpower the dry, stale wit and tired, ashen ironies that sap imaginative vigor in his weakest poems. Suicide, first sexual experience, loss of a limb in wartime—these subjects have an inherent immediacy that animates Shapiro's descriptive genius enough to counteract his digressive intellectualizing. Such poems avoid intrusiveness of thought not so much by quieting the thinking voice as by ensnaring all ideas into the matrix of the poem's design.

In sheer workmanlike virtuosity, Shapiro has never surpassed "The Fly." For this poem, all the early tools of his craft were perfectly honed. In his other best early work, he was divided between antipodal identities, leaning now to one, now to the other: the verbal voluptuary (the Hart Crane influence) of "Buick," "The Gun," rejoicing in the aesthetic beauty of the thing, an idolator of finely crafted instruments; the sardonic culture-iconoclast (the Auden influence) of "University," "Drug Store," eschewing the anti-human character of a thing-idolizing community. Lurking in each side of his personality was the hidden antagonist of the other: the anti-rationalist of "The Intellectual" versus the anti-sensualist of "The Glutton." His vacillation between the two is clearly mirrored in the reversal of his poetics from traditional to anti-traditional, and back again.

The main thrust of Shapiro's middle career has been the search for a technical means to liberate his passional nature from the overbearing rigor of his intellect. In his critical writings of this period, climaxing in his best prose work *In Defense of Ignorance,* the fury of self-liberation took the form of flogging his past taskmasters, Eliot and Pound, while glorifying the wild old wicked (if, for the past thirty years, thoroughly domesticated) reprobate of American letters, Henry Miller. In his poetry, his radicalism took the form of the prose poems of *The Bourgeois Poet.* Whatever the shortcomings of that book, we mustn't forget it is no small triumph to revolt successfully against a guaranteed blue-ribbon instrument for turning out the well-made poem. Merely to have closed the door, unalterably, on his celebrated old style and plunged into total risk of the new is a healthy mechanism for artistic survival. The book's positive force obtains from the impact of Shapiro's middle-aged personality on his youthful learned intelligence, as reflected in the contest between logic and the imagery of hysteria. Though he cannot always break the grip of his intellect, he consistently infuses hallucinatory intensity into the struggle. We witness in this poetry the drama of the critical intelligence, which knows too much for its own health, trying to free itself from insights that threaten to become self-devouring, and so attain a higher graciousness of loving selfhood. This conversion, when successful, is the essence that informs Shapiro's best writing. The freedom he has won for the subject, the image, the language of his poetry in *The Bourgeois Poet* is an astonishing breakthrough out of the fixity of his old constrictive forms. He has unleashed a kind of pure adventurousness of sensibility.

Now that I have read the beautiful love poems in Shapiro's newest volume, *The White-Haired Lover,* I would hazard the guess that his future work stands an excellent chance of merging the superior qualities of two opposite modes: the expressiveness of candid personal confession and the durability of significant form (the latter had been all but lost, for me, in Shapiro's prose poems), thereby demonstrating the long-range wisdom of an experiment that prepared its author to advance to a sphere of poetic resources—available raw materials for poetic art—that could never have been anticipated by the safely boxed-in, over-refined verses of his early career.

W. D. Snodgrass

Admirers of W. D. Snodgrass' early "confessional" poetry will be surprised to find that the best poems in his long-awaited second volume, *After Experience,* are the least personal ones. The opening thirty pages of the book reveal an artist helplessly trapped in a style which—there can be no mistake about it—has reached a dead end. All of these poems suffer by comparison with the brilliant "Heart's Needle" sequence, and most of them seem like so many feebly smoldering embers of a dying fire. The meters are limp, the forms pre-digested, and the despairing voice is halfheartedly one-toned.

"The Flat One" is an exception. It proceeds with the raw directness that is instantly recognizable as the Snodgrass manner, but it goes beyond any previous poem in its single-minded exhibition of physical agonies. The modern hospital ward is viewed as a medieval torture chamber in which a terminal cancer patient is kept alive, artificially, for

After Experience, by W. D. Snodgrass. (Harper & Row, 1968.)

seven months. The subject lends itself perfectly to the Snodgrass method of linking extreme feeling to a theme that must, thereafter, become forever wedded in the reader's memory to that emotion. In this poem, the feeling of repulsion from a body slowly dying—dying as a way of life—is endowed with ultimacy. One can hardly conceive of repulsion being carried to any higher pitch of envisioned pain and intensity of felt ugliness than in the art of "The Flat One." Snodgrass has a way of so utterly exhausting a subject like this one that no one can ever undertake it again without seeming outrageously derivative.

In the rich middle section of the book, we observe him experimenting with a variety of forms and styles, trying to cultivate a more versatile poetics. It is heartening to find that, in a number of ambitious new poems, he is able to fight free of obsolete habits of introspection that, in his early work, had fostered a magnificent power of structuring poetry, but in more recent work has inhibited his sense of structure. Snodgrass is at a crossroads in his art.

In "The Examination," the same grotesque ingredients as in "The Flat One," gothic horror-images lifted from modern surgery, are cast into a new mold—the mold of satire. Whatever the order of composition of the two poems, Snodgrass' art travels an immense distance between them. In "The Examination," the poet has all but removed himself from the field of the poem's drama. Descriptive detail, instead of seizing the reader by the throat and throttling him, achieves an emotional distancing; with Swiftean incisiveness, the description sets up a chain of ironic and bizarre correspondences between a surgical operation and the process it parodies—the quizzing of Ph.D. candidates. "The Examination" stands by itself as Snodgrass' single ambitious satire, but the added dimension to his descriptive power—a weave of allusiveness, radiating in many directions at once—carries over into the poems about paintings, which I take to be his most accomplished new work.

"Van Gogh: The Starry Night" is much the best of the poems about paintings. In form, it is an ingenious collage of statements from Van Gogh's letters enmeshed in passages describing portions of the painting. The operation of the poem's movement is fluid and halting, by turns, alternating between open and closed form, though there is a firm controlling hand in evidence throughout. The strongest moments are explosive word-bursts in which the lines of poetry attain a unique spiraling onrush that comes as close as any poetry I have read to resembling the spatial movement and texture—the soul-spatterings of color—that characterize impressionistic painting. Though it is theoretically impossible to convert the aesthetics of paint into a commensurable aesthetics of language, Snodgrass zealously explores in his style an astonishingly true poetic equivalent for the fiercely ordered chaos of the Van Gogh painting.

THE YALE REVIEW, 1968

Peter Viereck

The career in poetry of Peter Viereck, perhaps more than that of any other writer of our time, can be viewed as an experiment in the symbiosis of poetry and politics. "The New Cultural Blues," his best satire, draws on a complex linguistic and sociological intelligence. I can't recall when, if ever, these two cultures (language and social science) have been embraced by a more consolidating sensibility. His best satires are memorable events in the history of ideas, without loss of art.

Viereck's earliest poetry served him as an extension of political consciousness into a medium in which paramount ideas of our era could be abstracted from their worrisome contexts in international affairs and viewed freshly and intrinsically through the symbolic machinery of art. Poetry later became for Viereck a mind-style for escaping the risks of socio-political consciousness in playful, if ingenious, literary word-puzzles. But in his most recent work, in going still further beyond literal reality, Viereck returns to full human force and wholeness. Enacted before our eyes in "Five Walks on the Edge" is the drama of aspiring spirit in search of the mindlessness of supra-being, the poet attaining a larger totality of mind than ever before in "Counter-Walk, Reversals," the superb poem that ends the book. Foregoing his former escape of spiritual transcendence, there is a new toughness in immanence, identification with the in-dwelling natural forces in rivers, trees, cliffs, rock, mud. In "River," a voyage of man's spirit is symbolized, but an equal interest is generated in the sheer fun of letting the river be itself, speak its being, act out its life of surfaces, appearances: nothing *is* but what can be seen, touched, poured. If the poet's mental life, a seesawing fluid motion, is particularized and embodied in the river's cycles, his fascination with the actual properties of the river is so intense it threatens to steal attention away from its symbolic value. It is a vision in which we feel "body is not bruised to

New and Selected Poems, by Peter Viereck. (Bobbs-Merrill, 1967.)

pleasure soul," nor ideas lost to things. No portion of sensibility is sacrificed or compromised to any other. The political man is perfecting his anti-self in apolitical forms and spirits in nature.

I'm particularly struck with the original design of this book, the organization taking account of Viereck's development as a cyclic eternal return to key themes, an ascent along many separate spirals: not a mere chronology. This method of arrangement befits Viereck's work more than it would the work of most other poets, but all can profit by the example—especially in what it tells of a man's style of guiding the growth of his art over a thirty-year period.

POETRY, 1968

Robert Watson

Many poets writing today, who have flourished in the countries of their early good poems, renounce the privileges of citizenship as a debilitating luxury. The conscience of imagination sends them on intercontinental travels. Robert Watson's second book undertakes this voyage, but readers of his excellent first volume, *A Paper Horse*, will be disappointed with *Advantages of Dark*.

A writer's quest to revolutionize his technique is an act of total risk, of ultimacy. The nutrients he discards are often, gravely, more nourishing to his art than those which supersede them. To abandon utterly a successful and proven identity/style and throw oneself open to the chaos of the medium—the raw encounter between a poet, who has cast off his weapons, and the shark's teeth of language—is an adventure in the literary politics of lightning, which, say the wise, never strikes twice in the same soul. They're wrong. In poetry, often it does. At least three American poets in the sixties—W. S. Merwin, James Dickey, and James Merrill—have changed coats in their new books almost as decisively as did Yeats ("Song, let them [the fools] take it,/ For there's more enterprise/ In walking naked.").

Robert Watson's new book may well be an isthmus that will take *him* into a resourceful new continent of his art, but the book, in itself, is a retrogression of talents. The long storytelling poems in *A Paper Horse* are his best work. They are monologs of psychological complexity in which the delivery is so luminous that all of the poem's subtleties can be grasped at a single reading. Under a transparent surface of witty

Advantages of Dark, by Robert Watson. (Atheneum, 1966.)

conversation and high-toned gossip, the speaker develops a circuit of symbols that serve as an index to his character:

> I let him in my room, lock the door;
> Then lock the door of the room inside my head,
> Where he tinkers, puffing at the knob,
> Stoops peering at me on the bed,
> Peering for what he, what the world thinks I have hidden.
>
> ("Whore with Trick")

The speaker's free association of ideas is rendered in tones of voice that are so lifelike, the poems create the illusion that the reader is not so much reading as listening in, eavesdropping on private inner speech.

In the new monologs, the line is too open, slack, lacking the sort of tautness and texture the intensity of the speaker's voice requires for its release. Some of the individual lines are so uninteresting that they fall into a prosiness dull as lead: "Will anyone ever come to understand me," or "I don't know where to live, says Donald Hall." (These lines are repeated refrains.)

There are superb moments in the shorter poems, electric passages which leap from the page like exposed nerve-ends. But the poems in which they occur are usually left ungelled in a deliberate defiance of any sort of polish, as if Watson (who does not write for "an audience of professors, or other poets, or editors of little learned magazines") is flouting art to get closer to human experience in all its chaos, rawness, disunity. In the new poems, a reader is less struck with new virtues than constantly reminded of old rewards the poet is painstakingly, if not self-consciously, leaving out. He seems more preoccupied with checks and resistances to old habits than with evolving new strategies in their place. Perhaps we find in these poems an art in transition. We shall wait to see whether Robert Watson is indeed moving toward an apocalyptic breakthrough, or is stuck in the limbo of unregenerative mannerism, stalemated.

POETRY, 1967

Theodore Weiss

In 1939, by an absurd leap of faith, Yeats could look past the political nightmare of his time and take solace in those spiraling gyres, the

The World Before Us: Poems, 1950–1970, by Theodore Weiss. (Macmillan, 1970.)

cycles of history, to rebuild the fallen empires: "All things fall and are built again,/ And those that build them again are gay." In 1965, Theodore Weiss, foreseeing a catastrophe beyond all re-assemblage, disavows both the legacy of culture and the historical cycles that bequeathed it to us, "To hell with holy relics . . . More shambling about/ in abandoned clammy churches/ and I abjure all religion,/ even my own." Such towering disavowals—amounting to a self-incurred exile from the very language of his craft—come at a high cost to a scholar-poet who in his eminent work over the last twenty-five years as editor, professor, and man of letters has himself dedicated immense labor to perpetuating that bequeathal.

By his forty-ninth year, Weiss had reached a major aesthetic crisis and crossroads, as avouched in the poem "Ruins for These Times," which I take to be the pivotal statement of his middle career, a declared manifesto for the future. He had grown contemptuous of mining the ruins of the past:

> I, plundered, plundering,
> out of these forty odd bumbling
> years have heaped up spoils
> with spells compelling
> enough, my own.

"The Medium," another poem of the same period, is a humorous dialogue between He and She which, in developing a serious aesthetic philosophy through exchange of repartee, is Yeatsian. Through excesses in the discourse of the male speaker, Weiss parodies the ponderous allusive style of his early work. The poem is an act of conscious, painstaking self-criticism. It demonstrates Weiss's rage, in mid-career, to purify his language, to learn to listen for deeper voices in his psyche than those of his education, and to wait for the silence to deliver its speech. He must withhold his limitless verbal skill, his sprawling talent:

> Cleansed of words,
> my fears and doubts cast off, the fears
> that words invent, I see each thing, free
> at last to its own nature, see it free
> to say exactly what it is.

This poem challenges the integrity of language itself, as if the very essence of things is somehow beyond language, and the words, no matter how scrupulously they be used, somehow always corrupt and impurify beings, feelings, events. All things, to approach their pure essence, then, must escape, and thereby transcend, language. But what appears here as an attack upon all language as an unfit medium to transmit sacred or mystic experience in later poems is tempered to a quest for a raw, open, intimate, and direct language.

Weiss's most recent short poems have advanced to a more acute raw-boned gauntness of style than any earlier work, approaching stridency in some passages. The new poems resume Weiss's faith in the undiminished efficacy of today's language as a medium for poetry, a faith first voiced in the youthful poem "The Hook," the brilliant exemplar of his early style which introduces *The World Before Us,* this meaty selection—ample in bulk as well as substance—from four previous volumes, plus a complete book-length sequence of new short poems.

As I leaf through some three hundred pages which do not even include the superb long poem *Gunsight,* published as a separate volume in 1962, I'm reminded that Weiss's longest poems are usually his most impressive and memorable works. They form a continuing cycle, from book to book, and in them a reader may chart the milestones of Weiss's extraordinary search for a more viable poetic language:

> Read to him,
> his face among the pictures—the animals gentle
> in their alphabet—like something princely
> blossomed there, naming after me
> with first clear breath flowers, birds, and beasts.
> Day by day his mind more avid, lighting
> up whatever feeds and brightens it...
> (from "The Generations")

The genesis of all language—in the ear of the pre-literate child and, by extrapolation, in the ear of primitive man, the racial vestiges echoing in the modern voice—is in the *naming of things.* At the pure beginnings, the need to enchant (yes, a chanting!) the ear with beautiful names was indissolubly linked to the need to control things with words. The religious and aesthetic functions of language evolved concurrently with the physical, all collaborating in survival. Through language, self-preservation extended effortlessly and naturally from the hunt and the kill to the inner dream life. Weiss's poems, especially the long interior monologs—"The Generations," "Gunsight," "Caliban Remembers," "Wunsch-zettel"—re-enact this drama for us, as the poet participates with intense sympathetic involvement in the mental life of adventurers in language, following them through each stage of the love affair: from first infatuation with the sound and feel of words, through the deaths of language as it becomes cut off from its origins in natural process and man's dream life is divorced from his daily life of action, to those high, rare marriages of language and mission—the true calling—which come as a beatitude of fulfillment to the lucky few who fight their way back from exile (language abused banishes us from its country) to find the true heartland of the self in human love. The first poem in the series, "The Generations," appearing in Weiss's second volume, is trapped in the middle stage of this journey. The problem of losing and finding the language again is hopelessly entangled with the sin of self-righteousness. The iron-willed female protagonist is the sort of gardener who tramples her flower bed to keep the weeds from growing. This attitude extends to her method of child-rearing, as well as to books: "Silken words . . . Rip them out and rip though some good go." Her vision is monolithic, totalitarian— resembling the doctrines of Maoism as satirized in a new poem, "The Little Red Book"—and her lifelong failed genocidal war on the weed population carries over to her sons. She would tear the human tongue out by the roots rather than risk a few weeds in the garden of speech.

The gardening motif in "The Generations" is an obvious repetitive symbol. It operates mechanically and woodenly. The heroine is a flat character, doggedly obsessed and blind to her own deathliness: "This separateness./ It stretches through words, chores, my mocking steps./ Clutch as I may, will nothing bend to me?" Weiss masters the garden metaphor in the far superior recent poem in the same mode, "Wunsch-zettel." The art of gardening, like the art of mountain-climbing explored in the ambitious "Mount Washington," is a complex metaphor which both lends itself to a richly developed personality portrait and advances Weiss's theory of language arts. The heroine, a German war expatriate now living in New Hampshire, recalls a six-week stay in Switzerland during which she taught gardening to child refugees of World War II, many of whom had lost their families to the concentration camps: "Nature, I told them, can be/ trusted. Though how they, plucked from the wreck/ of Europe, could trust to trust me I do not know." Despite her skepticism, she succeeds in transmitting to the children her sensitive gift, learned as a child, for expressing a wide range of human feelings through plants, and she restores them to some measure of human community: "I've striven for this:/ A garden to be implanted in each mind,/ with fruits for others, blessed community." Thinking of the plight of the children, she recalls her own childhood in a passage that develops more exquisitely than in any other poem Weiss's remarkable theory of the way the healthy mind discovers language:

> Till three I said no single word. My mother
> worried, by the tinkling goat-bell father
> tied to me soon reassured.
>
> "That child,"

he smiled, "only when she can put her words
in perfect sentences will speak."

What other
namings needed I? Clear voices they were,
the animals, wings, petalings, voices
like the sun in heather loud. Each day
I took him to our flower-beds to show
each fragrant task the seedlings were performing...

Instinctively, the child knows the words must be held back. Words
must wait for the natural forms to choose them, to embrace them in
her own auditory imagination—the inner ear or mind's eye of the
poet. Namings are emblems rooted in the beings of plants and ani-
mals they inhabit, and the wise child, a poet in her way, knows it is best
to wait for her body's knowledge of living forms—"wings, petalings,
voices"—to unlock the mystery of words. The intimacies of touch,
allurements of the eye and ear, if learned first, carry over to the words
and endow them—for speaker and listener alike—with feelings. The
child knows how to wait for the life of feeling to resume the language
slowly in her ear; she discovers her own best pace for receiving the
seeds of language in the garden plots of memory. Then, when she
first takes hold of the words with her voice, she truly makes them her
own: they belong to her, find a new life in her use of them. They are
reknown and kept alive in her saying.

Language is sterile and lifeless if it is absorbed mechanically. A poet
must periodically rage to return the words from books to plant and
animal beings. A poet must be a gardener or a mountaineer first, a
word maestro second. Most of us learned the language too fast, and if
we get lucky, we spend the rest of our lives learning to slow down, to
wait for the words to reconnect with those avatars that enshrine them:
things of this world.

THE YALE REVIEW, 1971

Reed Whittemore

In so many of Reed Whittemore's poems, the ear is flawless. His voice
is perfectly pitched, immaculate, suave, urbane. There are no slips, no
mistakes—if he trips, it is always accidentally on purpose; he comes up

Poems: New and Selected, by Reed Whittemore. (University of Minnesota Press, 1967.)

smiling, and we smile with him, not at him. He is one of our dwindling few tasteful and intelligent satirists, and we don't dare risk putting him off on some other track; but we do wish he would surprise us a bit more.

When the good poem starts to unwind, to uncoil, it serpentines cunningly, and as the poem rises to a perfect little loop at the finish, and sticks its little forked tongue out at me, I am genuinely tickled and stung. But there is always a moment just before the finish when I want to slash through the poem's sleek hide and expose the rough second skin, and this devilishness of mine lingers with me as an aftertaste when I finish reading the poem. With ample selections from all his previous books before me, I am reminded that Whittemore's style, tone, manner, and range of targets had become too predictable. He has stuck to the same mode for so long, I had begun to associate only one type of poetry with him—the low, guttural chuckle of a highbrow Ogden Nash. Perhaps the comparison is unfair; his sensibility is sophisticated, closer to that of Jules Pfeiffer's cartoons.

In general, I think we enjoy reading Whittemore to the extent that he is in a pleasurable mood when he writes. When he seems hampered from within by a nondescript small poison that he can't rout out of his system, the tone becomes quizzical, self-chiding, and the poetry loses its charm, as in "The Philadelphia Vireo":

> It's a bad day and I feel like a fool out here with the birds,
> And now I'm writing these lines, dissonant things, and thinking bird
>   things,
> Because I'm a bloody professional bird and must damn well sing.
> So I sing: chirk, chirk.

Now and then, particularly in the recent poems, there is a nihilistic tendency to turn the eye of his wit back on itself, shaming him into a state of jaded withdrawal.

Among my favorites in the section of new work are the vivifying family poems, ranging from the explicit tenderness and father-son chumminess of "clamming" to the throwing of sardonic poison-pen-darts in "The Bad Daddy":

> And anyway you should know that your mother and I
> Really think you're a frightful bitch. Love, Dad.

> So now the bad Daddy feels much much more like himself.
> His typewriter pants pleasantly in its shed; the beast is fed.
> Down the long waste of his year he sees, suddenly, violets.
> He picks them and crushes them gently, and is at peace.
> Gettem all, bad Daddy, and sleep now.

The most memorable single poem is the caustic and wildly funny "Dear God," a mock heroic lampoon against foundation-supported American artists, exposing their moral grandiosity, as well as their leaning to opportunism and grantsmanship. But I am most taken with "Six Shaggy," a sequence of poems in which a new manner seems to be emerging. Halting rhythms, inverted syntax, a roughing around the edges of the line, more verbal texture and compression of effects—all add up to a significant redirection in Whittemore's art:

Once upon a time, a long time not ago, in Flint, Mish.,
Lived a man who was very affluent and well-to-do and rish
With six sweet children lovely and long shiny motor cars three
And a wife *charmante* and a home *charmante* and a thoroughly life happy,
When in the midst mist leafy of a Flint-gorgeous warful Fall
Pronto this man popped out with symptoms several of withdrawal.

At times there are knotty, gymnastic rhythms in these poems that seem difficult for the sheer sake of exercising the reader's ear to unravel them—devices that seem to be derived from the art of Berryman's *Dream Songs*—nevertheless, it is a fresh and promising tone frequency that could lead to a strangely alive new scale in Whittemore's art.

THE YALE REVIEW, 1968

Miller Williams

Miller Williams is a poet who has entirely secured his own line and his own idiom—a manner closely modeled from the rhythms of southern colloquial speech. He has a lively eye, wit, and an alert intelligence. His style is lean and spare, streamlined to add up a welter of fresh images and impressions at a remarkable velocity. "Cat You Do Not," the short poem which ends *So Long at the Fair*, rehearses the mental ritual of reductiveness, the habit of mind that propels Williams' art in his best work:

Cat
You do not mail letters
Cat
You do not go to funerals
You sleep

So Long at the Fair, by Miller Williams. (E. P. Dutton, 1968.)

across my lap
lying with everything shut
Cat
I am learning to sleep

One can feel him sinking into a quietude behind all life of action, dwelling there, lingering, keeping the warm spaces in himself empty, leaving everything out that is not lazy-serious, "lying with everything shut." Often his lines are delivered in a voice of indescribably low-pitched intensity, nimbly escaping, stolen from the hush of voiceless-ness—as in the lovely portrait of his daughter being put to bed:

In bed again
re-covered and re-kissed
she locked her arms and mumbling love to mine
until turning she slipped
into the deep bone-bottomed dish
of sleep

In a number of poems, mostly sketchier pieces in loose forms, Williams lets his structure go soft. In "Commencement," for example, his usual compactness and verbal tension are shattered by a rapid-fire sequence of wisecracks. But in the best poems, the ones that start and finish the book ("A Note to God," "Weatherman," "The Caterpillar," "The Widow," "Sale"), he fastens onto his line movement, and the plain speech rhythms and diction store up light and easy beauties with the sort of magical bluntness and swiftness that we admire in the early Hemingway. Williams is able to forge a burning, and often mystical, seriousness from lightness—of tone, of touch—a lightness that is never far from slipping over the edge into mere cleverness, but which in the best poems steadily glows with an impassive energy and strength.

THE YALE REVIEW, 1968

PART III

James Dickey and A. R. Ammons

THE UNBROKEN FLOW

James Dickey and A. R. Ammons are evolving a poetic line that works wonders in the extended lyric. In composing the longer poem, most poets rely on sectional subdivisions and distinct variations in form between sections to keep the poem from growing tedious. But in so doing they jeopardize the key advantage that Dickey and Ammons get from writing on a broad scale—the unbroken flow of language.

For Ammons, words on the page weave in and out like cross-currents in a calm river:

> ... shapeless, undependable
> powerless in the actual
> which I rule, I
>
> will not
> make deposits in your bank account
> or free you from bosses
>   in little factories,
> will not spare you insult, will not
> protect you from
> men who
>   have never heard of modes, who
> do not respect me
> or your knowledge of me in you;
>   men I let win,
> their thin tight lips
> humiliating my worshippers:
>
>   I betray
> him who gets me in his eyes ...

There is a quality of hesitation and search in the variable movement of the line down the page. The center of gravity in the lines shifts from left to right to center. In most of Ammons' poems, a sort of variable but recognizable stanza pattern emerges from the movement. In others, there is a relatively unbroken thrust down the page, as in the passage quoted.

Expressions of Sea Level, by A. R. Ammons. (Ohio State University Press, 1963.)
Helmets, by James Dickey. (Wesleyan University Press, 1964.)

Dickey's line plays upon regularity like the undulations of a stream over rocks in shallow water:

> When the rattlesnake bit, I lay
> In a dream of the country, and dreamed
> Day after day of the river,
>
> Where I sat with a jackknife and quickly
> Opened my sole to the water. . . .
> The freezing river poured on
>
> And, as it took hold of my blood,
> Leapt up round the rocks and boiled over.
>   (from "The Poisoned Man")

Dickey's regular three-beat line captures natural speech rhythms, and he is learning how to avoid monotony by shifting caesuras and balancing light and heavy accents within and between the lines. *Helmets* is much less one-toned than was his previous collection, *Drowning with Others*.

Many a contemporary poet handles language like a mason laying a foundation for a house—the words are so many concrete blocks to be cemented into a wall. Dickey and Ammons treat language with special attention to tone, modulation, and breathing space; all are suavely managed. Particular words and phrases rarely call attention to themselves; they must swing with the abiding rhythm and movement. It is hard to conceive of this poetry being composed slowly, word by word. There is too much continuity and rhythmic sweep. It is as though Dickey's voice were speaking through him; once the tone of voice has been adjusted, the versification moves along with a kind of flawless inevitability:

> He is gone below, and I limp
> To look for my clothes in the world,
>
> A middle-aged, softening man
> Grinning and shaking his head
> In amazement to last him forever.
> I put on the warm-bodied wool,
> The four sweaters inside-out,
> The bootlaces dangling and tripping,
> Then pick my tense bow off the limb
> And turn with the unwinding hooftracks,
> In my good, tricked clothes,
> To hunt, under Springer Mountain,
> Deer for the first and last time.
>   (from "Springer Mountain")

Both Dickey and Ammons tend to write very long, sweeping verse sentences that read quickly. There is more technical excitement for the reader of Ammons; I find myself moving down the page and weaving back and forth simultaneously, hunting the rhythmical center of each line. It's a poetry of cross-currents, and a reader finds he is rowing *with* the current and *into* the current at once.

A quality that makes both of these poets better able to work on a larger scale than most of their contemporaries is the extraordinary power of mind they bring to bear on experience in their poems. In both, the depth and breadth of concentration is astonishing. Surprisingly, neither poet suffers from abstractness or obscurity, two hazards that poetry which thinks very hard is usually prone to. Their poetry seems to think its way *into* experience and things in life, not *around* them, and never loses a close touch with the contours of creature, landscape, and seascape:

> ... here on the
> bottom of an ocean of space
> we babble words recorded
>   in waves
> of sound that
> cannot fully disappear,
>   washing up
> like fossils on the shores of unknown worlds ...
>   (from "Risks and Possibilities"—Ammons)

Ideas in the poems seem less important in themselves, more important as conveyors or conductors that lead the mind into the center of happening.

I think the extended lyric is one of the most fertile and inviting territories for the poet of today, and I hope we can look to Ammons and Dickey for more solid achievement in this genre. It will take some doing to offset the movement toward fragmentation of experience set in motion by the shorter lyrics of William Carlos Williams in the twenties, and to initiate a return to structures that are large enough to cope with our most important experiences.

THE ANTIOCH REVIEW, 1964

M. B. Tolson and A. R. Ammons

BOOK-LENGTH POEMS

Two unusually long (book-length) poems appear this quarter, *Harlem Gallery* by M. B. Tolson, and *Tape for the Turn of the Year* by A. R. Ammons. Both books immediately reveal the sort of technical virtuosity that commands a reader to keep on with it to the finish. Since readers of poetry, as a rule, have a rather short attention span, the usual repeated stanza form, or blank verse, grows tedious; it will not hold his interest for *two hundred pages*. Both Tolson and Ammons keep the eye moving down the page—from top to bottom—instead of horizontally. This gives the poems a forward-thrust of great energy and momentum. In *Harlem Gallery* all of the lines are centered on the vertical axis, and Tolson freely rotates long lines and short ones; in *Tape*, Ammons is confined to narrower (in both senses of that word) limits, since the entire poem was composed on a roll of adding-machine tape. In most other respects, the poems differ vastly, since *Harlem Gallery* was written over a period of ten or fifteen years, whereas *Tape* is a sequence of daily entries in a journal ranging over slightly more than a month in the poet's life.

Karl Shapiro, in his introduction to *Harlem Gallery*, makes the highest possible claim for Tolson: "A great poet has been living in our midst for decades and is almost totally unknown, even by the literati, even by poets." He says further that Tolson's art has been ignored mainly because he is an enemy to the " 'Graeco-Judaic-Christian' culture" of our ruling establishment: "He is, to use the term he prefers, an Afroamerican poet, not an American Negro poet accommodating himself to the tradition. . . . *Tolson writes in Negro.*"

It may well be that my problem in reading this book is that I am not Negro. Well, I have just spent a year teaching at the college in St. Thomas. The student body here is about 90 per cent Negro, and nearly every Negro land I can think of is represented, including Africa and the States. Though English is the mother tongue for nearly all of the students, there is so much variety of accent and dialect, I have to struggle to understand what they are saying in class (as indeed, they must struggle to understand each other). Africa is the land

Harlem Gallery, by M. B. Tolson. (Twayne Publishers, 1965.)
Tape for the Turn of the Year, by A. R. Ammons. (Cornell University Press, 1965.)
Corson's Inlet, by A. R. Ammons. (Cornell University Press, 1965.)

of *their* racial heritage, quite as much as it is Tolson's. I have tried to get the students—and some of them are promising poets—to become interested in reading Tolson's book. They do not understand him. He simply does not speak their language. How then can it be said that Tolson writes *in Negro?*

Perhaps this is an unfair criterion; it may be that poetry in our time is for The Few, and this handful of readers is an intellectual elite that prevails over racial or religious or national barriers. For my own part, as a reader, I feel that *Harlem Gallery* does have some of the hallmarks of an important work of art, and I share the sort of literary wishful-thinking that makes me want to support Mr. Shapiro's enthusiastic response.

The book has astonishing linguistic range, a vital new imagery, and much technical excitement. It is a strange hybrid of many dialects. But there seem to be only traces of *Negro* slang and dialect. The characters are literary oddities: they sparkle like ornaments in the vast mosaic of the poem. The book is weighed down with literary allusions; it is top-heavy with the tradition and special learning. While it is true that often Tolson successfully ridicules the cultural establishment from which he derives so much of his imagery, more often he is too steeped in that tradition to work against it. There are many passages that are cluttered with references to poets, painters, composers—and their works. Examples range from Homer through Shakespeare to the present. Some lines are so thick with allusions that they become opaque; a reader cannot find his way into their meanings, their sayings. The tradition that the poem supports *is* basically that of the "Graeco-Judaic-Christian culture," and not a distinctly Negro heritage. I think Tolson defines his own difficulty in breaking away from the dominant culture of America in a few lines of the poem:

> I was a half-white egghead with maggots on the brain.
> I ate my crow,
> for the unconscious of the artist
> cannot say to itself *No.*

The literary milieu which gave him birth now refuses to set him free.

The Trinidadians and Guyanese I have met in St. Thomas have a more seminal dispute with Western culture than any American Negro I have ever read, including Tolson and Baldwin. The Negroes of Trinidad and Guyana have had Western culture shoved down their throats by the United Kingdom at closer range than the American Negroes. Some of the more outspoken among them dismiss the entire civilization arising from the Greeks as barbaric, and favor an Egypt-oriented definition of our cultural heritage. However absurd their claim, they at least offer a possibility for a new major direction and tradition for the modern world. Tolson does not offer this, so far as I can see.

Harlem Gallery is intended as a prelude (*Book I: The Curator*) to a much larger work. There are some sections that suggest in their clarity and razor-sharp irony that Tolson has it in him to become, and may well be on the way to becoming, a satirist of the first order. If he can find his position and his voice more distinctly outside the cultural fortress he is failing to undermine from within, I will be among the first to cheer as the walls come tumbling down.

It is clear from the two collections of Ammons' shorter poems (*Corson's Inlet* was published concurrently with *Tape* by Cornell University Press) that this poet usually gets his best results when he varies his line-lengths over the widest possible range. Why, then, does he restrict himself in *Tape* to a limitation of form that cuts off much of his technical power? A reader's first inclination is to assume that he resorted to the gimmick of adding-machine tape to keep pace with the current fad of pop art. And certainly there is no harm in borrowing honestly from the other contemporary arts. But all this is misleading, for if there is a pioneer in the technique of poetry today, it is A. R. Ammons. *Tape* is a daring book. It takes valiant risks. At the time of its composition, the poet must have doubted whether the book would be able to attract and hold a single reader, much less a publisher:

> ... the denominator
> here may be too low: the
> lines may be
> too light, the song
>   too hard to hear:
>   still, it's not been
>   easy: it's
>   cost me plenty ...

Ammons has become dissatisfied with the poem that is small enough in scope to be worked into a perfected artifact through many revisions:

> ... lines that can be
> gone over (and over)
> till they sing with
> pre-established rightness ...
>   I've hated at times the
> self-conscious poem ...

He seems to feel that if a poem is re-worked too many times, it recedes from experience, loses its naturalness, the sense of life taking place on the page, now. He wants the movement of the poem to get directly in step with the turnover of experience in his mind, to capture the many sides of himself that work at cross-purposes in life, and embrace them in the process of dynamic interchange and imbalance, rather than contrive a sense of balance and comfortable order by squeezing a poem into a single dimension of experience. To give an accurate sampling of Ammons' *Tape*, I would have to suggest something of the bulging spans of emotion, the multiplicities of experience he is able to exhale, all of a piece, in each massive breathful of the poem.

In *Corson's Inlet*, the collection of shorter poems, Ammons is searching for a medium—a fabric of line and rhythm—that can assimilate into itself the most complex and intricate rhythms of nature: alterations in the shapes of dunes, feeding habits and migrations of birds— singly or in multitudes, tentacular shiftings and gropings of pea vines. His movement must remain fluid at all times to keep in touch with the actual phenomena adorned (never merely described) by the poem. He will not permit his medium to become fixed, not even to the extent of evolving consistent inconsistencies: "So that I make no form of formlessness."

All this Ammons has achieved with astonishing success in the title poem, "Corson's Inlet." I believe it is a poem of the first importance. Every block of language exhibits an arrangement that appeals to the eye and the ear, every passage is somehow different from every other, yet all passages partake of some basic rhythm or movement that permeates the poem as a whole. The problem of form is not solved until the poem is completed. The poet, with extraordinary nimbleness, discovers and re-discovers the movement of his line—and nothing can be preconceived, all must emerge instantaneously from the flux of language and the interplay of lines. The speaker in this poem is continually beset by pressures to take the easy way out, to settle for obvious solutions or tidy exits. But his vision overrides every hazard, as he continues to find in the natural setting a pattern for his thought as well as for the movement of his verse:

> I see narrow orders, limited tightness, but will
> not run to that easy victory:
>   still around the looser, wider forces work:
>   I will try
> to fasten into order enlarging grasps of disorder . . .

Many readers, and some good ones, reject nearly all free verse as an abdication of form. Ammons has adopted free verse in quest of a more meaningful and porous order than traditional forms could possibly allow. While this poem balances exquisitely between form and flow, between order and disorder, the poet's preference for the maximum freedom of movement and the minimum of constraint appears early in the poem:

> ... the walk liberating, I was released from forms,
> from the perpendiculars,
>   straight lines, blocks, boxes, binds
> of thought
> into the hues, shadings, rises, flowing bends and blends
>   of sight...

In a couple of poems, notably "Lines" and "Prodigal," there is a tendency to multiply abstract verbiage until it recoils upon itself. But most of the poems have a vivid and exuberant language, a memorable language that never becomes merely flat or inert. In a series of confrontations with nature, in various poems, Ammons expresses his distrust for the tendency of his own mind to violate the integrity of natural objects by transforming them into mere symbols for poetry, and he chides other poets for trying to superimpose aesthetic formulas on living experience ("no humbling of reality to precept") and for contriving melodrama out of natural events ("no arranged terror: no forcing of image, plan, or thought: no propaganda"). Usually Ammons maintains a saintly reverence before trees, birds, waters— and with a sort of fond protectiveness and self-derisiveness he cherishes their secret identities in the lines that conclude the book:

> ... so I look and reflect, but the air's glass
> jail seals each thing in its entity:
> no use to make any philosophies here:
>   I see no
> god in the holly, hear no song from
> the snowbroken weeds: Hegel is not the winter
> yellow in the pines: the sunlight has never
> heard of trees: surrendered self among
>   unwelcoming forms: stranger,
> hoist your burdens, get on down the road.

This poet is at his best as he moves between the worlds of fact and idea. The vivid extra dimension that each world imparts to the other, at such moments, is exceeded by the poet's luminous ambience as he journeys between them.

THE HUDSON REVIEW, 1965

W. S. Merwin and Anthony Hecht

RISKS AND FAITHS

If there is any book today that has perfectly captured the peculiar spiritual agony of our time, the agony of a generation which knows itself to be the last, and has transformed that agony into great art, it is W. S. Merwin's *The Lice*. To read these poems is an act of self-purification. Every poem in the book pronounces a judgment against modern man—the gravest sentence the poetic imagination can conceive for man's withered and wasted conscience: our sweep of history adds up to one thing only, a moral vacuity that is absolute and irrevocable. This book is a testament of betrayals; we have betrayed all beings that had power to save us: the forests, the animals, the gods, the dead, the spirit in us, the words. Now, in our last moments alive, they return to haunt us.

Merwin powerfully dramatizes states of disorientation, spiritual vertigo. The speaker in the poems is lost in time, lost to himself. He exists in stark disrelation. The sensibility of the persona is desperately trying to catch up with experiences—of self and the world—that have long since passed him by. The possibility of an inner life of spirit continues, as before, but we are helpless to embrace it: "Not that heaven does not exist but/ That it exists without us." The artist cannot save us, but he employs a heroic intelligence in the task of defining the exact conditions of our helplessness:

> I
> Am all that became of them
> Clearly all is lost
>
> The gods are what has failed to become of us
> Now it is over we do not speak
>
> Now the moment has gone it is dark
> What is man that he should be infinite
> The music of a deaf planet
> The one note
> Continues clearly this is

The Lice, by W. S. Merwin. (Atheneum, 1967.)
The Hard Hours, by Anthony Hecht. (Atheneum, 1967.)

> The other world
> These strewn rocks belong to the wind
> If it could use them
> (from "The Gods")

These poems speak to our sensibility from the corridors of sleep, and there are moments in the reading of them, or just after reading them, when we feel the odd wide-awakeness—the super-alertness—that we experience when a deep sleep is suddenly interrupted by a very disturbing dream and we spring upright in bed with an absurd sense of relief, in the certainty that all of our questions have been answered, even the ones we never knew enough to ask. This poetry, at its best— and at our best as readers—is able to meet us and engage our wills as never before in the thresholds between waking and sleeping, past and future, self and anti-self, men and gods, the living and the dead.

In "Is That What You Are," man's spiritual disorientation is queerly externalized: the spirits of the dead hover on the sill of man's consciousness, bewildered, waiting to be re-positioned in man's scheme of the universe. Now that man has lost his identity, they too have lost theirs; the dead stare at us across an abyss, and, by an ironic reversal of traditional roles, they pose unanswerable questions to us; and we can only stare back, a race of somnambulistic amnesiacs:

> New ghost is that what you are
> Standing on the stairs of water
>
> No longer surprised
>
> Hope and grief are still our wings
> Why we cannot fly
>
> What failure still keeps you
> Among us the unfinished . . .
>
> I did not think I had anything else to give

As this poem proceeds, the gap between the living man—who is in reality "the dying"—and the dead spirit, who clings helplessly to the living, narrows, and finally one cannot tell them apart. The twin conditions of death-in-life and life-in-death dramatized by Yeats in the Byzantium poems are viewed here in a strikingly new relation. Yeats had envisioned the passage of the living artist's spirit into the antiworld of the dead as being a gesture of great spiritual energy, a state from which the living spirit could return to this world enriched, spiritually nourished. In Merwin, the opposition between the spirits of the two worlds has grown feebler and feebler, since life and death have grown to resemble each other more and more. Loss of identity, in both cases, has resulted in loss of spiritual vitality, and both heaven and earth are moving toward extinction; like the American soldiers fighting in Vietnam, "Nothing they will come to is real/ Nor for long."

The most remarkable poems in this book are the ones in which the speaker confronts a strange alien being—a god, an animal, a dead spirit. The persona is the last man: he embodies what is left of the spirit of natural life-giving beauty in man. He has long since written off the question of survival, of saving anything for the future, as hopeless ("Today belongs to few and tomorrow to no one"). All that remains to him is to grace the obsequies of our passage into extinction with a few words of dignity and bitter truth:

> ... there are
> Occupations
> My blind neighbor has required of me
> A description of darkness
> And I begin I begin ...

Merwin, in this book, is a soul surgeon performing radical operations on modern man's failing spirit. The patient is on the critical list and the prognosis is very poor. In the bleakest poems, the patient has already died. The poet performs a spiritual autopsy: the anatomical findings reveal that the corpse had died many times over before being declared officially dead.

To learn to read any major poet correctly, we must train the ear to listen for nuances of language and line movement that may be as unfamiliar and inaccessible, at first reading, as those of a foreign language. These difficulties, and the rewards that may be earned by surmounting them, are larger in Merwin's new poetry than in the work of most other contemporaries. As we hunt the pauses we missed on first reading, we are forced to hesitate, and Merwin's mastery is nowhere more evident than in his consistent power to turn these inevitable hesitations to advantage. Nearly always, the reader finds that there are images with hidden meanings and statements with a potential doubling effect; ambiguities that were hidden on first reading somehow become perfectly available during repeated readings, since the rhythmical pauses left by elided punctuation are exquisitely timed in relation to moments of revelation waiting to be grasped in line and image.

The other main difficulty in learning to read these poems is the peculiar distancing of the voice. It is as though the voice filters up to the reader like echoes from a very deep well, and yet it strikes his ear with a raw energy—a sustained inner urgency—that is rare even in poetry of the direct and explicit type. It is as though the artist's spirit, in fighting free of his human personality, layer by layer, has won through to the frontier of great impersonal being, and, in poem after poem, his spirit stands before us and speaks in utter simplicity and nakedness with no loss of personal immediacy. And yet, the voice has a strangely disembodied quality: it seems to speak across a very great barren distance. The poems must be read very slowly, since most of their uncanny power is hidden in overtones that must be listened for in silences between lines, and still stranger silences within lines.

Though the style of *The Lice* is little more than a continuation of the successful technical experiment in Merwin's last book, *The Moving Target*, the later book goes beyond the former in an important way. In reading the first book, I felt that each of the best poems was self-contained and bore little relation to the other poems in the volume. The new book is pervaded by a consistent and continually developing vision of modern man's moment in the world. Symbols—such as stars, ashes, hands, doors, windows, shadows, walls—are used repeatedly in poem after poem, and, as in the later Yeats, a cross-fertilization of meanings occurs between a group of poems employing the same symbols. The comprehensiveness of the author's vision is authenticated by the solidarity of these symbols, which a reader senses are never just self-referring. They point beyond themselves to a frame of reference, a vision of life, that seems to be everywhere interfused. This is a sure mark of art of the highest order.

Anthony Hecht's new poetry is a powerful synthesizing art. In the best poems, he stringently resists his earlier habit of analyzing and interpreting the subject for the reader, and would now confront us with nothing short of the totality of experience, by raw exposure to what he calls the "brute fact."

> The contemplation of horror is not edifying,
> Neither does it strengthen the soul . . .
> Fear of our own imperfections,
> Fear learned and inherited,
> Fear shapes itself in dreams
> Not more fantastic than the brute fact.
>   (from "Rites and Ceremonies")

If to encounter the horrors of modern war directly is to be overwhelmed by unthinkable facts, to encounter them in major art *may* "strengthen the soul," and I urge that horror is the principal subject that releases explosive energy in Hecht's best work.

Modern art usually takes the mind into the reality of unbearable pain through the side door of symbolism. The hazard of the symbolist's art is the difficulty of returning the reader from the comfortable aesthetic remove of the symbol's refining grace to the raw ugliness of political atrocity. W. S. Merwin enables the reader to negotiate the return trip from symbol to fact with unusual efficacy, partly because he seems to live much of the time in a state of intimate communion with the impersonal associative centers of the mind which constitute a common ground—a spiritual bridge—between the reader's experience and his own. Perhaps this is why so many of his symbols instantly strike the reader as being the mirror complement for moments in his own life. Hecht has chosen a more direct, though no less hazardous, route to the same end: the providing of a complement to match, or counterbalance—in imagination—the brutality of our age. His method combines the strengths of narrative and dramatic art, and fuses them in the compact medium of the lyric.

At first acquaintance, Hecht's art may seem to be a retreat, or withdrawal, from modernism. In his method, he leans more to realism than to symbolism, and he is an insistent moralist—his poems carry an unfashionably large freight of message. Though Merwin's poems make similar moral designs upon the reader, he is instantly recognizable as a modernist; the contents of his poems come at the reader obliquely, across a mental distance that the reader must make a conscious effort to cross before he can feel that he has entered the life of the poems at all. The images are the central vehicles of Merwin's poetry, and, like Lorca's images, they resemble the symbolism of dreams. Hecht directs the reader's attention mainly to the facts of the story he is telling. In "The Hill," "Behold the Lilies of the Field," "More Light! More Light!" and parts of the long sequence "Rites and Ceremonies," Hecht's style has so much conversational ease and fluency that we begin reading with the illusion that the poem is merely giving a journalistic account of the events.

In "The Hill," the extreme risks taken by Hecht's method are more evident than in other poems. The reader is initially so aware of the poem's intentional deprivations of style that he finds himself wondering how the poet can possibly offset the studied bareness of his medium. Whereas the symbolist's difficulty is the risk of moving too far from literal experience to be intelligible, Hecht's art takes the risk of moving in too close. We see the events as clearly as through the camera eye—there seems to be no blurriness, even at the edges of the scene imaged, no ambiguities. In contrast with the ornate style of many of Hecht's earlier poems, the new work is characterized by starkly undecorative—and unpretentious—writing. He relies, to a valiant degree, on the power of quiet overtones to transmit the intense emotional experience hidden below the casual surface; the undemonstrative vocabulary, low-keyed meters, and rhythms often accumulate, as in the closing lines of "The Hill," into a withering revelation of truth and pain.

At times, Hecht's new style grows too flat and prosy, one-toned. All verbal tension is dissipated by the studied dullness of rhythms. In an extreme effort to pare down his verse to essentials, and to omit any embellishments of style that might attract the reader's attention to themselves and away from the serious human statement, the technique backfires. In "Message from the City," I find myself going over the same passages again and again—not so much to probe any opacity of meaning as to find points of emphasis in sound or rhythm to guide my ear, in design to lead my eye:

> It is raining here.
> On my neighbor's fire escape
> geraniums are set out
> in their brick-clay pots,
> along with the mop,
> old dishrags, and a cracked
> enamel bowl for the dog . . .
>
> Yesterday was nice.
> I took my boys to the park.
> We played Ogre on the grass.
> I am, of course, the Ogre,
> and invariably get killed.

When the line flows too easily and unobtrusively, it offers no settling resistance to the reader—the hesitations that significant form always imposes on the mind's ear—to free him from style and release his thought into the urgencies of subject. This is the risk Hecht takes when he trims his style too close, but only rarely does he over-refine.

Hecht's most consistently masterful device is to juxtapose stories from history, ancient and contemporary (or scenes from his personal life, present and past), generating a powerful religious and political moral from collision between them. In "Behold the Lilies of the Field," he constructs his vision from a reading of history, his own and the world's, interwoven. In "More Light! More Light!" and "Rites and Ceremonies," the interlocking of dramas mercilessly batters the reader's sensibility with excoriating facts, and judges his conscience. The scissoring movement between story and story provides the reader's nervous system with a series of shocks, a jackknifing of emotions, comparable to that produced by the interplay of plot and subplot in *King Lear*, and in some story sequences of the Old Testament. I don't know any other poetry in English, outside poetic drama, that creates anything like this effect.

John Berryman, William Stafford, and James Dickey

THE EXPANSIONAL POET: A RETURN TO PERSONALITY

No fewer than three of the best current volumes of poetry seem decisively committed to the full expression of the writer's personality in his art. *Berryman's Sonnets*, written over twenty years ago and now published for the first time, demonstrate the brilliant, though uneven, beginnings of a serial, cumulative art form that later produced the monumental *Homage to Mistress Bradstreet*—a small masterpiece—and, more recently, the savagely comic *Dream Songs*. In *The Rescued Year*, William Stafford has outdistanced his earlier work, particularly in the sequence "Following the *Markings* of Dag Hammarskjöld," a movement of poetry that builds quitely into a triumph of self-transcendence. James Dickey's new volume contains the best work of his four earlier books, all published in the sixties, and a book-length section of new poems. Several of the new poems surpass his many previous successes in sheer magnitude of vision. (It is evident, too, that with each succeeding volume Dickey has markedly advanced his art, producing at each stage some poems that clearly exceed the best work of the previous volume, though there are more outstanding whole poems in the middle book, *Helmets*, than in any other single collection.) In all three instances, some of the writer's newest work is the best he has ever produced. And this, in itself, is an event which should give us pause. Further, in the development of these artists, the human personality felt through the poetry has grown steadily more vivid, more intensely present.

"The progress of an artist is a continual self-sacrifice, a continual extinction of personality.... Poetry is ... not the expression of personality, but an escape from personality." In his classic essay, "Tradition and the Individual Talent," T. S. Eliot gave us the best definition we have today of the relation between the poet and the poem, subsequent to the first revolution of poetry in the period we call modern.

Berryman's Sonnets, by John Berryman. (Farrar, Straus & Giroux, 1967.)

The Rescued Year, by William Stafford. (Harper & Row, 1966.)

Poems, 1957–67, by James Dickey. (Wesleyan University Press, 1967.)

The books under consideration here convince me that "the second birth" has definitely arrived. We are witnessing a return to personality—and more, an about-face: the mystique of one's self.

The usual argument against writing about oneself, or strictly out of one's own experience, is the risk that once the writer has exhausted his unique experience as subject matter for his art, he may reach a dead end, coming to a creative standstill. This is largely true, especially in the case of "the confessional poet," but every artistic direction poses grave hazards, and it is the rare poet working in any mode who can continue to develop his art, and to keep his genius alive into full maturity. "His earliest (and best) work" has become a catch phrase to describe most modern American authors, from Hemingway to Robert Lowell, and I'm afraid T. S. Eliot himself was no exception to this trend. The one poet writing within the framework outlined by Eliot and Pound who conspicuously rounded out a full career of continued growth was, of course, Yeats. And, strangely, there is an emergence of what could be called personality in the later Yeats, though I much prefer Richard Ellmann's term, "identity," which more accurately identifies a personality that served Yeats as little more than an over-cultivated literary stage prop in his poems.

"The more perfect the artist the more completely separate in him will be the man who suffers and the mind which creates." Again, Eliot's dictum is borne out by the example of Yeats: the suffering ego projected in Yeats's later poems is no more than a mask; rarely, in Yeats, even in his most nakedly explicit moments, do we sense that his actual human personality touches us directly. Rather, Theodore Roethke is the poet in whose art we feel the nearest approach to the man who suffers, the man who knows joy. He is the first major poet to continue, throughout his career, to deepen and intensify his total personality in his art.

Berryman, Stafford, and Dickey are all writers whose chief recognition has come in the sixties, relatively late in their careers, a reliable indication that their art—like Roethke's—ran against the grain of literary fashion (though in Dickey's remarkably swift rise following the publication of his first book seven years ago, there was hardly time to take note of this). Also, each was a proud, solitary worker who stood aloof from literary movements and the self-advertisement that usually accrues to those.

In the best new work of these three poets, nearly every line resonates with the passion (Eliot asks, too, that the poet be passionless) of a remarkable being aspiring to claim his full due as a human personality. To read their new poetry is to be struck with an expansional flowering of personality. Expansional poetry is not to be confused

with confessional poetry: the work of Sexton, Snodgrass, Lowell in
Life Studies. The confessional poets are limited to writing autobiog-
raphy, and their work is largely one-dimensional, all surface. The
expansional poets are projecting—not merely "expressing"—the sum
total of vivid personality in their work. At the same time, their poetry
is a medium for discovering, or creating, a sensibility. In reaction to
Eliot's plea for depersonalization, they animate their art with hyper-
personalization. Berryman's Henry in *Dream Songs*, Stafford's variants
of Dag Hammarskjöld, Dickey's sheep child and the stewardess in
"Falling"—all are simultaneously symbolic projections of the author's
personality and self-transcendent dream-beings: the persona becomes
a medium through which the author can release and realize pos-
sibilities in the self which are thwarted or blocked in his daily life.

These poems are similar to the work of confessional poets in one
way only: both prescribe a religion of selfhood; fidelity to the human
being—to the uniqueness of personality behind the poem—is pri-
mary; perfection of the art, secondary. In this regard, both types are
staunchly opposed to Eliot, who prescribes the extinction of personal-
ity. But the confessional poet restricts his range, narrows his focus of
vision, to literal events in his life—usually morbid autobiographical
data. The expansional poet plunges into an unfamiliar field of ex-
perience in the poem, a field that can widen and deepen his personal-
ity and stretch his intelligence.

The daring imagination of John Berryman in *Dream Songs*, and to a
lesser degree in the *Sonnets*, is constantly en route between the bizarre
melodrama of a loser-in-love—with all that world's particularity of
detail—and the hallucinatory dream-world of his inner life. We keep
traveling back and forth between these two poles, and Berryman's
sensibility is so rich, his imagery so fresh and varied, he never repeats
himself, even though he seems to be covering virtually the same
ground again and again. The possibilities are endless, inexhaustible,
always unpredictable. The circuit between dream and reality is a
pliant, limber, ever-adaptable medium for expressing what may well
be the most tantalizingly resourceful personality in contemporary lit-
erature. Many of the poems gravitate too near one pole or the other:
those that are explicitly confessional, almost journalistic, tend to be
outlandishly slapstick, corny, self-pitying, or indulgently freakish.
Others sail away in dream-clouds of smoky obscurity. In fact, I find
very few of the poems to be altogether successful. Nearly all are
flawed in some lines; some are cluttered with glaring blemishes. So
often, Berryman tries to mix irreconcilables: classical references,
squibs in French or German, insolubly diverse metaphors. A key fail-
ing that taxes believability in the sonnets, but less frequently mars the

dream songs, is over-fixation on self-gloom:

> who am I? a scum
> Thickens on a victim, a delirium
> Begins to mutter, which I must explore.

Berryman deliberately maintains a state of sterile depravity so he can sniff around in the scummy surface and record the data of his glum inspection. A lot of the whines and howls strike me as being trumped-up self-preenings.

A number of clues to Berryman's later development are to be found in the sonnets, mostly in stray lines or phrases explicitly commenting on the logic behind his innovatory style. Inversions and other oddities of syntax are evidently intended to transmit emotional quirks, sudden reversals of feeling:

> Crumpling a syntax at a sudden need,
> Stridor of English softening to plead
> O to you plainly lest you more resist.

Berryman's verse movement proceeds by word-and-image increments, searching for a sound-clash that will truly echo the jangle of inner voices:

> I prod our English: cough me up a word,
> Slip me an epithet will justify
> My daring fondle, fumble of far fire
> Crackling nearby, unreasonable as a surd,
> A flash of light, an insight.

When the technique fails, his phrasing suffers from redundancy, imprecision, word-thickness. When it succeeds—more often than not, surely—each element in the cluster of meanings seems like an irreducible fragment of the inner state of personality, and the successive words and phrases connect horizontally, if not vertically, in a chain which, though discontinuous at points, vibrates uniformly. The characteristic tone frequency of Berryman's poetry is a superarticulate mental wail. The accumulative effect of the *Dream Songs,* as well as the *Sonnets,* is overwhelmingly powerful. One must read Berryman by the bookful. Then one is struck by the ceaselessly self-risking explorations of levels of pain and frustration in modern life, and, in addition, his marvelous capacity for laughing at himself whenever the poetry verges on studiously earnest self-torture. As in the art of Groucho Marx, the slapstick comedy veils a keen, self-piercing intelligence. Berryman is our shrewdest clown.

William Stafford's grip is always loose, his touch light—almost feathery. Often a very good poem slips through his fingers, slides away from him in the closing lines; and this is the risk he takes by his unwillingness to tighten his hold to protect his interests. If the reader feels let down, disappointed, he also senses the poet is content to have lost the poem to save the quiet tenderness of the human voice weaving through it. If we read on, we learn that a few poems end with a magic and bewitching mysticism that is a perfect arrival, a blossoming and fulfillment of the poet's voice, one of the strangest in our literature:

> So I try not to learn, disengage because reasons
> block the next needed feeling. While others
> talk, all of my tentative poems begin
> to open their eyes, wistful . . .

These intensely memorable lines are of a quality we have seen nowhere else. All of Stafford's poems may be viewed as hopeful voyages toward those few deeply religious moments. His best lines don't necessarily have the ring of inevitability: rather, they are on exactly the right wavelength, in the right tone of voice. They could as easily have been other lines, we feel, but we know they have been intimately listened—not worried!—into being:

> Today drinking coffee I look over the cup
> and want to have the right amount of fear,
> preferring to be saved and not, like him [his father], heroic.

In these lines from "Parentage," there is a cautiousness, an apparent narrowing and reduction of soul response, that is deceptive. Actually, it is the fixing of a scale of thinking that will allow Stafford's deeper mind to move steadily—if carefully, safely—into the dark reality behind experience: a reality in the world and in the mind. The scale chosen may disturb the reader, since it automatically restricts itself to the limitations of a softly whispered one-man's viewing, but we are never led to doubt that Stafford has perfectly secured his most telling angle of vision. The style of seeing is usually the mover behind the poem's subject, not the reverse; and the poem becomes a way of creating a sensibility, not just discovering one already inherent in himself: a way of shaping a manner of feeling, wording inner responses and fitting them to the world. There is a religion here of the right response: the poem is praying for feelings, lines, ideas, phrases, that are true to the mind's touch:

> Reader, we are in such a story:
> all of this is trying to arrange a kind of a prayer for you.
>
> Pray for me.

Not accidentally, these lines end the book.

But it is the sequence "Following the *Markings* of Dag Hammarskjöld" that radically extends Stafford's personality outward, for the first time perhaps, by absorbing and transmitting through his own mental apparatus the mystical workings—*Markings*—of the mind of a magnificent human Other being. In most of his poems, it appears that Stafford has let himself become somewhat too rigidly, or programmatically, confined to a studiedly low-keyed temperament:

> In scenery I like flat country.
> In life I don't like much to happen.
>
> In personalities I like mild colorless people.
> And in colors I prefer gray and brown.

But as he self-mockingly reveals later in the same poem ("Passing Remark"), he also has an ungovernable weakness for his colorful opposites:

> My wife, a vivid girl from the mountains,
> says, "Then why did you choose me?"
>
> Mildly I lower my brown eyes—
> there are so many things admirable people
> do not understand.

And it is not so much his attraction to his opposites as his greater resiliency, in recent poems, to allow himself to be sympathetically drawn into the mind of another person for whom he feels great spiritual affinity, that saves him from a protective insularity of being.

His poems to his father, some of which are re-collected in this volume from his first book *West of Your City,* demonstrate his early leanings in this direction; but his father's mind is too much an incorporated part of his own personality for the experience of identification to extend the boundaries of his immediate consciousness very much. However, merging his thought with the mind and spirit of Dag Hammarskjöld lifts him entirely out of that insular self and expands his personality as never before. I can imagine Stafford training and disciplining his mind for months—patiently quieting and muffling his mental habits of years, to prepare a fertile mental soil in which seeds wafted from the mental field of his newly adopted alter ego, Dag Hammarskjöld, firmly took root. How else can he so decisively and conclusively have expanded himself? I have to strongly differ with the critic Hazard Adams, who admonishes Stafford to adhere, fixedly, to writing poetry in a nostalgic personal mode. I agree most of his best work has been done in that mode, but that mastery is precisely the reason it is time to go beyond.

In his characteristic mode, Stafford, making a powerful effort to resist the usual habits of his senses, slowly discovers the remarkable

hidden beauty in ordinary low-keyed experience. The world is some-
how to be learned by arduously and freshly observing average
experience—not extreme or fantastic experience. In this sense, he has
been developing in a direction opposite to James Dickey's, though
both writers have been richening a personal and mystical vision.

The subject of Dickey's new poetry is being in extremity, being
stretched to the outer—or inner—limits of joy and terror. Dickey, at
his best, is now able to give us the radically new experience in poetry
that D. H. Lawrence superbly demonstrated to be America's most
singular contribution to world literature, particularly in his essays on
the art of Melville and Whitman. Dickey's radicalism is most extreme
in two poems, "Falling" and "The Sheep Child." The persona in these
poems is "beginning to be something/ that no one has ever been and
lived through." As the stewardess nears death, toward the end of her
tragic fall, her erotic dream fantasy withstands a collision with intense
rival counterimages of hard, cold reality. Her inner life of dream-
being attains, finally, a more impervious solidity and stability than the
great ultimates of death and time we cling to in the real world:

> she must
> Do something with water   fly to it   fall in it   drink it   rise
> From it   but there is none left upon earth   the clouds have drunk it
>   back
> The plants have sucked it down   there are standing toward her only
> The common fields of death   she comes back from flying to falling
> Returns to a powerful cry   the silent scream with which she blew down
> The coupled door of the airliner   nearly   nearly losing hold
> Of what she has done   remembers   remembers the shape at the heart
> Of cloud   fashionably swirling   remembers she still has time to die
> Beyond explanation.

Such clarity and intensity are characteristic of Dickey's most achieved
vision, and can only have been earned by a monumentalizing of being.

In tracing the genesis of "Falling" and "The Sheep Child" in Dick-
ey's earlier work, we find that each poem has a number of anteced-
ents. In each case, Dickey has been trying, in poem after poem, to
find a way to project into his art a central experience of his life which
played a large role in the shaping of his personality. His experience of
hunting with bow and arrow, as well as his experience of flying aircraft
in combat missions—the world of the hunter and the world of the
fighter pilot—are two key rooms in the dream-world of Dickey's per-
sonality that continually open new doors into his poetry.

Dickey's flying experience (first dramatized extensively in two di-
verse "poems of the air"—"The Firebombing" and "Reincarnation 2")
combines with his experience of sky-diving and parachuting to pro-
duce the incredible interior drama of the stewardess in "Falling."

While her mental state ranges between extremes of terror and joy, the poem projects the sensation of complex body-movements, to a degree unprecedented in Dickey's work, through a series of ingenious kinesthetic images. In the turbulent space-flux of her fall, her tumbling body learns control, develops a ballet in air, and ascends, finally, into a transcendent cosmic dance of love:

> She is hung high up in the overwhelming middle of things   in
> her
> Self in low body-whistling wrapped intensely   in all her dark
> danceweight
> Coming down from a marvellous leap with the delaying, dumbfounding
> ease
> Of a dream . . .

The intimacy Dickey feels for hunted animals led him to conceive and participate in the dream life of animals, and to nourish the growth in his personality of an inhuman—subhuman and superhuman, at once—speaking voice in a series of poems: "The Heaven of Animals," "Fog Envelops the Animals," and "Springer Mountain," to name a few. In these poems, his being voyages between the human and animal poles, but nowhere does he achieve a stranger verisimilitude of fusion than in the soliloquy of the sheep child:

> I saw for a blazing moment
> The great grassy world from both sides,
> Man and beast in the round of their need,
> And the hill wind stirred in my wool,
> My hoof and my hand clasped each other,
> I ate my one meal
> Of milk, and died
> Staring.

In the poetry of Berryman and Stafford, the line is the pivotal unit of measure. Only Roethke exceeds Berryman in the variety and frequency of lines that stand up from the page—alluring and wildly strange. Stafford's best lines, slow-paced and quiet, owe much more to the field in which they occur, gathering a curious vividness from silences in other parts of the poem. In Dickey's poetry, the phrase is the unit that draws attention to itself, cutting imperceptibly across the surging, unstoppable rhythm; rarely does the word or line interrupt the poem's flow to create a surprising locus of interest. Dickey's sound accrues from the swift adding up of memorable phrases in the reader's ear, phrases that multiply into a trance-like, massive sound-aggregate; the reader is often astonished to find that his ear has been able to assimilate so much vivid imagery so quickly. The momentum rolls through the poem, as in Dylan Thomas, but whereas in Thomas the rapidity of flow is often self-defeating because of the opacity of argument, in Dickey's best work speed of reading enhances the delivery of meaning, since the poems are fantastically lively and crystalline on the surface.

The aesthetics of expansional poetry sketchily outlined below are mainly derived from my reading of these three poets. The expansional poet has learned to liberate his personality—not just his experience—in poems: he is free to discover all levels of his personality, all hidden selves coming into play. The man who suffers, in Eliot's phrase, contains many other men. They are all truly himself, or parts of himself. He isn't just a catalyst, or neutral medium through which mystery voices speak ("the platinum . . . has remained inert, neutral, and unchanged. . . . The mind of the poet is the shred of platinum"—Eliot). Those voices he is able to release though self-expansion in the poem are themselves the substance and make-up of his total personality. The poems he writes enlarge his personality, in fact, to the degree that he enlarges his experience of humanity—or ultrahumanity—in the writing of them. The expansional poet has learned to harness his personality, to make it run at full gallop in the poetry, to open it up and let it flow outward into the world, constrained neither by experience it has already mastered in life, nor by traditional forms and meters. For the expansional poet, form is developmental, self-discovering. The expanding self is constantly hunting a new sound to liberate its new emotions. The following remarks were Dickey's reply to a question put to him about "Falling," in an interview with the poet at about the time that he was at work on the early drafts of the poem:

> Too early to talk about it. I think I've got a new kind of sound again, another beat, a halting, hesitant, stuttering kind of sound. I haven't really made it go yet, but occasionally I can hear a halting voice saying amazing things.

The expansion begins in the ear as a new rhythm, a sound the poet has never heard before, but the transport he feels makes him know a new birth in the self is starting. Everything is beginning again!

THE YALE REVIEW, 1968

William Stafford and
Frederick Morgan

THE SHOCKS OF NORMALITY

The shocks of normality. Of healthiness. To be an ordinary man today. To be alive now, to spring awake in the night, what a lucky coincidence! It is the great reward, the greatest privilege of all:

> Sometimes we wake
> in the night: the millions better than we
> who had to crawl away! We borrow their
> breath, and the breath of the numberless
> who never were born.

In William Stafford's poems, the shocks of steadiness, the great stillnesses of his quiet, reserved voice—innocently surprised at its own depths of silence—are just one step, one line of verse, one breath away from registering the whole earth's shudder as our own:

> When the earth doesn't shake, when the sky
> is still, we feel something under the earth:
> a shock of steadiness. When the storm is gone,
> when the air passes, we feel our own
> shudder—the terror of having such a great
> friend, undeserved.

One of the rich, unexpected rewards of Stafford's maturity was the discovery that the many years of cultivating a bare, plain idiom capable of the widest range of expressiveness in the lowest registers of the quiet tones of language—the low-pitched key of our human voice (consider the narrow range of the bass viol, but the unearthly overtones sung by the instrument in the hands of a virtuoso performer!)—have produced a medium in which his own great calm would be a fit conductor for violent hidden movements of the earth, quaking in concert with deep temblors of the human spirit. Stafford celebrates the common bonds—the mediating site—between the earth and the single frail human vessel, astonished to find that any one of us in depths of "our stillness" can *contain* such magnitude of subterra-

Someday, Maybe, by William Stafford. (Harper & Row, 1973.)
A Book of Change, by Frederick Morgan. (Scribner's, 1972.)

nean currents:

> We know the motions of this great friend,
> all resolved into one move, our stillness.

Stafford is inundated with the ecstasy of beautiful surging commu-
nion with the land, and he is so stubbornly committed to thinking
himself an average simple person, his experience ordinary and shared
by everyone, by anyone else—any reader, certainly—why, he peti-
tions, isn't each one of us this very moment out running on the hills of
night, of day, to become swept up into this love affair with our great
benefactor, this marriage to our most faithful patron:

> Why is no one on the hills where they
> graze, the sun and the stars, no one
> clamoring north, running as we would
> run to belong to the earth. We come, we
> celebrate with our breath, we join on the curve
> of our street, never lost, the surge of the land
> all around us that always is ours,
> the beginning of the world and the end.

Stafford's voice is so quiet, so low-keyed, that his taciturnity may be
mistaken for frailness, timidity; his humble cries for self-diminish-
ment, or self-depreciation. Yet he makes the highest possible claims
for his humanity and his art. He is a man who knows how to stand
utterly alone and let the heart of the world shudder through him.
In the most intimate communion between one soul and the earth,
there is no friend, no companion, no beloved who can follow or
accompany this pilgrim, *"Oh friends, where can one find a partner/for the
long dance over the fields?"* That path is immitigably a lonely one (this is
his poem "So Long" in the earlier volume *Allegiances*):

> At least at night, a streetlight
> is better than a star.
> And better good shoes on a
> long walk, than a good friend.
>
> Often in winter with my old
> cap I slip away into the gloom
> like a happy fish, at home
> with all I touch, at the level of love.
>
> No one can surface till far,
> far on, and all that we'll have
> to love may be what's near
> in the cold, even then.

This poem is aimed at the unpeopled zones of the planet. There is an
arctic chill lining the verses. In this book, as in the others before it,

Stafford is of two minds: a loving, generous, outgoing brother to all human fellows, dear ones and strangers alike—not accidentally, he addresses remarks in his poems to *friend,* or *stranger,* by turns; or a militiaman of the wilds, a guerrilla woodsman constantly in training to *provide, provide* for a foreseen era of extreme shortages of supplies, an age of severe poverty and drought (guess how soon, reader). On one wavelength, all the saying favors a life of giving and belonging to the human community. On the other, he would give himself up irrevocably to the wilderness:

> At caves in the desert, close
> to rocks, I wait. I live
> by grace of shadows. In moonlight
> I hear a room open behind me.
>
> At the last when you come
> I am a track in the dust.

Stafford's enduring resources of human warmth and personal intimacy are revealed in the short masterful poem, "Father and Son":

> No sound—a spell—on, on out
> where the wind went, our kite sent back
> its thrill along the string that
> sagged but sang and said, "I'm here!
> I'm here!"—till broke somewhere,
> gone years ago, but sailed forever clear
> of earth. I hold—whatever tugs
> the other end—I hold that string.

The kite metaphor skillfully mediates between the worlds of paternity and authorship. In so few lines, aptly low-keyed, undertoned, Stafford merges the two aesthetics—the siring of poems, of sons—and demonstrates with effortless grace and agility the stark interwovenness of his vision. The trick is to keep holding the string years and years after it breaks, and to keep feeling the infinitesimally faint—but invaluable—tugs from the lost kite of fatherhood through the feeble, paltry conductor of thin air. To continue to traverse that gap across a near-vacuum in the thinning filial atmosphere is a feat of mental radar, thoughts and feelings so delicately balanced and held by so light a grasp, contact with the other being—father to son, writer to reader—is maintained by subtle echo-location.

A large unwritten chapter of the book of our "Origins" is locked in the racial memory of our hands—the key site, or locus, of our body's subconscious mind passed over by Jungian psychologists:

> So long ago that we weren't people then
> our hands came upon this warm place on a rock

> inside a high cave in the North, in the wilderness.
> No light was there, but "Homeland" glowed in that dark. . . .
> Now along walls, over quilts, by locks, our hands
> retell that story. Wherever touch finds hope again,
> these hands remember that other time: they are lost;
> they hunt for a place more precious than here.
> *Who will accept us wanderers? Where is our home?*

In many new poems, Stafford explores the frontiers of the hands' powers of remembering. A friend of mine, an expert craftsman of the short story, doggedly insists on the rule of thumb—not of tongue—"I never know what I think about anything until my hand tells me." Stafford is a poet who espouses that aesthetic. His art is lavishly extemporaneous and unpremeditated. He is poetry's zealot of improvisation. Moreover, with a childlike innocence, he profoundly trusts what his hand tells him is true:

> This is the hand I dipped in the Missouri
> above Council Bluffs and found the springs.
> All through the days of my life I escort
> this hand. . . .
>
> Summits in the Rockies received this diplomat.
> Brush that concealed the lost children yielded
> them to this hand. Even on the last morning
> when we all tremble and lose, I will reach
> carefully, eagerly through that rain, at the end—
>
> Toward whatever is there, with this loyal hand.

Stafford's lines of verse are felt to be a perfect extension of his hand's natural moves and gestures, as exhalations of our breath are inescapably tinged with our lungs' odor. The lines charmed and escorted across the page by the maestro's conducting hand are the intensest and most irreducible expression of our human reality. They are *the authentic*:

> The authentic is a line from one thing
> along to the next . . . It holds
> together something more than the world,
> this line. And we are your wavery
> efforts at following it. Are you coming?
> Good: now it is time.

To live well in the world, to write the poem that rings true, follow the hand's right leads, the hand's wisdom. Aristotle was a great thinker because he correctly assessed the hand's sensitive intelligence. Its genius inheres in its flexibility, the instinctive rightness of its moves, not in its power—athletic or military prowess, a lesson which his student, Alexander, failed to learn (from *Allegiances*):

> Aristotle was a little man with
> eyes like a lizard. . . .
>
> He said you should put your hand out
> at the time and place of need:
> strength matters little, he said,
> nor even speed.
>
> His pupil, a king's son, died
> at an early age. That Aristotle spoke of him
> it is impossible to find—the youth was
> notorious, a conqueror, a kid with a gang,
> but even this Aristotle didn't ever say.

William Stafford has continued, unwaveringly, for the last thirteen years, following the publication of his first volume of poetry at age forty-six, to develop and refine one of the most delicate supersensitive recording instruments in our poetry. He has been training himself to hear and feel his way back in touch with distant places, ages, epochs. Like some stones, there are men "too quiet for these days," and a part of themselves hangs back, lingers, dreams its way to other eras, universes. But it's not bodiless imagination, pure enchanted spirit, that negotiates the leaps across thousands of years, billions of miles. It is, rather, an act of the senses, a superkeen listening, a reaching of the hand via its magical powers of touching for immanent—but deeply buried—crypts of reality hidden in the rock, the walls of a cave:

TOUCHES

> Late, you can hear the stars. And beyond them
> some kind of quiet other than silence, a deepness
> the miles make, the way canyons
> hold their miles back: you are in the earth and
> it guides you; out where the sun comes
> it is the precious world.
> There are stones too quiet for these days,
> old ones that belong in the earlier mountains.
> You put a hand out in the dark of a cave and
> the wall waits for your fingers. Cold, that stone
> tells you all of the years that passed without knowing.
> You think of caves held in the earth, no mouth,
> no light. Down there the years have lost their way.
> Under your hand it all steadies,
> is the world under your hand.

It is the transcendent grace of the hand's gentlest touch, and of the listener's marvelously intense hearing, that achieves penetration into

spheres of reality the mind cannot enter. The hand's touch can re-
cover any lost world.

Touches. The shocks of a normal hand. In our homes and families,
by common daily routines, we connect with the spirit of all that lives
across the planet ("At the sink I start/ a faucet; water from far is/
immediate on my hand"), the whole world rescued and transmitted in
each natural human gesture, and these are the events most worth
publishing to a readership; the simple motions of our body's saying
them at home are the true miracles, the noteworthy headlines of each
day's life. The poem aspires to catch the exact uniquely marvelous
twist of each never-to-be-repeated human event of watching this bird
now, glimpsing the moon between buildings at a special new angle,
improvising a new story to a child at bedtime, seeing the light (". . .
any light. Oh—any light.") come on again in the child's eyes, or in his
late father's intricately remembered words. These occurrences, then,
are Stafford's alternative to what newsprint "an eighth of an inch thick"
offers as world news (from *Allegiances*):

> That one great window puts forth
> its own scene, the whole world
> alive in glass. In it a war happens,
> only an eighth of an inch thick.
> Some of our friends have leaped
> through, disappeared, become unknown
> voices and rumors of crowds.
>
> In our thick house, every evening
> I turn from that world,
> and room by room I walk, to
> enjoy space. At the sink I start
> a faucet; water from far is
> immediate on my hand. I open our
> door, to check where we live.
> In the yard I pray birds,
> wind, unscheduled grass,
> that they please help to make
> everything go deep again.

Stafford chronicles *his* global highlights in the form of lean verses,
messages offered to the world for minimal daily unction, so many
"small acts of honesty, to use like/ salt pills, one at a time, at need."
Stafford always localizes himself by starting from the small indigenous
happenstance whereby he feels solidly anchored and centered in his
person (from *Allegiances*):

> Like a stubborn tumbleweed I hold,
> hold where I live. . . .

> We ordinary beings can cling to the earth and love
> where we are, sturdy for common things.

If the poem always stays within hand's-reach of pedestrian daily events, it finds its life mainly in collecting the inner resonances. How quickly and adroitly Stafford can step back from the life of action, himself the tree abruptly engulfed in fog, given over completely to the inner storm of mirrorings and reverberations ("that far flood/ Inside"), without losing his grasp of the bare, plain, earthy quantities— mortal or inanimate particularities—that touched off the inner chain of correspondences (from *Allegiances*):

IN FOG

> In fog a tree steps back.
>
> Once gone, it joins those hordes
> blizzards rage for over tundra.
>
> With new respect I tell
> my dreams to grant all claims;
>
> Lavishly, my eyes close between
> what they saw and that far flood
>
> Inside: the universe that happens
> deep and steadily.

Stafford's calm, mild-mannered voice dances lightfootedly, the nimble steps half-masking the scrupulous rigor of his thought and toughness of his vision. Many readers fail to grasp how much concentrated force of mind—a shrewd, energetic intelligence—is mobilized to support his mild soft-spokenness, those lines that would "breathe a harmless breath." Stafford would make his lines imitate the effortless floating ease and drift of the falling snowflake ("what snowflake, even, may try/ today so calm a life,/ so mild a death?"). Words and phrases, as in a dance by Fred Astaire, swish and glide and float across the page—lightest footfalls, a delicate, thin, relaxed saying that approaches a condition of pure breath, all easefulness:

> This whole day is your gift:
> hold it and read a leaf at a
> time, never hurried, never waiting,
> Step, step, slide; then turn,
> dance on the calendar,
> reach out a hand, give lavish
> as anyone ever gave—all.

The lines imitate the smooth, easy gestures of a dancer, or those of any great musical performer whose instrument—violin, piano, cello,

his own body or voice—seems to vanish, to disappear, to melt away
into the serene flow of pure, entranced rhythm. There is a quality of
relaxed arbitrariness by which Stafford lazily coaxes—or coaches—
so many of his best lines and images out of the depths of his solitude,
such that the lines seem to lean backward, half-clinging still to the
lovely voiceless silence of his frequent late-night strolls. By a most
rigorous artifice, he establishes the fleetingly accidental human im-
pulse, the feeling of this moment, as *the* viable human occasion most
tractable for grafting into his art: he celebrates, above all, each acci-
dental next passing fancy, notion, hunch, guess, chance remark. He
must learn to be always on the alert, on his mental toes so to speak, to
select fertile items from the always available and swiftly unfolding
agendas of sensory and cerebral data that flicker upon the screen of
his rich imaginative life, and he proceeds with an unprecedented
good faith that the inexhaustible stockpile of such treasures of infor-
mation is readily accessible to the poetry-making process at any mo-
ment of our waking lives, and it will be fully replenished every next
moment. Luck is a helpful catalyst which we can train ourselves—
always on the run, in the midst of flow—to seize upon as an indispens-
able ally to creation, and some moments are inherently more propi-
tious to the creative eye than others.

We are persuaded by the sheer weight of swiftly mounting evi-
dence, as we move from poem to poem, that William Stafford's day-
to-day life is perennially aglow with constellations of tiny momentous
events, meetings, exchanges, transferrals of mystical energies between
Stafford and the world. We witness in him a chosen person whom the
world makes thousands of careful moves daily to reward:

> Oh, I thought, how hard the world has tried
> with its wind, its miles, its blundering
> stumbling days, again and again, to find my hand.

To receive the many gifts, he need only restore in himself daily the
condition of availability and receptiveness.

In the Staffordian psychic Elysium, it appears that anyone who
simply cultivates the spirit of lowliness, one who trains daily the fac-
ulty of bowing down before the world's delicate beauties ("'A great
event is coming, bow down.'/ And I, always looking for something
anyway,/ always bow down"), enhances the world's power to bestow
them. Stafford is not, as might appear to some, offering himself as a
candidate for sainthood; speaking for the common chosenness in us
all, he locates and canonizes a site in himself that is shared by all of
common humanity, and perhaps this is why William Stafford, to a
keener pitch than any other American contemporary, raises in his

voice the accents of a statesman's speech. He would re-endow our poetry with a Frostian vernacular, a level directness of delivery of sufficient plainness to win back to the reading of verse a wide readership of unsophisticated caring humans. He is a civic manager legislating urban renewals of the heart. Stafford is our poetry's ambassador to the provinces.

On nearly every page of Frederick Morgan's *Book of Change*, I feel that I come into touch with a lively, warm human being through the poetry. Though in some sections of this ambitious and expansive poetic sequence the pressure of human feeling overtakes the formal structuring of lines and stanzas, how refreshing it is to read a premiere volume in which the sheer quantity of erupting life overwhelms the literary boundaries, at times, after so many recent first books of verse in which the self-conscious stylistic mannerisms of this or that school squelch the sense of life.

Morgan, who, as founding editor of *The Hudson Review*, has been regarded for many years by William Stafford, A. R. Ammons, and other central poets of our day as being a profoundly influential guiding mentor to contemporaries, has shifted the focus of much of that energetic brilliance—in mid-career—from the editorial platform to the swift unfolding of a full-fledged mature poetics of his own. Though for some twenty-odd years Morgan had written, intermittently, successful—if undistinguished—original verse and some passable translations, his poetic art has taken a breathtakingly sudden upswing in the last few years, and he leaps into prominence in this first collection as an important writer in the current scene. Perhaps following the lead of the senior poet Stafford in the richly human articulateness and candor of his style, Morgan's zest and unguarded forthrightness of delivery insure the distinctiveness of his voice and measure. He appears to have assimilated an impressive blend of influences and orthodoxies without strain: so many ideas and presences, epiphanies and personages and beings—demonic, angelic, and mortal—are falling all over each other in the struggle to be born, any derivative elements of Morgan's style are burned away as he amplifies his medium and stretches the skin of the work to contain so much eruption of newly awakened life:

> At this fresh dawn in the middle of my life—
> [Oh Lord] . . . steady my steps along the road,
> help me abate my rage and fretfulness,
> this energy of yours, help me control it!
> Strong and in order let the good words sound.

Morgan's outburst of creativity—which appears to have taken its author by surprise with the unforeseen violence of a seizure or a visitation—was evidently prompted by the sudden tragic death of his son John, followed mercifully by the birth of the revitalizing love relation with Paula, Morgan's present wife:

> Dear son, you died three years ago today.
> I died too, and have risen from the dead
> and take you with me in my blood and bones
> through a new life.—Poor boy, what was there left?
> Your corpse, part-decomposed when it was found,
> sent home for burial; your clothing, books,
> letters, snapshots—a suitcaseful shipped home.
> Sad remnants, John. . . .

In "The Smile," as in a number of the other best love poems to Paula, Morgan achieves a rare discipline, the power to step back far enough into oneself—during moments of profound intimacy—to pass through the self and move beyond into a condition of spirit in which even the beloved may be witnessed purely, freshly, and accurately. At such moments, a supernatural radiance lifts the usual film of haziness from the lover's eyes, and all is seen with a final clarity—even those humans closest to us—such as we suppose may be afforded only to ghosts returning from the dead. Our eyes seem to pass through themselves into another life, beyond sight into a second seeing:

> Your hands were deft. Your face, intent
> above that work you do so well,
> took on a gentle, abstract smile.
> . . . the true beauty, grace of one
> at home with her desires and powers.
> I treasure it, and always shall,
> that smile of yours above the flowers.

His abstracted vision is half human, half trans-human, modeled after the smile described. Second sight has sprung up within love, but passes beyond into a solitary and lonely life of its own. The poet has witnessed this capacity for purely independent self-possession in the beloved, of which her smile is both manifestation and emblem. The poem had begun by ridiculing Byron's betrayal of his true affections in poetry by a heavy-handed submission to convention. Dante's adoration of Beatrice is the closest prototype in literature for the exalted love portrayed, but for all Morgan's struggle to escape the falsities of convention, he establishes a more subtle artifice in which the relation between lines of verse and human moments they mirror approach photographic realism. However, his warring against the inbred artificialities of the medium infuses most of his poetry with the quality of utmost ingenuousness.

Morgan's plain, lucid style—all openness and transparency—

endues the infrequent occasions of modest stylistic glamor with surprising power and resonance. His relaxed highlighting is always suavely compatible with the prevailing forthrightness of voice, virtues of a kind that the density and compression of a grand style could never support:

> In last extremities of pain and fear
> when you are all alone with nothingness
> and clench your teeth on it and taste despair,
> if you remember this is each man's fate
> and God's fate, too, as far as we are he,
> and let your inner substance rest on it
> and merge with it as with a summer sea—
> then comes the Change. You have become the pain
> and all at once attained the further shore.
>
> (from "Pain Poems")

How much power he gets from the inescapable hard-earned honesty of these plain findings—the language not invented, adorned, reveled in muscularly, but simply received and guilelessly transmitted to the reader. His many poetic forms, like his style, approach the purity of a natural expressive instrument superbly well synchronized with the widely varied dimensions of his mind and art.

Though Morgan has a strong predilection for condensed nuggets of wisdom—the axiom, the adage, the proverb—his comic spirit saves him from any leanings toward pedagogy:

> The wise old man said, "He's a fool
> who tries to live his life by rule,
> but if you think to get to heaven
> by rules, I'll gladly give you seven.
>
> First, *be healthy*: because, you know,
> your body's you, it's where you grow
> and meet the real world, opening.
> Don't treat it like a foreign thing. . . ."

This poem exhibits a cunning of self-parody. Much of the thematic content of the book is presented in the form of refined epigrammatic thought-capsules, but Morgan always escapes self-conscious didacticism, since his philosophic baggage is lightly held. His voice has, unfailingly, the authentic ring of a man thinking on his feet, soliloquizing in the heat of passion, or conducting a sensual wrestling bout with his god, displaying all the tactile intimacy of Donne's *Holy Sonnets*:

> Letting go into God is almost physical . . .
> like letting your body slide into a quarry pool
> deep in the woods. It's summertime—hot sun, green trees—

but the water is dark and chill, and there is no one watching.
You slip from the edge—a shock of cold—and then you're free!
Indeed, if you died that instant, free for ever
because you've given your self. . . . But the heart stops at last.
The truth is in the shock and the surrender.

Throughout *A Book of Change* Morgan's late-blooming youthful exuberance, surging as if for the first time in a man of fifty, combines freshness with reserve, lighthearted optimism with an earned austerity of command in drawing upon his prodigious reservoir of neglected intellectual resources: he both achieves an attractive synthesis of wisdom of the ages—extracted from classical works of theology, philosophy, and mythology—and produces a full-scale self-portrait. But the work is not diaristic, after the fashion of *Notebook* or *The Dream Songs*, though the four-part structure is punctuated with recurring confessional motifs. The book's overall design unfolds by such a natural rhythm of disclosure of key moments and upheavals, selected from the flux of ongoing human experience, that the semi-narrative episodic form wears the guise of conventional autobiography. But the thin veneer of chronological narration masks a consistent grasp of inner spiritual cycles which truly dominate the vision, and which are skillfully reinforced by the internal arrangement of poems within each of the four sections.

The slow, irreversible growth of a second mental life—the fruition of a totally new sensibility—hiddenly evolving within the dried-out husk of a middle-aged man's former collapsed identity is the remarkable adventure recounted in *A Book of Change*. If the book's formal design seems scattered, from time to time, its level of craft and style of execution uneven, with each re-reading of the work one is inescapably struck by the cumulative power of a sustained vision of human regeneration. This is a book of awesome metamorphosis.

Derek Walcott and Michael S. Harper

THE MUSE OF HISTORY

Miasma, acedia, the enervations of damp,
as the teeth of the mould gnaw, greening the carious stump
of the beaten, corrugated silver of the marsh light,
where the red heron hides, without a secret...
where the pirogue foundered with its caved-in stomach
(a hulk, trying hard to look like
a paleolithic, half-gnawed memory of pre-history)...
let the historian go mad there
from thirst. Slowly the water rat takes up its reed pen
and scribbles. Leisurely, the egret
on the mud tablet stamps its hieroglyph.

The explorer stumbles out of the bush crying out for myth.
The tired slave vomits his past....
the mummified odour of onions,
spikenard, and old Pharaohs peeling like onionskin
to the archaeologist's finger—all that
is the muse of history. Potsherds,
and the crusted amphora of cutthroats....
                                       The astigmatic geologist
stoops, with the crouch of the heron,
deciphering—not a sign.
All of the epics are blown away with the leaves,
blown with the careful calculations on brown paper;
these were the only epics, the leaves.

—Derek Walcott

In St. Lucia, B.W.I., all secrets of the past are burrowing deeper and deeper under "miasma, acedia, the enervations" of the slow lassitude of the West Indian temperament and metabolism, languishing beneath layers and layers of mold for want of the one true artist-historiographer to discover and interpret the myth of history. To found the myth of history is an act of creative discovery, a courting of the muse; it is, above all, an act of bravery, austere honesty, and searching imagination. The historian, the archeologist, the geologist—

Another Life, by Derek Walcott. (Farrar, Straus & Giroux, 1973.)

Debridement, by Michael S. Harper. (Doubleday, 1973.)

all are ill equipped to deliver the myth of the life of past eras, of lost epochs.

Two outstanding new books by black poets immediately advance their authors to the front ranks of poets writing in English today, and challenge afresh the misnomer "Black Poetry," given such widespread currency by the proliferating institution of Black Studies programs in the universities and by chief spokesmen for the black cultural establishment alike. Since both of these volumes boldly defy the rigid limits ordinarily ascribed to the genre, perhaps they will help us to dislodge not only the name of the so-called Black Poets School, but our specious fixed ideas of the black man's potential scope of vision in the poetry of our language as well. The prevailing trend in poetry criticism is to greet the better work of black poets either with polite silence or, worse, with deadening overpraise, an undiscriminating rave notice that invariably demeans the book under review by suggesting, patronizingly, that though the work is the best of its kind, critical allowances—of an order equivalent to a handicap for second-class entrants in a golf tournament—are automatically extended to black artists.

Luckily for our apprehension of contemporary poetry's range of vitality, neither Derek Walcott's *Another Life* nor Michael Harper's *Debridement* can be conveniently pigeonholed. These are fourth—and best—volumes by both authors. Walcott's reputation in this country has grown slowly, but steadily, since the appearance here of his *Selected Poems* in 1963. He is the one distinguished poet-playwright of the West Indies to have acquired, early on, an assured niche in the mainstream of contemporary poetry. Harper, a younger poet in an earlier stage of development, who divided his childhood between Brooklyn and Los Angeles, has produced work of very high quality at the rate of one book per year since 1970. Both poets, noted for a musical richness and density of style in the short, compact lyric, have suddenly exploded their technical resources and extended their range by venturing into the broader landscape of the imagination of history. Walcott's book-length autobiographical narrative is the issue of seven years' labor. Harper's *Debridement* is a trio of poetic sequences, each exploring the life of a key figure in the black man's valiant struggle to achieve an American identity, and representing three different eras in United States history: John Brown, Richard Wright, and "John Henry Louis," a persona for the black Congressional Medal of Honor winner who was murdered in Detroit.

Both Walcott and Harper, recognizing that the crucial breach in the cultural identity of the black Westerner dates back to the epoch of total blackout of consciousness (the many decades of slavery with their legacy of namelessness: racial and cultural amnesia), set about to fashion a poetic instrument with the efficacy to fill the void of the historical interregnum. Both poets, writing in an alien, bartered language and lacking a viable tradition in poetry of their race to build upon, sought mentors in early career from the sister arts. Harper, in his first volume, *Dear John, Dear Coltrane,* pledging himself in spiritual apostleship to the great jazz master, modeled his rhythms and verse measure after Coltrane's music. His debt to the music was evidently far more pertinent to the annealing—a tempering and toughening—of his own distinctive line and meters than to any literary influences. Walcott struggled for many years of failure as a seascape painter in the company of his gifted friend Gregorias, a painter of impulsive genius, his first master in the arts; together, they paid homage to Saints Vincent (Van Gogh) and Paul (Gauguin). Despite the collapse of his abortive career in pictorial art, he had served his apprenticeship and made inestimable headway in exploring the artistic sensibility that would support his poetry. Later, he would revivify in his poems the early credo to which he and Gregorias swore their vows: they would transmit into paint or words the natural lineaments of their native place, the Island of St. Lucia:

> But drunkenly, or secretly, we swore,
> disciples of that astigmatic saint,
> that we would never leave the island
> until we had put down, in paint, in words,
> as palmists learn the network of a hand,
> all of its sunken, leaf-choked ravines,
> every neglected, self-pitying inlet
> muttering in brackish dialect, the ropes of mangroves
> from which old soldier crabs slipped
> surrendering to slush.

Subsequently, this creed was appropriated into Walcott's mature poetics as a ritual first step in the process of recovering the lost history of the native peoples, and forging a poetic craft informed by history and the vitality of its correlative mythos. Already, in these fledgling years, he had unknowingly become conscripted in the service of the muse of history, "that astigmatic saint," whose vision is always impaired, doubled, until the artist unlocks the hidden second life— *another life*—sealed within the memory of events and unblurs her sight.

The youthful Walcott and Gregorias saw themselves as pioneers undertaking, for the first time, the task of naming the forms of life in their habitat:

> For no one had yet written of this landscape
> that it was possible, though there were sounds
> given to its varieties of wood;
>
> the *bois-canot* responded to its echo,
> when the axe spoke, weeds ran up to the knee
> like bastard children, hiding in their names,
>
> whole generations died, unchristened,
> growths hidden in green darkness, forests
> of history thickening with amnesia . . .

The birth of Walcott's art, then, may be traced to his terrible foreboding that, like the many generations of black slaves—his forefathers—who vanished into a void of namelessness, the generations of native flora, too, would fall into extinction with no record, no history, no trace of a past for lack of a language—in words or paint—to christen them and preserve their memory. The modest goals outlined here barely hint at the immense ambitiousness of Walcott's full-scale undertaking, the high claims he would make for his art in the course of this impressive work. The islands of the West Indies were originally populated by tribes of Arawak Indians, and, later, legions of blacks imported from Africa: both cultures, strains of a common stock, were hopelessly cut off from each other by "the estranging sea." To re-envision the events of black history, Walcott is faced with the perplexity of trying to sort out myths and traditions spread out over a scattered island chain:

> There was a life older than geography,
> as the leaves of edible roots opened their pages
> at the child's last lesson, Africa, heart-shaped,
>
> and the lost Arawak hieroglyphs and signs
> were razed from slates by sponges of the rain,
> their symbols mixed with lichen,
>
> the archipelago like a broken root,
> divided among tribes, while trees and men
> laboured assiduously, silently to become
> whatever their given sounds resembled,
> ironwood, logwood-heart, golden apples, cedars . . .

His early vow, a spiritual pact with the land, to render into words the beauties of the natural habitat of a single island would later grow into a quest for cultural solidarity—a unified identity—for all of the islands, viewing the voluminously widespread Indies as a single interconnected archipelago, an aspiration that, not incidentally, parallels the thrust in recent years by many of the separate island governments to achieve political sovereignty and independence from the colonial

empire state—England, France, the Netherlands—and to seek a fed-
eration of liberated island republics.

Gregorias had an initial advantage over his friend, since the paint-
er's medium was more natural and direct. The colors and pigments
posed less difficulty than the finding of a language for the poet, whose
medium was pervasively tainted and impure, impossibly overladen
with the baggage of English literature, the dialectic and oratory of
political diplomacy, the stuffy grammarianism of the British public-
school system with its attendant colonial snobbishness and condescen-
sion to blacks. All of this freight stuck to the language in his ear, and
before he could purge the alien elements from his medium, before
"the tired slave vomited his past" in Walcott's psyche, he had to submit
himself to many years of indentured service to the smutched instru-
ment of the white culture's hand-me-down mother tongue. He and
the painter shared a common objective, to achieve a wholly indige-
nous Carib-black's art, but the poet would have to arrive at the goal
obliquely.

In the first of four sections of this autobiographical work, "The
Divided Child," he returns to the abandoned house of his childhood
in search of "Maman"—his dead mother, and he discovers her essence
at last in the touched edges of objects she always carefully arranged in
their home:

> Finger each object, lift it
> from its place, and it screams again
> to be put down
> in its ring of dust, like the marriage finger
> frantic without its ring;
> I can no more move you from your true alignment,
> mother, than we can move objects in paintings.
>
> Your house sang softly of balance,
> of the rightness of placed things.

He must touch the household utensils, the knickknacks, take them up
in his hands again and again since they are deeply tinged with his
mother's being, her presence. The magic vessels "assess us," and se-
cretly mediate between us in our homes and families, and if our
"radiance of sharing extends to the simplest objects,/ to a favourite
hammer, a paintbrush, a toothless,/ gum-sunken old shoe," they, too,
in their turn, extend us, and the touch of ourselves clings to them long
after we have left them behind. The sacred objects imbued with us-
as-we-were embalm and preserve our lost ambrosias, our scents of
self: they are the secret crypts and vaults of memory, both in the
private life—the intimacy of family and friendship, and in the public
life—the lineage of race and community. The key he discovered in

search of "Maman" finds its wider application, then, in his search for
the lost memory of his race. The lineaments of racial memory may
best be traced, heritage and authentic myth reconstructed, by con-
necting with the simple objects, natural or man-made, that shared the
life-space of the earlier peoples. They embody the spirits of the dead.
This passage in Section One prefigures the radiant climactic passage
of Section Four, celebrating the recovery of lost identities, personal
and communal: a litany of holies addressed to Walcott's small son—all
illuminations—of the simple elements of setting that surround the
Rampanalgas River:

> I was eighteen then, now I am forty-one,
> I have had a serpent for companion,
> I was a heart full of knives,
> but, my son, my sun,
>
> holy is Rampanalgas and its high-circling hawks,
> holy are the rusted, tortured, rust-caked, blind almond trees,
> your great-grandfather's, and your father's torturing limbs,
> holy the small, almond-leaf-shadowed bridge
> by the small red shop, where everything smells of salt,
> and holiest the break of the blue sea below the trees,
> and the rock that takes blows on its back
> and is more rock,
> and the tireless hoarse anger of the waters
> by which I can walk calm, a renewed, exhausted man,
> balanced at its edge by the weight of two dear daughters.

Via the familiar landmarks of his own childhood—hawks, trees, old
bridge, aging shops, and finally rock and sea—he is inundated with a
vision of history, hidden and secretly waiting in the river and the
objects adjacent to it. All meanings of the past, buried with a people
who kept few written records, if any, of the crises and trials of identity
as they crossed the sea and plunged deeper into the anonymity of
slavery, all salvageable history is to be found in the permanent endur-
ing objects—physical structures or natural phenomena—of the locale.
To rescue that history, to come into possession of its surviving trea-
sury of myths, is to get sensitively into touch with these living things; if
he can charm them, invite them into the music of the poem, translate
them into a language and, above all, release the song of their names,
they will breathe their wisdom into his pages, effortlessly.

No other West Indian poet, to date, approaching Walcott's stature,
has succeeded in nourishing a consistently developed art under the
inhospitable conditions and hostile social climate of the island culture.
Which was the more insuperable obstacle to the artist's enterprise, a
reader is prompted to speculate: the despotism of the British ruling

class and their collaborating native flunky ministers of state; or the monolithic indifference of the poet's fellow countrymen, who refused to be shaken out of their stereotypic image of the artist as one of society's derelicts, who ought properly to die young, his early promise unfulfilled, his body to be found in the slum gutter? There are moments in the work in which the contempt which Walcott evidently feels for his own countrymen, "a people with no moral centre," appears to become an obstruction to his mission. In a number of passages toward the end of the book, the unrelieved stridency of his anger devalues the quality of the writing, his tirades lacking resonance or evocative overtones. This vituperative tendency culminates in the nightmarish imagery of Chapter 19, in which he consigns his enemies to perpetual suffering in an updated version of one circle in Dante's *Inferno*:

> ... I enclose in this circle of hell,
> in the stench of their own sulphur of self-hatred,
> in the steaming, scabrous rocks of Soufrière,
> in the boiling, pustular volcanoes of the South,
> all o' dem big boys, so, dem ministers,
> ministers of culture, ministers of development,
> the green blacks, and their old toms...

The chapter is a shattering indictment, but the overt analogy to Dante's masterwork seems pretentious and overtaxes the poetry. The poet arouses expectations in the reader far beyond the rewards that the modest dimensions of the images and pictures in this section can possibly deliver. The diffuseness of materials works to disadvantage, in contrast with Dante's relentless compactness and his pictorial genius; also, Walcott's moralizing tone suggests a pomposity in the author, who appears to be brandishing his credentials in a masquerade of self-importance, as if the linkage to Dante will automatically invest his scene with an elevation, a dignity, and a relevance that is not forthcoming from his poetic resources themselves. Characteristically, the strength of the passage inheres in those lines which draw on the indigenous experience. Walcott is at his best when he exercises novelistic skill in presenting his gallery of West Indian characters, an inexhaustible storehouse of types and classes. The physical details selected in his adroit portraits add up the historical indictment and sociological exegesis with amazing economy. When he lets the journalist-insider's eye speak out directly, he irresistibly persuades the reader. But his baggage of literary allusions and classical references are often stultifying, and they dissipate the driving primal force and energy of his firsthand experience.

For example, the vignette on the wealthy merchant Manoir, a former peasant turned "liquor baron," is perhaps the best of many fine compact story-capsules fitted into the matrix of the predominantly chronological narrative. The story of Manoir's death is a brilliant fable, a moral exemplum with an allegorical impact akin to the psychology of the medieval morality play. Walcott's gift for theatric characterization, an expertise acquired in his very substantial work in the drama, shows to best advantage in these capsule portraits. Whatever his debt here to English tradition, the mode is wedded with such dexterity to his West Indian subject that he both reanimates a dying form and exhibits a firmer grip on the crucial raw materials of his common humanity than is in evidence in most parts of the poem. Conversely, the interlude in the mode of Dante's cantos recoils upon itself, due to the striking contrast with the austerer majesty of the model. The superior style of the Manoir cameo portrait can be illustrated by the close-up of Manoir's hands:

> His hands still smelled of fish, of his beginnings,
> hands that he'd ringed with gold, to hide their smell,
> sometimes he'd hold them out,
> puckered with lotions, powdered, to his wife,
> a peasant's hands, a butcher's,
> their acrid odour of saltfish and lard.

The two identities in Manoir's divided psyche are well dramatized here. His tragedy derives from the way his assumed identity, which governs his lifestyle, obliterates the nobler identity that is permanently stamped on—etched into—his body. Manoir's hands remember the whole man he was. The portrait symbolically reiterates Walcott's central thesis in this book: the muse of history resides invisibly in the body's memory: the human's body, land's body, sea's body, domestic implement's body. Taken together, they are memory's body. There is no unbodied memory. To survive, a race's, or culture's, history and myth must be bodied in art—words, paint, stone.

A final metaphor, near the end of the book, most perfectly gives body to Walcott's vision of his own destiny:

> I wanted to grow white-haired
> as the wave, with a wrinkled
>
> brown rock's face, salted,
> seamed, an old poet,
> facing the wind
>
> and nothing, which is,
> the loud world in his mind.

Balancing at the sea's edge, half-white half-brown, like wave-foam splashing over rock, he would embody and merge the two moieties that are warring in his soul: the inner rock of his African blood, of race; the outer wash of Western culture, art, language.

Derek Walcott emerges in this book-length poem as one of the handful of brilliant historic mythologists of our day, though he is, as yet, a far less accomplished technician than Robert Lowell, who is surely unsurpassed in his genius for imagining the mythos of our historical moment. For many years, Walcott was haunted with intimations of guilt in having betrayed his best friends, his first love, and the very colors and contours of his native land—he felt trapped and somehow victimized by his unstoppable gift for transforming memory into metaphor. Until recently, he imperfectly understood the long-term virtues and rewards of his extraordinary power to crystallize personal memory and public history into myths which carry an astonishing ring of truth in the dense, rich music of their utterance. He has yet to learn to assimilate into a recognizable stylistic blend his synthesis of the spectacular medley of styles and stylizations, manners and mannerisms, vernaculars and dialects, mystiques and mystifications that he has drawn from the tradition of English poetry, the vocabularies of cinquecento Italian art, modern impressionist painting, and West Indian Gothic architecture, as well as the idiomatic "calypso" English of his fellow countrymen. I anticipate his next book, in which it is to be hoped that his conflicting "disciplines might/ by painful accretion cohere/ and finally ignite" in a fully controlled distinctive voice, and he will become immeasurably more adept at his enterprise, much as the present volume has surpassed his previous work, both in breadth of perspective and in magnitude of human vision.

Michael Harper finds his medium and mouthpiece in John Brown, that rare, Ibsenesque hero in the chronicles of history who can stand utterly alone, and whose consciousness will not be compromised or defined by any partisanship outside the inner dictates of his blazing moral passion. When we find him at the end of his career, his resources depleted, his family in jeopardy, there is not a trace of indulgence in the tepid imagination of martyrdom, or self-pity; he continues to take inventory of his accounts in the accustomed plain bare style—the items of bankrupt supplies, the items of peak spiritual capacity, listed side by side with the same dry efficiency:

> I am without horses, holsters,
> wagons, tents, saddles, bridles,
> spurs, camp utensils, blankets,
> intrenching tools, knapsacks,

> spades, shovels, mattocks, crowbars,
> no ammunition, no money
> for freight or travel:
> I have left my family poorly:
> *I will give my life for a slave*
> *with a gun my secret passage.*

Harper's language in this book is amazingly free of emotive words, his style approaching a tone of dispassionate quietude, in jarring contrast with the intensity of his subjects. He appears to have adopted the same code for dealing with both literary tradition and black American history: learn from the past, but most lessons are formulas for not repeating past mistakes. The words must be the irreducible few cues, signals, cries, instant messages, dead-center bull's-eye exchanges between men, "rifle ball words/ on rifle ball tongue." The language of sentimentality and melodrama has been stripped from Harper's finely attuned medium, but his deadpan style is deceptive; when it most wears the guise of expressionless immobility, just under the chilled surface a cunning of insurgency lurks to spring:

> We made our own "constructive
> treason" at "Dutch Henry" settlement
> in the Swamp of the Swan:
> death by broadswords.
> I took my instruments
> into their camp . . .
> mistook-mapmaker for slavery:
> Owen, Frederick, Salmon, Oliver:
> chain carriers, axman, marker.
> One Georgian said:
> "them damned Browns over there,
> we're going to whip, drive out,
> or kill, any way to
> *get shut* of them, by God"
> while I made entries
> in my surveyor's book
> to strike the blow.

Much as John Brown posed as a surveyor, his tools weapons in disguise, the crisp, spare units of Harper's verse imitate the form of maps, itineraries, blueprints, charts; their contents—plans, messages, orders, directions. All is presented with the spare economy of data, itemizations, agendas. A day's agenda becomes a year's, a movement's ("The Great Black Way"), a generation's, a race's agendas. The author's passions, like his protagonist's, are ordered, shaped, controlled by intelligence; rage, or pain, transfigured by vision. Emotions, as by a

woodsman's discipline, are reduced to lean physical details. The poem
unfolds with the clean, unwavery succinctness of a ship's navigator's
recording logs, as Brown plans the next steps of rebellion, gauged to
match the storms in the quick-changing racial weather.

Harper admires the work of Richard Wright, but with strong reser-
vations about his "uneven wattage." He loves Wright's "soulful heart,"
but inveighs against his inadvertently subscribing to romantic
stereotypes of black sex and black violence, myths which act as a
cornerstone still in white America's most prevalent image of the black
man's identity:

> That parable of black man, white woman,
> the man's penis slung to his shin,
> erect, foaming in that woman's womb,
> the ambivalent female with smirk-shriek,
> daylights of coitus stuck together,
> through the nights the razored solution;
> that the black man is nature,
> the woman, on her drilled pedestal, divine,
> the man with razor an artisan
> in symmetry steel and sharp blades—
> let him melt into his vat of precious metal,
> let the female wipe her face of sperm,
> let the black man's penis shrink to normal
> service, let the posse eat their whips instead.

While Harper gives Wright his due both as a man and artist, he im-
pugns him for misrepresenting black history as "hallucination"; his
vision contains too much hysteria, not enough clear-sightedness. The
novel in English, Harper seems to suggest, is *ipso facto* an unfit medium
for the black artist today. Due to deep-rooted propensities bred into
the mode, even in the hands of a substantial writer like Richard Wright,
both the form and the novelistic language automatically fall prey to
formulas that betray the black man, trap him into misreadings of his
history. The black novel is handicapped by a thrust—largely uncon-
trollable—to appropriate into its vision images and psychologies,
myths and stereotypes, that are current in the cinema and popular
newspapers. Even a superior black novelist may unwittingly set back
by many years the black man's struggle to discover the accurate facts
and undistorted raw materials of his usable past, the core of authentic
history that is needed as a scaffolding to his art. Harper's vision is,
above all, a moral passion because the instrument seems relatively free
from innate bonds to conform to idols of the marketplace.

"Debridement," the third and final poem, moves into the present
historical moment. It recounts the death of one "John Henry Louis,"

a Congressional Medal of Honor winner who was paraded as a war
hero by the government and business corporations in Detroit for as
long as he was willing to debase himself by making a sales pitch to
prospective black army recruits. After he resigned from the tour in
disgust, the government abandoned him; subsequently, he was shot
down in the street by a white shopkeeper who owed the black man
money, and claimed that he tried to burglarize his store.

In many sections of "Debridement," Harper experiments with a
unique poetic language. In "Operation Harvest Moon," the key seg-
ment of the sequence, he employs a "found" poetry, a pure cross-
section of language chosen from the vocabularies of emergency mili-
tary surgery and the hospital operating room. At first reading, this
unit creates the illusion of merely presenting data from the medical
chart and log of an operation, set up arbitrarily in the form of Harper's
typical spare, short lines of verse. He is adamant in his refusal to make
explicit comment in the body of the poem, steadfast in his assertion
that the raw data will speak for themselves; he need merely exhibit
them, cleanly and luminously:

> Venous pressure: 8; lumbar
> musculature, lower spinal column
> pulverized; ligate blood vessels,
> right forearm; trim meat, bone ends;
> tourniquet above fracture, left arm;
> urine negative: 4 hours; pressure
> unstable; remove shrapnel flecks.

When you compound the language of the military with that of
modern surgery, the descriptions of massive human casualties sound
as inert, lifeless, and mechanical as the instruction kit for assembling a
model rocket ship. The abiding sting of this poetry in the reader's ear
is the implication that the dehumanizing vocabularies of the war
bureaucracy will be fatal to us if the war wounds are not.

In "Debridement," Harper alternates short prose sections in italics
with the verse units. The poem reads somewhat like a film in the
mode of *Citizen Kane*: frequent bulletins of prose newsreel are played
off against the longer verse passages which re-create the crises of
human personality and character that are hidden behind the public
data and public scenes. The form creates a dialogue, or counterpoint-
ing, of the two voices: history and its metaphor. The form separates
and clearly delineates the two major dimensions in Harper's long,
semi-documentary genre. This is a brilliantly appropriate strategy,
since the poem's essential subject is dramatized as much by the work's
structure as by its content. In fact, a major aspect of the subject is an

investigation into the process whereby crucial human events in the public sphere are misinterpreted and distorted by social critics who fail to adequately sift fact from fantasy, sanity from hallucination. This theme underscores Harper's thesis that the first task of the poet as historian is to acquire the trustworthiness and objectivity of a good journalist.

The form of "Debridement" follows roughly a chronological linear scheme. The interaction between news bulletins and resonating human episodes invests the poem's unfolding drama with dynamism. We move at the thresholds, the sensitive border zones, between history and poetry as we observe firsthand the delicate exchanges between objective and subjective orders—and Harper never lets us forget that the healthy imagination, the aspiring self, of the artist imposes a higher order on his materials in the shaping of form. "Debridement" is easily the best of the three long poems that comprise the volume, largely because the form is wide open and invites the reader to witness directly the secret workings of the poet's medium. In parts of the other two poems, the form lacks multi-dimensional rigor. But all three poems mask an unswerving blooded vision behind the quiet consistency of simple dutiful reportage, events reflected in the cool restraint of Harper's style which is so unobtrusive, at times, in its recording of the bare historical data—the act of notation—that a hasty reader may miss the abiding qualities of the art which selects and rescues the salient moments—quiet urgencies—of history automatically yielding up its metaphor, as the facts are salvaged by the careful eye and ear informed by a remarkable imagination which balances the American present and past.

THE YALE REVIEW, 1973